Hybrid Cloud for Developers

Develop and deploy cost-effective applications on the AWS and OpenStack platforms with ease

Manoj Hirway

BIRMINGHAM - MUMBAI

Hybrid Cloud for Developers

Commissioning Editor: Vijin Boricha
Acquisition Editor: Rohit Rajkumar
Content Development Editor: Sharon Raj
Technical Editor: Mohit Hassija
Copy Editor: Safis Editing
Project Coordinator: Virginia Dias
Proofreader: Safis Editing
Indexer: Mariammal Chettiyar
Graphics: Tom Scaria
Production Coordinator: Shantanu Zagade

First published: April 2018

Production reference: 1190418

Published by Packt Publishing Ltd.
Livery Place
35 Livery Street
Birmingham
B3 2PB, UK.

ISBN 978-1-78883-087-4

www.packtpub.com

I dedicate this book to my lovely daughter, Pavitraa, who has been my constant source of energy.

Mapt

Contributors

About the author

Manoj Hirway has extensive industrial experience on various cloud and virtualization technologies. He is currently working as a solutions architect in a fast-growing start-up at Pune. He acquired a bachelor's degree in computer engineering from Pune Institute of Computer Technology. He loves to explore new technologies. He wishes to help our readers by sharing his knowledge about the tech trends on the market.

This book would not have been possible without the support of my publisher, Packt Publishing. I wish to especially thank Sharon Raj and Rohit Rajkumar for their guidance in creating this book.

I am also grateful to my wife, Bhakti, my brother, Pankaj, and my parents, Mala and Nagesh for supporting me throughout the journey of this book.

About the reviewers

Neelesh Gurjar, working as a DevOps lead, helps organizations to automate their software development phases, along with designing and implementing cloud infrastructures in various cloud service providers. He has more than 13 years of experience in IT. He is an expert in AWS, Google Cloud, DevOps, and Linux. He is AWS Certified Solution Architect Professional.

Vaibhav Bhatkar is an infrastructure, automation, and a security expert. Throughout his career, he has been deeply involved in designing, developing, and deploying on-premise/cloud/hybrid infrastructures, monitoring, and storage. He has consulted various start-ups at different growth stages to provide guidance on their data center and infrastructure hosting strategies. He is an EC council certified ethical hacker and a security analyst. He is currently leading the infrastructure team at a start-up.

Packt is searching for authors like you

If you're interested in becoming an author for Packt, please visit `authors.packtpub.com` and apply today. We have worked with thousands of developers and tech professionals, just like you, to help them share their insight with the global tech community. You can make a general application, apply for a specific hot topic that we are recruiting an author for, or submit your own idea.

Table of Contents

Preface

In the past decade, cloud computing has emerged as a leading technology that is now used widely across different industries. Depending on the business need, different cloud computing models emerged. Enterprise applications now run on the cloud platform. As the requirements grew, there was a need for a hybrid cloud computing model. Cloud applications are now required to be cloud independent, and they should be able to run on any cloud. This was the main motivation of this book.

This book mainly focuses on hybrid cloud platforms. It introduces the reader to the hybrid cloud environment and teaches how to develop effective, robust, and flexible hybrid cloud applications. It talks about the migration techniques, best practices, and troubleshooting skills required to effectively manage a hybrid cloud platform.

Who this book is for

If you are an IT professional, developer, or a DevOps engineer looking to develop and manage your applications on the hybrid cloud platform, then this book is for you. This book will also benefit beginners to hybrid cloud computing. Developers looking to build applications using AWS or OpenStack services will benefit from this book.

What this book covers

`Chapter 1`, *Introducing Hybrid Clouds*, will cover the basic concepts of cloud computing. You will get familiar with the terminology used in cloud computing, types of cloud, and the advantages that cloud offers.

`Chapter 2`, *Exploring AWS Cloud*, will make you familiar with the **Amazon Web Services** (**AWS**) cloud and the various features, such as EC2 and EBS, that it offers. You will learn how to leverage the AWS technology in your day-to-day project requirements.

`Chapter 3`, *Exploring OpenStack Private Cloud*, will help you learn about the open source OpenStack platform. You will get familiar with various OpenStack components, such as Nova, Cinder, and Neutron.

`Chapter 4`, *Developing AWS Cloud Applications*, will teach you to set up the development environment for building AWS applications and develop AWS applications using the SDKs provided by Amazon.

`Chapter 5`, *Developing OpenStack Applications*, will enable you to start building OpenStack applications using the OpenStack SDK and REST APIs.

`Chapter 6`, *Cloud Migration*, will discuss migrating your applications across clouds. It talks about various considerations to be made while migrating applications.

`Chapter 7`, *Hybrid Cloud Best Practices*, will talk about the best practices to be followed while developing and working with hybrid cloud environments.

`Chapter 8`, *Monitoring and Troubleshooting Hybrid Cloud*, will discuss various monitoring and troubleshooting techniques for AWS and OpenStack clouds.

`Chapter 9`, *Hybrid Cloud Security*, will discuss the security implications to be considered on a hybrid cloud environment (AWS and OpenStack).

To get the most out of this book

Although this book is suitable for any IT professional who wishes to explore the hybrid cloud platform and develop applications, to get the most out of this book, the reader is expected to know basics of cloud computing and object oriented programming. Familiarity with C# or Python will be very helpful to understand the code examples in this book.

To try out the code in this book, the reader must have a PC with standard configuration with basic knowledge of running C# or Python programs.

Download the example code files

You can download the example code files for this book from your account at `www.packtpub.com`. If you purchased this book elsewhere, you can visit `www.packtpub.com/support` and register to have the files emailed directly to you.

You can download the code files by following these steps:

1. Log in or register at `www.packtpub.com`.
2. Select the **SUPPORT** tab.
3. Click on **Code Downloads & Errata**.
4. Enter the name of the book in the **Search** box and follow the onscreen instructions.

Once the file is downloaded, please make sure that you unzip or extract the folder using the latest version of:

- WinRAR/7-Zip for Windows
- Zipeg/iZip/UnRarX for Mac
- 7-Zip/PeaZip for Linux

The code bundle for the book is also hosted on GitHub at `https://github.com/PacktPublishing/Hybrid-Cloud-for-Developers`. In case there's an update to the code, it will be updated on the existing GitHub repository.

We also have other code bundles from our rich catalog of books and videos available at `https://github.com/PacktPublishing/`. Check them out!

Download the color images

We also provide a PDF file that has color images of the screenshots/diagrams used in this book. You can download it from `https://www.packtpub.com/sites/default/files/downloads/HybridCloudforDevelopers_ColorImages.pdf`.

Code in action

Visit the following link to check out the code in action:

`https://goo.gl/xmbUzE`

Conventions used

There are a number of text conventions used throughout this book.

`CodeInText`: Indicates code words in text, database table names, folder names, filenames, file extensions, pathnames, dummy URLs, user input, and Twitter handles. Here is an example: "Invoke this function by calling it from the `main()` function."

A block of code is set as follows:

```
public static void Main(string[] args)
{
    createS3Bucket(); // invoke the method to create an S3 bucket
    listS3Buckets(); // invoke the method to list all S3 buckets
    Console.ReadKey();
}
```

When we wish to draw your attention to a particular part of a code block, the relevant lines or items are set in bold:

```
public static void Main(string[] args)
{
    createS3Bucket(); // invoke the method to create an S3 bucket
    listS3Buckets(); // invoke the method to list all S3 buckets
    Console.ReadKey();
}
```

Any command-line input or output is written as follows:

```
[ec2-user ~] # aws s3 cp s3://<bucketname>/<path to file>/<filename>
myfile.txt
```

Bold: Indicates a new term, an important word, or words that you see onscreen. For example, words in menus or dialog boxes appear in the text like this. Here is an example: "Next, click on **Continue** to select your **Support Plan**."

Warnings or important notes appear like this.

Tips and tricks appear like this.

Get in touch

Feedback from our readers is always welcome.

General feedback: Email `feedback@packtpub.com` and mention the book title in the subject of your message. If you have questions about any aspect of this book, please email us at `questions@packtpub.com`.

Errata: Although we have taken every care to ensure the accuracy of our content, mistakes do happen. If you have found a mistake in this book, we would be grateful if you would report this to us. Please visit `www.packtpub.com/submit-errata`, selecting your book, clicking on the Errata Submission Form link, and entering the details.

Piracy: If you come across any illegal copies of our works in any form on the Internet, we would be grateful if you would provide us with the location address or website name. Please contact us at `copyright@packtpub.com` with a link to the material.

If you are interested in becoming an author: If there is a topic that you have expertise in and you are interested in either writing or contributing to a book, please visit `authors.packtpub.com`.

Reviews

Please leave a review. Once you have read and used this book, why not leave a review on the site that you purchased it from? Potential readers can then see and use your unbiased opinion to make purchase decisions, we at Packt can understand what you think about our products, and our authors can see your feedback on their book. Thank you!

For more information about Packt, please visit `packtpub.com`.

1
Introducing Hybrid Clouds

Welcome to the world of hybrid cloud computing. This chapter introduces you to the basic concepts of cloud computing and the fundamentals of the hybrid cloud landscape. It also talks about the architecture of a hybrid cloud and the advantages of using a hybrid cloud.

The following topics are covered in this chapter:

- Understanding hybrid clouds
  - What is cloud computing?
  - Basic types of cloud: Public, private
  - Technologies used by cloud providers
  - The hybrid cloud
- Hybrid cloud architecture
- Advantages of a hybrid cloud
- Factors to consider before moving to a hybrid cloud
- Understanding the DevOps methodology

Understanding hybrid clouds

Before we delve into the world of hybrid clouds, it is necessary to discuss some fundamental concepts of cloud computing.

What is cloud computing?

In the last few years, cloud computing has become a popular technology for acquiring and providing computing, network, and storage infrastructure that provides elastic, scalable, and reliable resources. Cloud computing also helps in outsourcing parts of the organization's IT infrastructure to highly-automated commercial data centers. Large companies such as Amazon, Google, and Microsoft have reliable and scalable infrastructures that they have opened for public use by providing cloud services. Cloud computing technology thus emerged, along with supporting technologies such as virtualization, containerization, and software-defined networking.

In today's world, individuals use cloud technologies for various daily activities. For example, Google Drive is used to store files, Google Photos is used to store web albums, and so on. Similarly, organizations also use cloud computing platforms extensively. For computing, resources such as servers, storage, databases, networks, software, and so on are required. These resources can either be dedicated to a user's system or can be provided by an external source. **Cloud computing is thus a delivery of services such as infrastructure, computing, storage, database, networks and software from a consolidated platform over the internet**. The companies that provide such services are called **cloud providers**.

Cloud providers typically provide three layers of service :

- Software-as-a-Service (SaaS)
- Platform-as-a-Service (PaaS)
- Infrastructure-as-a-Service (IaaS)

Lets discuss these models in brief.

Software as a Service

Software as a Service (SaaS) is a cloud service that provides access to software such as Microsoft Office, Google Apps, and so on. It allows the user to connect to and use the software application over the internet. Most SaaS applications can be accessed directly using a web browser with a plugin, and without performing any large downloads or installations. For example, companies such as Salesforce, Google (Gmail), Microsoft (Office 365), and so on, are all SaaS providers.

Users need to subscribe to the SaaS provider to use their services. The subscription costs are lower than the cost of purchasing the software license and then installing and maintaining it. Using SaaS, organizations are able to mobilize their workforce since users are able to access SaaS applications over the internet.

Platform as a Service

Platform as a Service (PaaS) provides a platform on which software can be created and launched. It is mostly used by software developers to access a development platform and provision computer infrastructure. Users can then create software applications through software components that are created in the PaaS.

The main advantage of the PaaS model is that all applications built on this platform inherit all the characteristics of the cloud. Software development, testing, and launching are also much faster on PaaS, as it requires lesser coding and helps in migrating applications to hybrid clouds. Users can manage servers, storage, and networking more efficiently using a PaaS.

Examples of PaaS services include AWS Elastic Beanstalk, Windows Azure, Heroku, Salesforce, Google App Engine, and Apache Stratos.

Infrastructure as a Service

The **Infrastructure as a Service (IaaS)** cloud computing model enables automated deployment of compute, storage, networking, and networking services. Using this cloud mode, users can build a virtual data center in the cloud with as many resource capabilities as found in traditional data centers. In addition, users can create their private data centers in the cloud and establish a VPN connectivity with their local data centers.

IaaS also provides **Application Programming Interfaces** (**APIs**) for software developers to access cloud resources programmatically.

Thus, users don't have to invest in hardware and are able to leverage the cloud resources and then be billed based on consumption. Cloud providers such as **Amazon (AWS)**, Microsoft (Azure), Google (GCP), and so on, are examples of companies that provide IaaS.

The following diagram summarizes the differences between IaaS, PaaS, and SaaS:

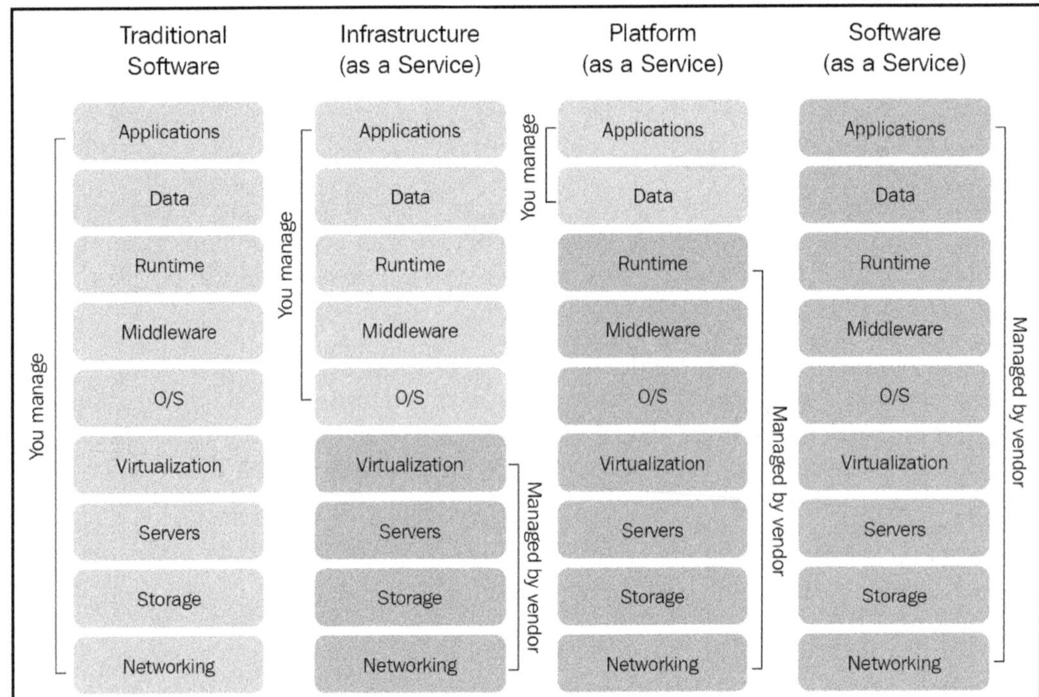

As shown here, in traditional software deployments, the entire stack is managed by the organization that implements the system. IaaS reduces the burden of managing the **Networking**, **Storage**, **Servers**, and **Virtualization** layers by owning and managing them. Thus, the user no longer has to worry about these layers and can focus on the software applications.

PaaS further relieves the user from managing the Operating System, Middleware and Runtime layers, thus leaving only the application management and data management responsibilities to the user.

Finally, a SaaS provider will own and manage the entire stack and the user just has to log in to the host to perform their activities.

Characteristics of a cloud

A cloud service should have the following characteristics:

- **On-demand service**: The user of the cloud should be able to provision resources on their own without any human action or intervention from the cloud providers.
- **Wide network accessibility:** The cloud resources should be available over the network to users either using a thick or thin client.
- **Resource pooling:** Cloud resources such as servers, disk storage, and so on should be dynamically allocated and de-allocated to users based on the demand. The same resources can be shared or pooled between users, giving them a virtually isolated instance of the resource.
- **Rapid elasticity**: Resources should be easily scalable. Based on the user's requests, resources should be scaled up and scaled down, giving an impression that there are more than enough resources available at a given point in time.
- **Measured service:** A cloud should also have the ability to measure the consumption of resources, as well as automatically control and optimize those resources.

Types of cloud

There are two fundamental types of cloud models:

- Private cloud
- Public cloud

A combination of these two types of cloud yields a third type of cloud, called a **hybrid cloud**.

Private cloud

The cloud platform can be deployed and hosted privately on organizational premises. The services of such a cloud platform are made available to internal users of the organization. This cloud is referred to as a private cloud.

A private cloud shares many of the characteristics of public cloud computing, including resource pooling, self-service, elasticity, and pay-by-use, delivered in a standardized manner with the additional control and customization available from dedicated resources.

OpenStack is an open source cloud operating system that can be deployed within an organization and hosted as a private cloud. We will cover OpenStack in detail in `Chapter 3`, *Developing AWS Cloud Applications*.

It's common to store data on cloud storage using **Software Defined Storage** (**SDS**) technologies. SDS helps in decoupling the storage hardware, such as HDD and SSD, from the software that is used to manage the storage. This provides the ability to abstract and consolidate the storage capacity in a cloud. It also allows users to scale beyond the underlying hardware limitations.

Two of the most widely used software-defined storage solutions are Ceph for structured data and Gluster for unstructured data. **Ceph** is popular for its scalability. It also provides a programmable storage system that works well with the OpenStack cloud platform because it integrates object, block, and file storage into one pool of resources. Similarly, Gluster is popular for handling traditional file storage and works well with provisioning and managing elastic storage for container-based applications. OpenStack Swift is another object storage solution that is popular today.

Advantages of a private cloud:

- Reduced cost of usage
- More control over services, data, and users
- Higher security as the cloud platform resides within the organization's network
- Higher performance as the cloud is on the local network

Disadvantages of a private cloud:

- High infrastructure cost
- High maintenance and administration costs
- Proper resource utilization is administrator's responsibility

Public cloud

When IT resources such as computing servers, storage, development platforms, applications, and so on are made available as a service over the internet and can be provisioned on demand using a publicly available self-service portal, such an offering is called a public cloud. Public clouds offer rapid elasticity and limitless scalability. They provide a measured service in which users are billed based on their usage.

Public clouds are hosted and managed using datacenters that belong to cloud service providers. The resources can be shared by multiple customers. This feature is called multi-tenancy. Sharing resources helps in reducing costs. However, there is reduced control over the resources in a public cloud than in a private cloud, because the underlying infrastructure is owned by the service provider. The level of control depends on the specific cloud delivery model.

There are many public cloud providers on the market, such as **Amazon Web Services** (**AWS**), Microsoft Azure, and **Google Cloud Platform** (**GCP**). We will be covering the AWS cloud in detail in this book.

Advantages of a public cloud:

- No administration and maintenance costs
- Simple and easy to use
- Quickly available on demand

Disadvantages of a public cloud:

- Security is a concern as data goes to a public network
- Lack of full control over the cloud

Technologies used by cloud providers

A **cloud platform** is a combination of various technologies tied together to create a hyper-converged platform. The three basic technologies that lay the foundation of a cloud are as follows:

- **Hypervisor:** A **hypervisor** is a combination of software, firmware, and sometimes hardware that is capable of running a virtual machine. A hypervisor that is capable of running a virtual machine on bare metal hardware is referred to as a Type 1 hypervisor. For example, VMWare ESXi server and Microsoft Hyper-V server are Type 1 hypervisors. The hypervisors that run on an operating system are referred to as Type 2 hypervisors. For example, Oracle VirtualBox, and VMWare Workstation are Type 2 hypervisors. OpenStack uses the Type 2 QEMU/KVM hypervisor as the default hypervisor. Similarly, AWS uses the Type 1 XEN hypervisor.

- **Storage: Cloud storage** is based on a virtualized storage infrastructure, which provides elasticity, multi-tenancy, scalability, and metered resource usage. Cloud storage mainly comes in object storage and block storage solutions. The OpenStack component that provides object storage is called Swift and the one that provides block storage is called Cinder. The AWS component for object storage is called S3, whereas for block storage is called EBS.
- **Software Defined Networking (SDN):** Most of the networking is managed by networking software such as OpenContrail, OpenVPN, and so on. AWS provides features such as Virtual Private Cloud, DirectConnect, and so on, which are provided by SDN. Similarly, OpenStack has a component called **Neutron** that can be used to configure OpenStack networking such as DHCP, DNS, Gateway, and so on.

Introducing hybrid cloud

As organizational business grows, there is a need to extend the enterprise operation along with the IT infrastructure. In other words, the onsite data center needs to be extended by adding more servers and resources to fulfill business demands. There is also a need to optimize and perform efficient utilization of available resources. High-end servers can't be left underutilized, as this will be a waste of the available resources. Purchasing more and more IT equipment increases the organizational infrastructure costs. Also, large servers tend to occupy more and more space in data centers. This becomes a problem and there is a need for a flexible and scalable model that will allow on-demand infrastructure scale-up and scale-down.

One solution is to use a private cloud that provides on demand scaling up and scaling down of the infrastructure by spinning up virtual machines. A private cloud will certainly solve the problem of flexible scaling and efficient utilization of resources. However, since a private cloud resides within the data center, it still requires large amounts of physical resources, which must be owned by the organization. Despite efficient utilization of resources, if the organization needs more infrastructure, a private cloud doesn't completely solve the problem, as the cost of owning the infrastructure must still be borne by the organization.

So, the other solution is to migrate the entire data center to a public cloud such as AWS or Azure. A public cloud will ensure that we have ample resources that can be scaled up and down based on requirements. Organizations don't have to worry about purchasing large servers and arranging floor space for accommodating them in their private data centers.

However, there are many downsides to using a public cloud. Migrating existing applications to the cloud is complex. There are portability problems as system architectures differ. Also, as the resources are scaled up and the data center expands, the costs can climb significantly. The overall costs of using a public cloud are high. Moreover, there are security concerns. Since organizational data could be confidential, putting it on a public network would not be liked by the IT security teams. Thus, using a public cloud alone doesn't solve the problem either.

Since both public and private cloud models have their pros and cons, there is a need to combine both the models and create a more suitable platform for the organization's needs. A cloud platform that is a combination of private and public clouds, and connected using an encrypted network, is referred to as a **hybrid cloud**. The **National Institute of Standards and Technology** (**NIST**) defines a hybrid cloud as follows: "*A hybrid cloud is a combination of public and private clouds connected together using a standardized network link that enables portability of data and applications.*" It could be a combination of a private cloud inside an organization with one or more public cloud providers, or a private cloud hosted on third-party premises with one or more public cloud providers.

A typical use case of the hybrid cloud model is a combination of customer facing systems (such as mobile phones) and systems of record management. For example, an e-commerce organizations might leverage their data center to manage transactions made by their customers using the frontend that is running on a public cloud. In other words, the frontend running on a public cloud will be connected to the datacenter. An organization might also use a third-party cloud service that verifies the credit of customers who choose to pay using the EMI option. They may also use the public cloud to expand their servers in case of high network traffic during online sales and holiday periods.

The hybrid cloud is thus becoming a widely used cloud model that adapts to rapid changes in technology and business in terms of networking, storage, and computing requirements.

Hybrid cloud architecture

As discussed in the previous section, a hybrid cloud is a combination of public and private clouds connected together using a secure connection. The following diagram shows a high-level overview of a typical hybrid cloud architecture. A simple hybrid cloud model involves one private cloud that is tied to the organization's data center and one public cloud, which is located offsite.

Both these clouds are connected using an encrypted network connection by VPN. An encrypted connection can be established using any of the available VPN applications, such as OpenVPN:

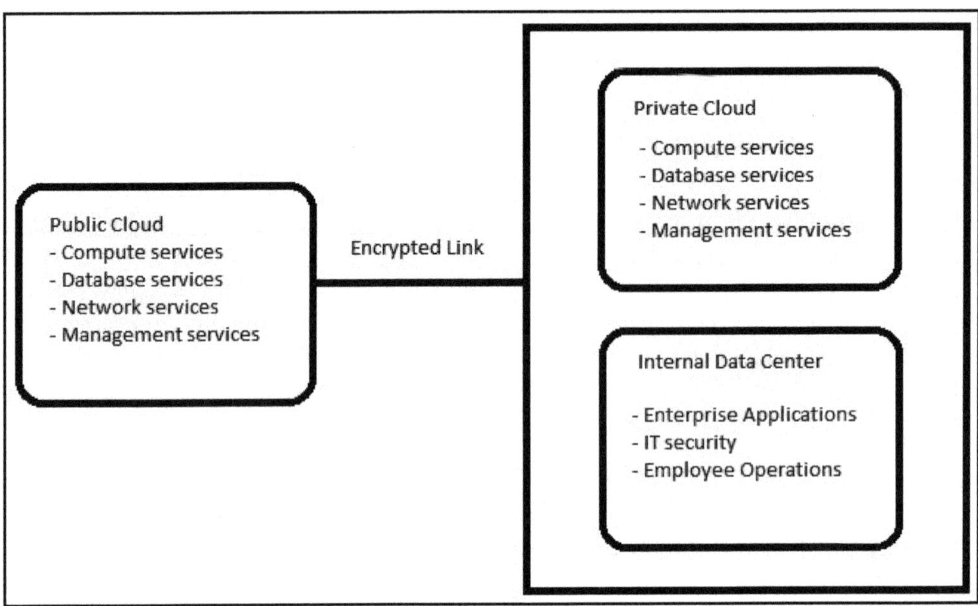

Fig 1.2: A typical hybrid cloud architecture

The public cloud could be any of the available cloud providers, such as AWS Cloud, Microsoft Azure, and so on. Similarly, a private cloud could be one of the most widely used open source cloud platforms, OpenStack, or a custom-built private cloud.

Hybrid cloud using OpenStack and AWS/Azure/GCP

The following diagram shows a hybrid cloud architecture created using the OpenStack private cloud and public clouds such as AWS, Azure, or GCP. The combination of these two clouds creates a hybrid cloud environment:

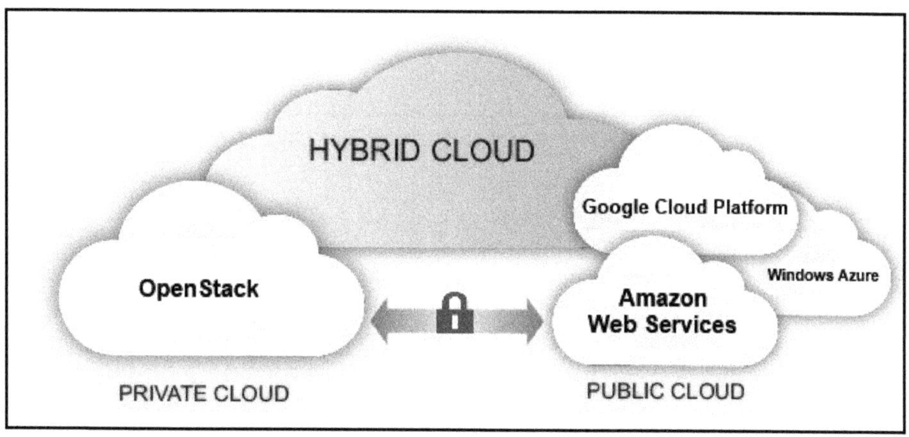

Fig 1.3: Hybrid cloud architecture created using the OpenStack private cloud and public clouds

Combining public cloud services with private clouds services along with the data center, thus creating a hybrid model, is needed in modern computing. Many companies now combine public cloud and private cloud services to create value.

If you have more than one cloud environment (public and private), then it is a good approach to have a management platform that spans these environments. If each of these clouds is managed separately, there is a duplication of efforts and the operations are prone to human error.

There are several startups and established companies that have developed software that allows users to centrally manage both private datacenters and public cloud infrastructure and applications. Managing virtual machines, storage, databases, and other resources can be done using a single console, which makes it easy to administer the entire operations on a hybrid cloud.

The following diagram shows another perspective of a hybrid cloud architecture using OpenStack:

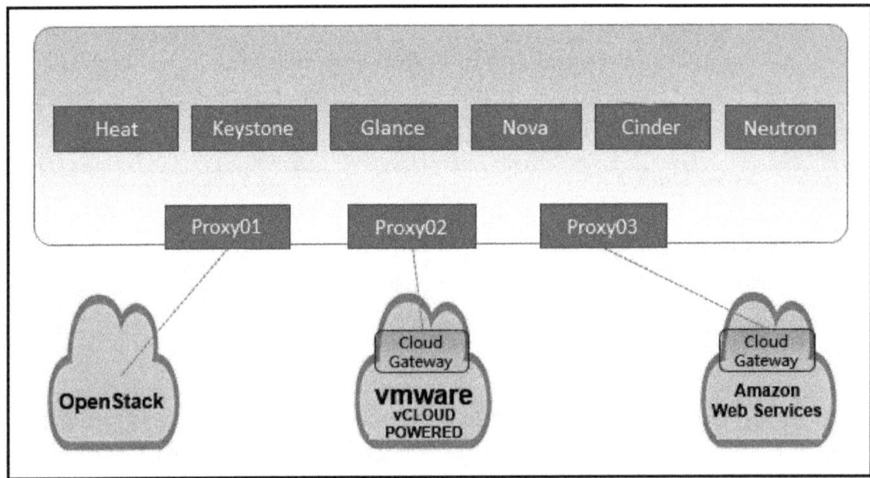

Here, the OpenStack components exist inside the boundaries of the organizational network. They use a proxy server for interfacing with the external public cloud providers. These proxy servers may act as a mediator between the public and private cloud environments.

Various OpenStack components such as Cinder, Neutron, and Nova collaborate with each other and also interact with the external public cloud to create a hybrid cloud architecture. OpenStack will be discussed in detail in later chapters.

What qualifies as a hybrid cloud?

There are certain conditions that must be met for a cloud to be qualified as a hybrid cloud.

A cloud is hybrid if:

- The organization data center is connected to the public cloud and sends/receives data from the public cloud
- An organization leverages a number of SaaS applications and moves data between private or data center resources
- An organizational business process is designed in such a way that it leverages the use of private and public clouds

A cloud is not hybrid if:

- Only a handful of people in the organization use the public cloud for deploying or testing applications, and it is completely disconnected from the data center
- An organization is using a SaaS application for a project, but there is no movement of data from that application into the organization's data center

The following diagram summarizes the characteristics of public, private, and hybrid clouds:

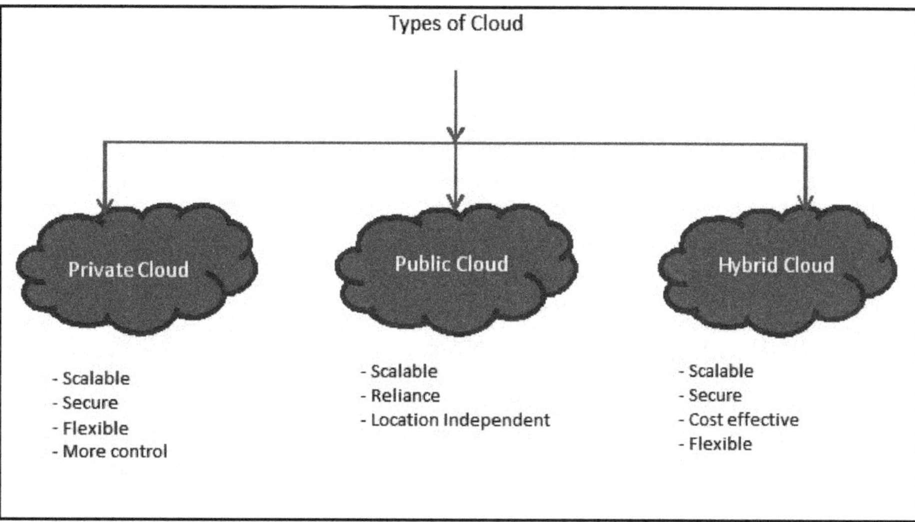

Cloud bursting in a hybrid cloud

Cloud bursting is one of the most important features of a hybrid cloud. It helps in scaling applications across public clouds.

Consider an application that is running in a private cloud or a local computing environment. Suppose a situation arises where the application needs additional resources such as computing power, storage, memory, and so on. In such a scenario, the application can *burst* into the public cloud and use the resources available there to ensure continuity and smooth operations. In other words, the application can expand itself to start using the resources of the public cloud on demand. This is called cloud bursting.

However, this can add complexity to the application design and special skills are required to design the application to leverage cloud bursting capabilities. There are vendors that provide hybrid cloud solutions that facilitate taking advantage of cloud bursting.

Advantages of using hybrid cloud

As discussed in the previous sections, a hybrid cloud offers the cost and scale benefits of public clouds, while also offering the security and control of private clouds. In this section, we will highlight some of the business benefits of hybrid clouds.

Cost savings

Since the high-end infrastructure is outsourced to the public cloud provider, there is a cost saving.

Temporary IT and development projects require temporary resources. For example, IT companies keep performing several **Proof of Concepts** (**POC**), which requires IT resources only till the duration of the project. These resources can be easily created and destroyed in the private or private cloud without spending too much.

An application may require different kinds and levels of resources during its life cycle. For a production grade environment, a public cloud can be used, whereas, for testing phases, a private cloud will suffice.

High-end servers have maintenance costs and their vendor contracts must be renewed periodically. Large applications that require high-end servers can be migrated to the public cloud and thus maintenance costs and effort can be saved.

Flexibility

A hybrid cloud offers the flexibility of control of a private cloud and at the same time, the agility of a public cloud. The private cloud component of the hybrid cloud can be customized as per the needs of the organization.

Also, when an organization requires additional computing resources, a public cloud can easily scale-up and satisfy additional needs.

Speed

High-end servers and computing resources can be spun up in a matter of minutes to satisfy organizational needs quickly on public clouds. High-speed internet links can also be established between data centers, thus delivering high performance.

Portability

By leveraging container technology such as Docker, applications can be containerized and made portable across several cloud platforms. For example, a containerized application can be easily migrated from the OpenStack private cloud to the AWS public cloud.

Security

Since an encrypted link or VPN is established between the public and private cloud of the organizational data center, confidential network data can be safely transferred across clouds.

Factors to consider before moving to a hybrid cloud

As discussed previously, moving the organization's data center to a hybrid cloud offers several advantages. However, changing the IT infrastructure of the organization could be a complex task. It may also be expensive. Hence, the following factors should be considered before choosing to migrate the infrastructure to a hybrid cloud environment:

- **Skilled engineers**: A hybrid cloud setup can become very complex, depending on the organization's IT infrastructure and customization. Highly skilled and experienced IT engineers must be available to perform the cloud migration and maintenance.

- **High bandwidth for data transfer**: To set up a hybrid cloud, a large amount of data may have to be moved from the private cloud to the public. This may involve high bandwidth utilization and may also affect the productivity of the existing engineers. Organizations should also be prepared to incur higher costs involved in large amount of data transfer.
- **Resource management**: Since hybrid cloud resources are scalable, all the resources must be utilized efficiently. The usage of CPU, memory, and storage should be monitored to ensure resources are not wasted.
- **Compliance**: Organizations that deal with sensitive and critical data have their own compliance policies. When moving to the hybrid cloud, periodic audits should be done to ensure that the cloud platform meets requirements.
- **Load balancing**: Appropriate load balancing techniques should be considered so that a single machine doesn't get overloaded with resource requests.

Now that we know the fundamentals of hybrid clouds, lets turn our attention to the software development methodologies that are suitable for working on cloud platforms.

Understanding DevOps methodology

Historically, many software companies followed the waterfall model of software development. The waterfall model involved the following stages:

1. Requirement analysis
2. System design
3. Implementation
4. Testing
5. Deployment
6. Maintenance

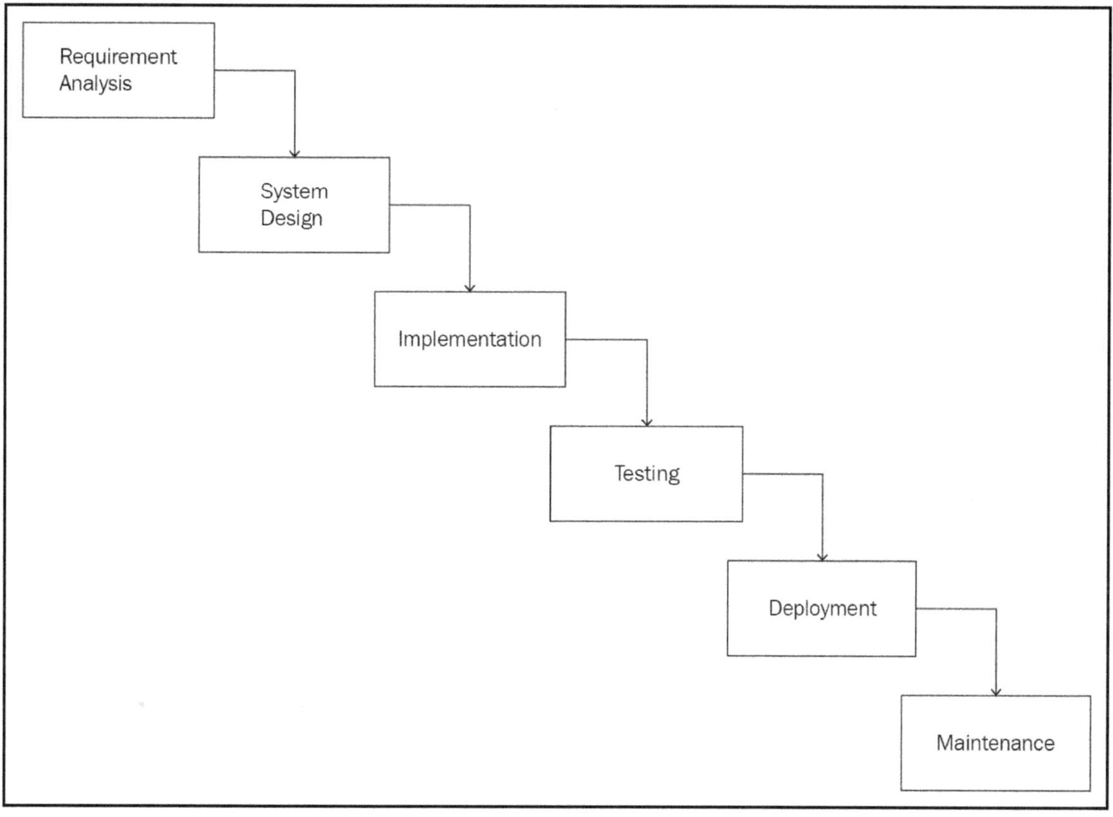

In this, each stage was virtually isolated and was mostly performed by a different set of people. It had poor integration between development, infrastructure, security, and support teams. Moreover, the teams working on each stage would report to different organizational structures with different corporate goals and philosophies. The primary goal of developers was to build the software, whereas the operations team had the goal of deploying software and ensure stability and reliability. This mismatch of goals would cause conflicts and ultimately the business would also suffer. Hence, there was a need to have more collaboration and communication between the software development teams and the operations teams.

The Agile software methodology addresses these concerns, and a modification to the agile model gave rise to DevOps.

DevOps is a faily new methodology that primarily focuses on improved collaboration, communication, and integration between software developers and IT operations. It is not a system, but a philosophy, cultural change, and paradigm shift in the way organizations' work.

The following diagram depicts a DevOps approach to software development.

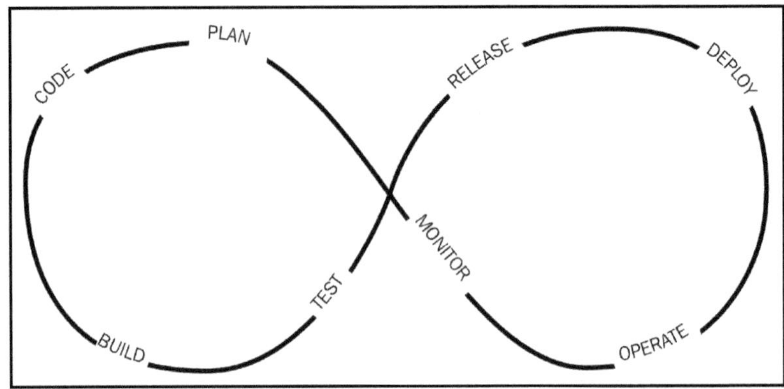

The different between the Agile model and DevOps is that Agile software development primarily focuses on the collaboration between the business and its developers, whereas the DevOps model focuses on the collaboration between developers, IT operations, and security teams.

IT operations include system administrators, database administrators, network engineers, infrastructure architects, and support engineers. The DevOps methodology means different things to different teams. For application developers, DevOps focuses on code building, code coverage, unit testing, packaging, and deployment. For IT operations teams, DevOps focuses on provisioning, configuration, orchestration, and deployment. But the basic principles of DevOps remain the same, irrespective of the teams and tasks being worked on.

The following are six important DevOps practices that are widely used by organizations who have chosen to adopt this methodology:

- Collaboration
- Automation
- Continuous integration
- Continuous testing
- Continuous delivery
- Continuous monitoring

Collaboration

As we discussed, the fundamental need from which the DevOps model arose is the lack of collaboration between software development teams and IT operations teams. The DevOps methodology not only implements effective collaboration between these two teams, but also to every other stakeholder of the software.

Automation

DevOps puts a heavy emphasis on automation. All possible tasks, such as software testing, infrastructure provisioning, software deployment, and so on, must be automated. This can be achieved using automation tools. There are several automation tools available in the market. **Jenkins** is one such tool, which can be used to automate several tasks such as code compilation, software testing, and so on.

Continuous integration

Continuous integration forces software developers to integrate their work with other developers. This exposes any integration issues much earlier than the release date and hence helps in fixing problems earlier. This approach definitely requires developers to communicate with each other and discuss their work and integration approaches.

Continuous testing

Continuous testing involves testing of the software code with every code change that is merged into the codebase. Developers should not only make sure that they deliver error-free code, but also provide test datasets to the testing teams and help them in configuring the testing environment so it is as close to the production environment as possible.

Use of automation testing tools reduces the cost and time of testing and frees up engineers to use their time more effectively.

Thus, in order to make the journey to the cloud efficient and effective, software companies must adapt the DevOps methodology for their software development and IT infrastructure deployment strategies.

Summary

Hybrid cloud proves to be helping tremendously in building an agile and future-ready hybrid IT environment. Backed by the advantages of public and private clouds, which involve a comprehensive and integrated suite of cloud resources, a hybrid cloud environment helps organizations leverage the flexibility and scalability of public clouds, along with the security and control of their own private infrastructure.

Using a hybrid cloud model, organizations can create a highly optimized IT environment, where they can leverage their own physical resources in their data centers to deploy mission critical applications, and put the non-critical apps on the public cloud. Organization now have the flexibility to choose between different cloud models, based on scalability, performance, and security requirements.

In the next chapter, we will start exploring the AWS public cloud.

2
Exploring AWS Cloud

In the previous chapter, we discussed the different types of cloud, such as public, private, and hybrid. We also mentioned public cloud providers, such as AWS, Google Cloud, and Microsoft Azure. In this chapter, we will start exploring AWS Cloud in more detail. We will also guide you through the process of creating a new AWS account. Finally, we will be launching an EC2 instance, creating an EBS volume, and an S3 bucket.

The following topics will be covered in the chapter:

- Introduction to AWS Cloud
- Creation of an AWS account
- Amazon **Elastic Compute Cloud** (**EC2**)
- Amazon **Elastic Block Storage** (**EBS**)
- Amazon **Simple Storage Service** (**S3**)
- Amazon **Virtual Private Cloud** (**VPC**)

Let's begin with a brief introduction to the AWS public cloud.

Introducing AWS Cloud

Amazon released its public cloud on March 13, 2006, in which they offered a storage service called **Simple Storage Service** (**S3**). This storage service allows users to upload files such as photos, videos, spreadsheets, and so on. Users were able to read, edit, and delete these files on the cloud using the console provided by Amazon. However, this service was only offered in the US. It wasn't available to the other parts of the world. However, as years progressed, Amazon started expanding and providing its services to the other regions and now offers its services to the entire world. The S3 service also matured and provides several more additional features such as encryption, logging, high availability, and so on. Users can now upload files with a size of up to 5 TB.

After the success of S3, Amazon also started a Queue Service called SQS or Simple Queue Service. This service provides software developers with a way to transfer messages between different software applications or programs. SQS can be used by software programs within the AWS environment and also outside AWS.

Later, Amazon started one of its most significant services of hosting a virtual machine inside the cloud. This service is called Elastic Compute Cloud or EC2 and is now very popular among AWS users. The EC2 service offers virtual machines with the required operating systems on demand, within a few seconds.

Amazon provides its own web interface to access its services. It also provides REST APIs and SDKs for software developers to access the services using software applications. We will discuss some of the features that AWS provides.

Amazon Web Service features

The AWS Cloud platform provides a bunch of different services to its users. Discussing all the services that AWS offers can be exhaustive and can easily fill up several books. We will discuss the most significant AWS services that can be leveraged in a hybrid cloud development process.

Following are the most important and commonly used AWS services:

- **Amazon EC2**: The Amazon EC2 service provides on-demand virtual servers that can be quickly launched in a few minutes by selecting the template provided. Amazon provides a ready-made VM template called **Amazon Machine Image (AMI)**.
- **Amazon S3**: The Amazon S3, is a cloud-based storage service that provides unlimited storage space to its users. S3 users can use the web console, CLI, or the S3 APIs to upload and download all types of files to the S3 storage.
- **Amazon Elastic MapReduce**: The Amazon Elastic MapReduce service provides a Hadoop framework that runs on the EC2 instance and S3 storage. It allows the user to process a large amount of data and thus perform data mining and analysis in the cloud.
- **Amazon CloudFront**: CloudFront provides an easy way for its users to distribute data through high-speed networks and are optimized to work with EC2 instances and S3 storage. It also delivers static content and streams web content using edge locations worldwide.

- **Amazon SimpleDB**: Amazon SimpleDB is a non-relational database service that is optimized for performance. Users can use this database service to store data from their applications and websites. Data stored in this database is automatically replicated for high availability.
- **Amazon Relational Database Service (RDS)**: Amazon RDS offers its users a highly scalable relational database located in the AWS Cloud, which can be easily accessed using a web service. This database is identical to the traditional relational database, and all tools that use the SQL language that work with a MySQL database, also work seamlessly with the RDS database. The database is periodically patched so that a database administrator does not have to worry about maintaining the database engine. Regular backups are also taken to ensure data protection.
- **Amazon SQS**: The Amazon SQS provides a queuing service that can be leveraged by distributed applications to pass messages between different components. This provides an asynchronous mechanism to communicate between SQS applications without losing any messages even if any of the components are not available.

- **Amazon Simple Notification Service (SNS)**: Amazon SNS allows its users to send notifications either using email or text messages. It uses the push mechanism to delivers messages to subscribed users. Users can thus use this service to get notified about the events happening in their cloud environments.
- **Amazon CloudWatch**: Amazon CloudWatch provides its users a monitoring facility for their EC2 and other Amazon cloud services. Users can thus select the EC2 instances they want to monitor, and CloudWatch fetches and monitors them to provide the required statistics such as disk throughput, CPU utilization, network traffic, and so on.
- **Amazon Virtual Private Cloud (VPC)**: VPC provides a way to create a safe and secure cloud environment respective to the user, which can act as a bridge between the user's data center or IT infrastructure and the AWS public cloud.
- **Elastic Load Balancing**: Elastic Load Balancing is a service that helps in balancing network traffic of your EC2 instance by automatically distributing the network across multiple EC2 instances. It can also launch an additional EC2 instance (if required) to balance the network traffic efficiently. Users can use this service within a single availability zone or even across multiple availability zones. One of the important use cases of this service is that it detects unhealthy EC2 instances and reroutes traffic to other healthy instances.

- **Amazon Elastic Block Store (EBS)**: The Amazon EBS service provides its users the ability to create block level storage volumes. These volumes do not need an EC2 instance to function. They can exist independently and can also be mounted to an existing EC2 instance as a volume.
- **AWS Import/Export**: The AWS Import/Export tool provides the ability to transfer data at very high speeds by bypassing the internet. It uses the company's internal high speed network link and storage devices to transfer the data. Users can transfer the high volume of data using this method with good transfer speeds.

AWS has expanded its presence across the world and the previously mentioned features are just a few of the services offered by AWS. We will be using the EC2, S3, and EBS services to demonstrate their uses in the hybrid cloud environment. Let's get hands-on experience of the AWS cloud. Let's start by creating a new AWS account.

Creating an AWS account

The following steps must be followed to create or sign up for an AWS account. When an AWS account is created by signing up, the account automatically includes all services in the AWS Cloud. However, you are billed only for the services that you consume:

1. Type `https://aws.amazon.com/` in your browser and then choose **Create an AWS Account**.

Note that this page might not be available in your web browser if you have signed into the AWS Management Console in the past. If this is the case, click on the **Sign In to the Console** button and select **Create a new account** and then follow the online instructions. The sign-up procedure also involves answering a phone call and you may have to enter a PIN using the phone keypad.

2. Enter all the address related information in the fields provided:

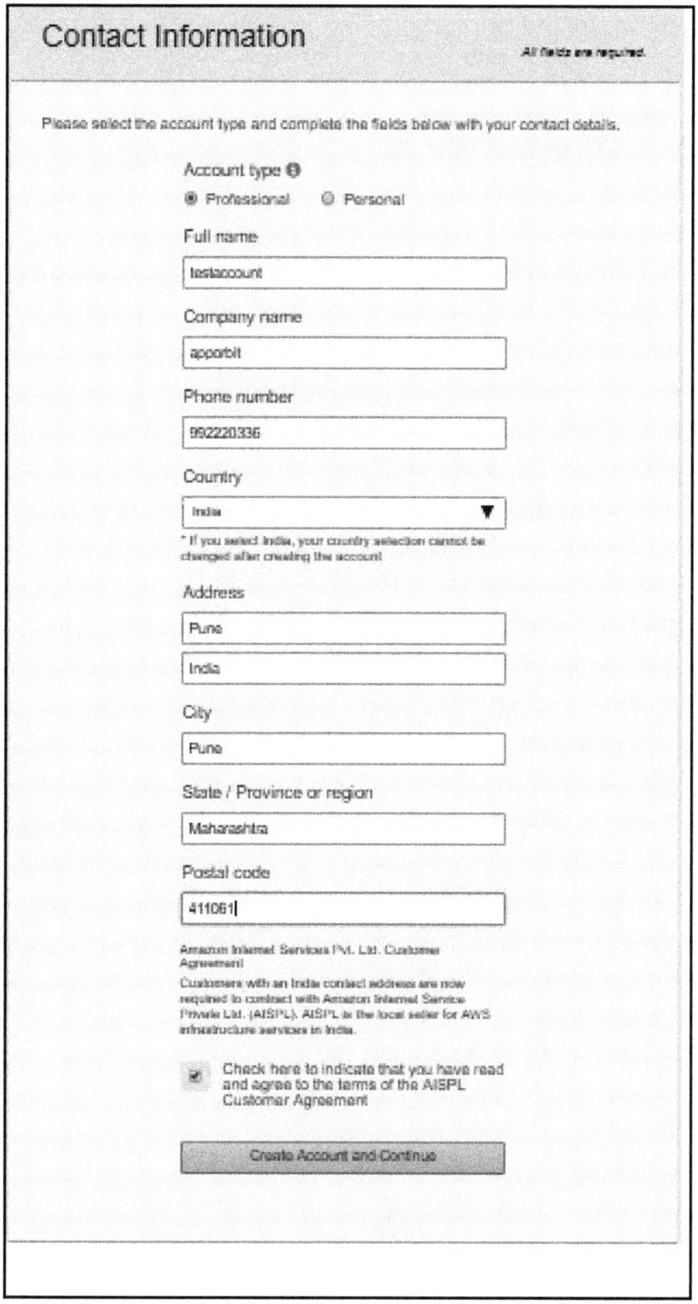

Contact Information

All fields are required.

Please select the account type and complete the fields below with your contact details.

Account type

◉ Professional ○ Personal

Full name

testaccount

Company name

apporbit

Phone number

992220336

Country

India

* If you select India, your country selection cannot be changed after creating the account

Address

Pune

India

City

Pune

State / Province or region

Maharashtra

Postal code

411061

Amazon Internet Services Pvt. Ltd. Customer Agreement

Customers with an India contact address are now required to contract with Amazon Internet Service Private Ltd. (AISPL). AISPL is the local seller for AWS infrastructure services in India.

☑ Check here to indicate that you have read and agree to the terms of the AISPL Customer Agreement

Create Account and Continue

3. Enter your payment information. You will be billed on the credit card information that you enter here:

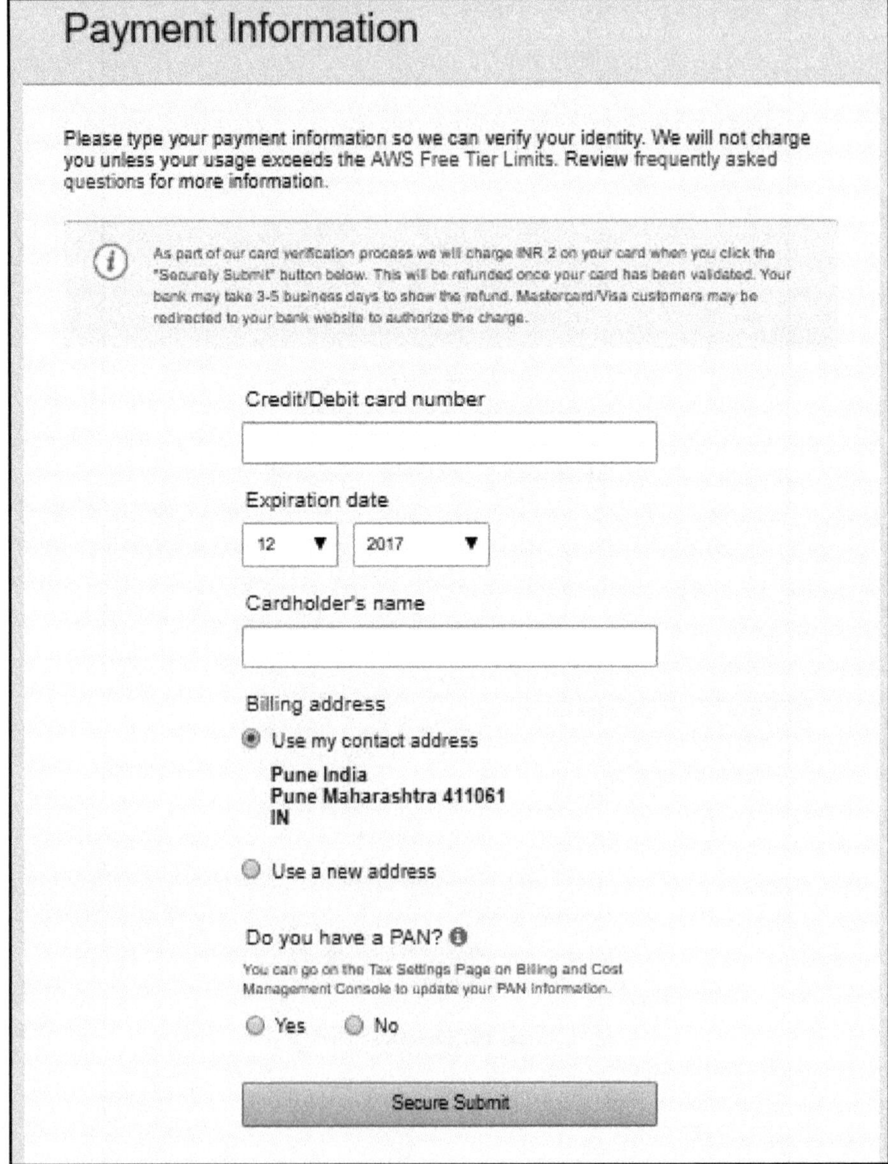

4. Verify your phone number by typing it on the **Identity Verification Page**. This is the number that you can use to answer a phone call from Amazon. When you're ready to answer the phone call, choose the **Call me now** option. Once you do that, an automated calling system will call you. Type the provided PIN using your phone's keypad.
5. Next, click on **Continue** to select your **Support Plan**. On the **Support Plan** page, choose one of the available support plans, and then choose **Continue**. You may find more information about the support plans on the AWS website.
6. Once you choose your support plan, a confirmation page will display which will indicate that your account is being activated. Usually, accounts will be activated within a few minutes, however, some accounts may take 24 hours to be fully activated.

When your account is fully activated, you will receive a confirmation email from AWS.

Once you have created your AWS account, it's time that we explore various AWS services in detail.

Let's begin by exploring the EC2 service that provides virtual servers to its users.

Amazon EC2

The Amazon EC2 service offers elastic and scalable computing servers in the AWS cloud platform. Amazon EC2 can be used to launch virtual machines with the required configuration. It also provides the ability to configure security parameters, along with networking. You can also manage storage.

Since this service is elastic, you can scale up and scale down your server resources based on the requirements. For example, if your network traffic increases, you may require additional servers that can be quickly launched in a matter of a few seconds to balance the traffic.

Amazon EC2 provides the following features:

- Virtual machines called EC2 instances that run various operating systems. They are launched using certain templates called AMIs. The AMIs define the operating system and the additional software that the instance will have.
- The ability to configure the EC2 instance properties such as number of CPU cores, amount of memory, disk storage type, disk storage size, and networking capacity.
- Secure login to your instances using SSH key pairs. The public key is stored on the AWS side and the private key is provided to you.

- Temporary disk volumes that can be attached to the instances. Since these volumes are temporary, the data does not persist across reboots and gets deleted when the instance is stopped.
- Permanent storage volumes for storing persistent data. The EBS service provides these volumes.
- The ability to launch the EC2 instance on different geographical locations where AWS data centers are located. These locations are called regions and availability zones.
- A configurable firewall that can allow or disallow various protocols, ports, or IP addresses. These firewalls are called security groups.
- The ability to assign public static IP addresses to the virtual machines, called elastic IP addresses.
- The ability to assign metadata to the virtual machines, which can be used for identification. This metadata is called a tag.
- Virtually isolated networks within the AWS Cloud in which virtual machines exist. These are known as VPCs.

We will now discuss some important features and terms used in the AWS EC2 environment.

AMI

AWS provides templates for virtual machines. The template is preconfigured for the type of operating system and it can be used when launching the instance. The template includes the following:

- The root volume that must be used by the operating system.
- The AMI permissions. These permissions determine who can use this template.

Users can create an AMI template from an existing EC2 instance. This allows users to create customized AMIs.

EC2 instance types

AWS provides different types of EC2 instances depending on the resources they consume. The naming convention for instance types is based on the number of CPU cores, memory size, disk size, and so on. Depending on these parameters, instances can be named `nano`, `micro`, `small`, `medium`, `large`, `xlarge`, `2xlarge`, and so on.

These instance types are classified into five categories: General Purpose, Compute Optimized, Memory Optimized, Storage Optimized, and Accelerated Computing.

The General Purpose category of instance is suitable for hosting websites, creating development environments or build servers, source code repositories, and so on.

The Compute Optimized category of instances can be used for CPU intensive tasks and applications such as high processing web servers, scientific modeling systems, data analytics, deduplication servers, and so on.

The Memory Optimized category is suited for memory intensive applications. For example, an instance of this category can be used to host a SAP HANA database, which is an in-memory database.

The Storage Optimized instances are well suited for file system specific operations that involve a lot of reads and writes to the storage disk. For example, Hadoop servers or Map Reduce servers can be installed on such instances.

EC2 instance IP addressing

The EC2 instances can be assigned either a static IP address or a dynamic IP address. AWS provides an option for both. It also provides DNS hostnames for the EC2 instances. The DNS names differ depending upon where the instance is launched. The instance launched in the EC2-Classic platform may have different DNS configuration as compared to the instance launched in the VPC.

Though an EC2 instance is assigned an IPv4 address by default, both VPC and EC2-Classic platforms support the IPv6 IP addressing schemes. When creating a VPC, the user must specify the IPv4 CIDR block that must be used to derive IP addresses to assign to the EC2 instance launched in that VPC. EC2-Classic platform does not support IPv6 format.

EC2 instance security groups

A **security group** is a firewall that is associated to one or more EC2 instances running on the AWS Cloud. It defines a set of rules that determine how network traffic flows to and from the instance.

Security groups provide the ability to set customized firewall rules based on the protocol, port, or IP address.

The following are the characteristics of security group rules:

- The default security group allows all outbound network traffic
- The security group rules for outbound traffic of the instance launched under the EC2-Classic platform are fixed and cannot be modified
- If an instance is associated with more than one security group, all the rules are combined and applied to the instance

A rule that is defined in the security group has the following three main parameters:

- **Protocol**: The protocol to be allowed/disallowed, such as TCP, UDP, ICMP, and so on
- **Port range**: For the selected protocol, the range of ports to allow or disallow
- **Source or destination**: The source and destination to which the network packet belongs

Launching an EC2 instance from the web console

To launch an EC2 instance, perform the following steps:

1. Log in to your AWS account and go to the AWS EC2 console at: `https://console.aws.amazon.com/ec2/`.
2. From the console, click on **Launch Instance**.
3. From the available choices, select the AMI that is to be used to launch the instance:

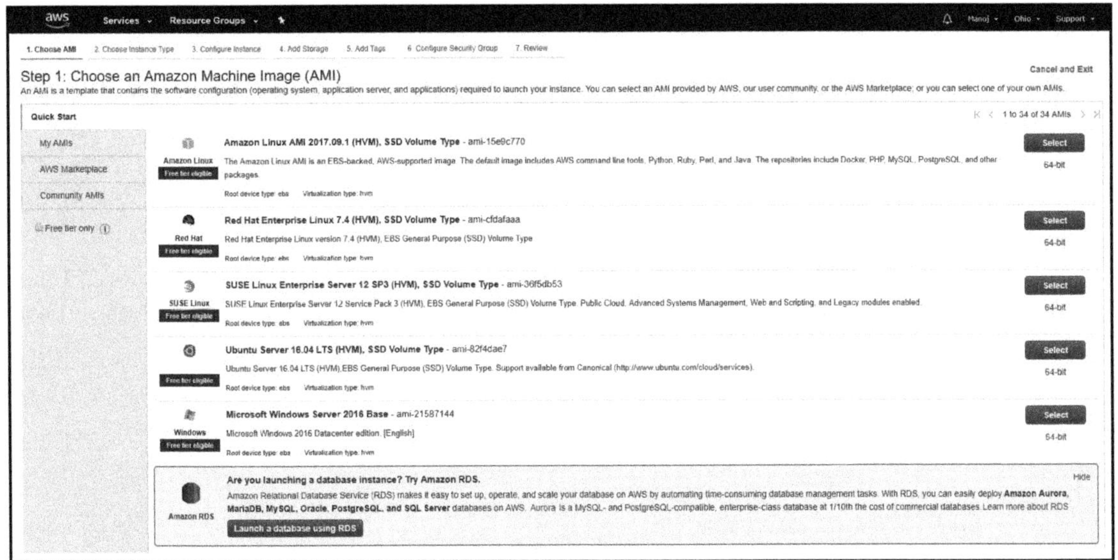

4. Select the instance type based on the number of CPUs, the memory required, and so on (we described instance types in the previous sections):

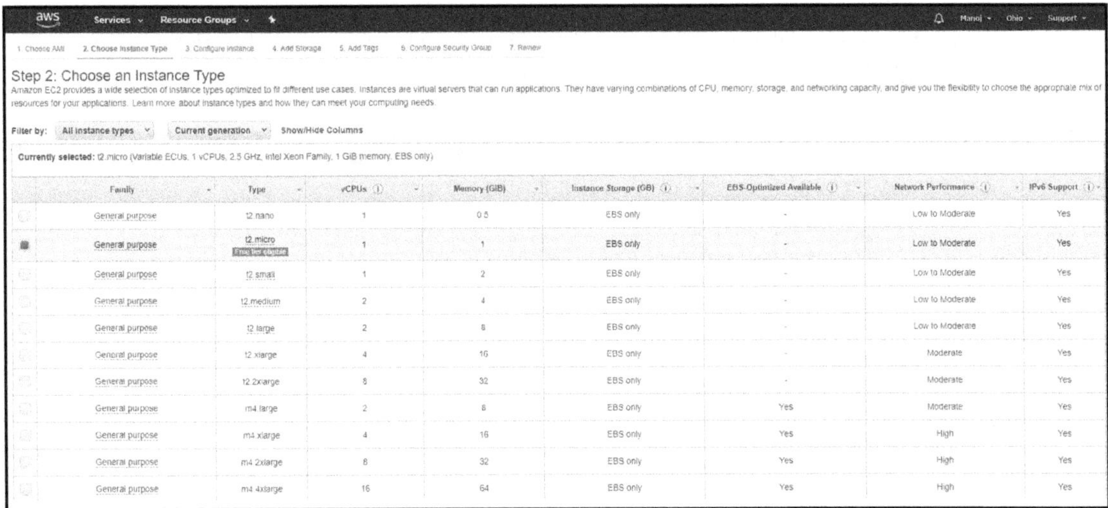

5. Specify the network and subnet to be used to launch the instance:

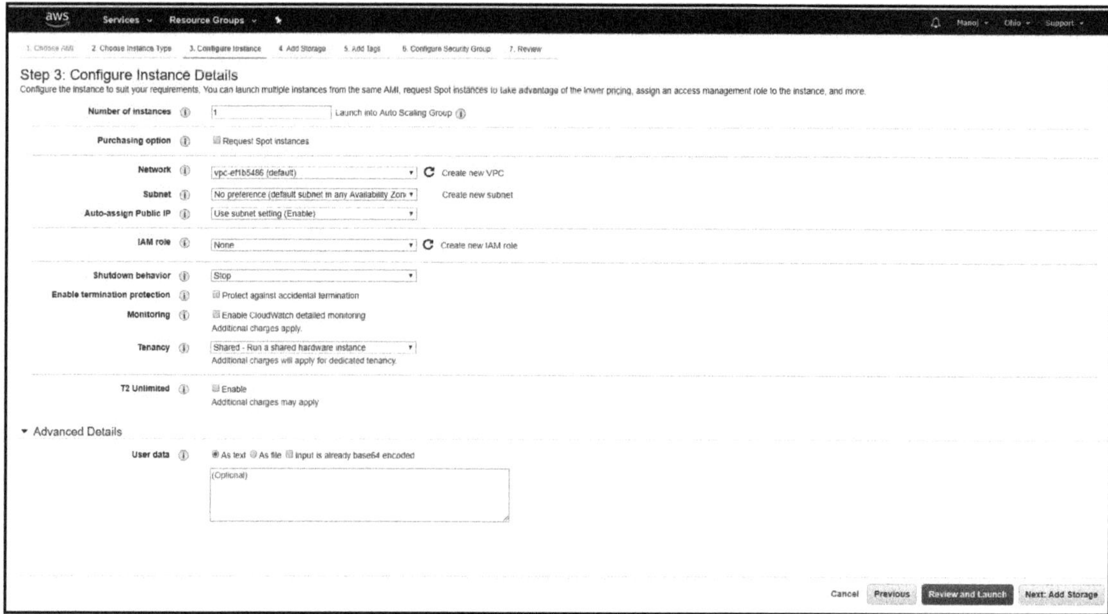

6. Specify the size of the storage volume that is to be added to the instance by default. One or more volumes can be added to the instance:

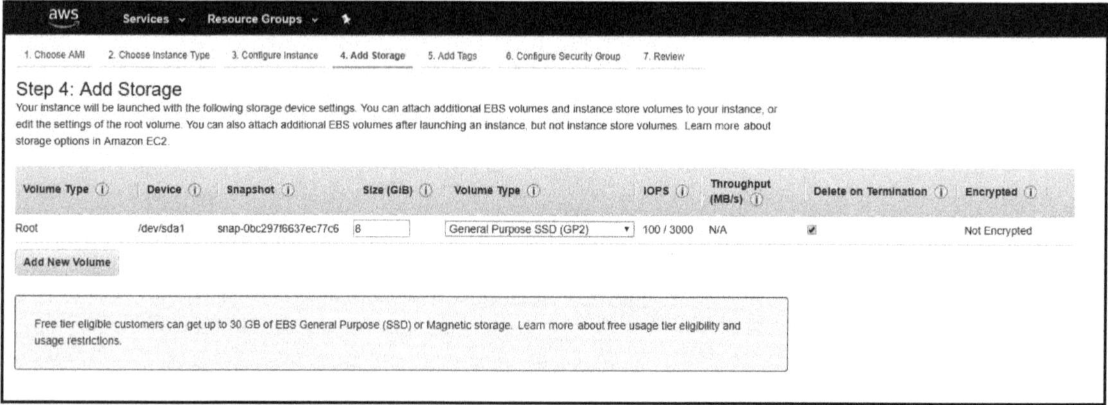

7. An instance can have metadata associated with it in the form of key value pairs. This metadata is added by using 'tags' to the instance. (this is optional):

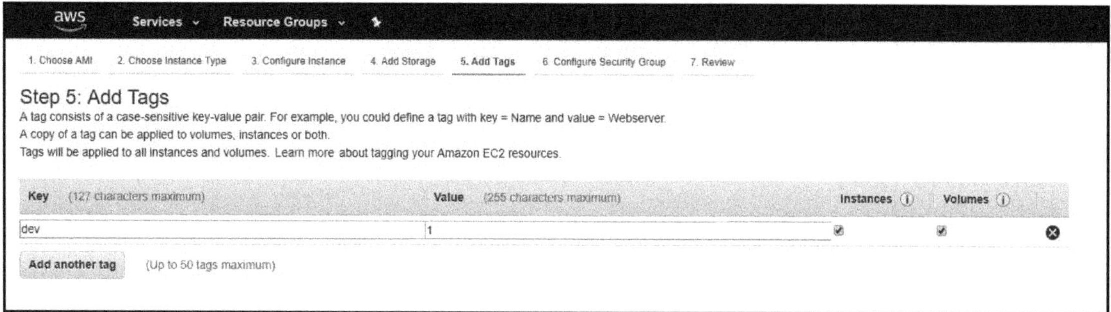

8. From the available security groups that are configured, select the security group to use and click on the **Review and Launch** button to launch the instance. You can also choose to add more rules to the security group:

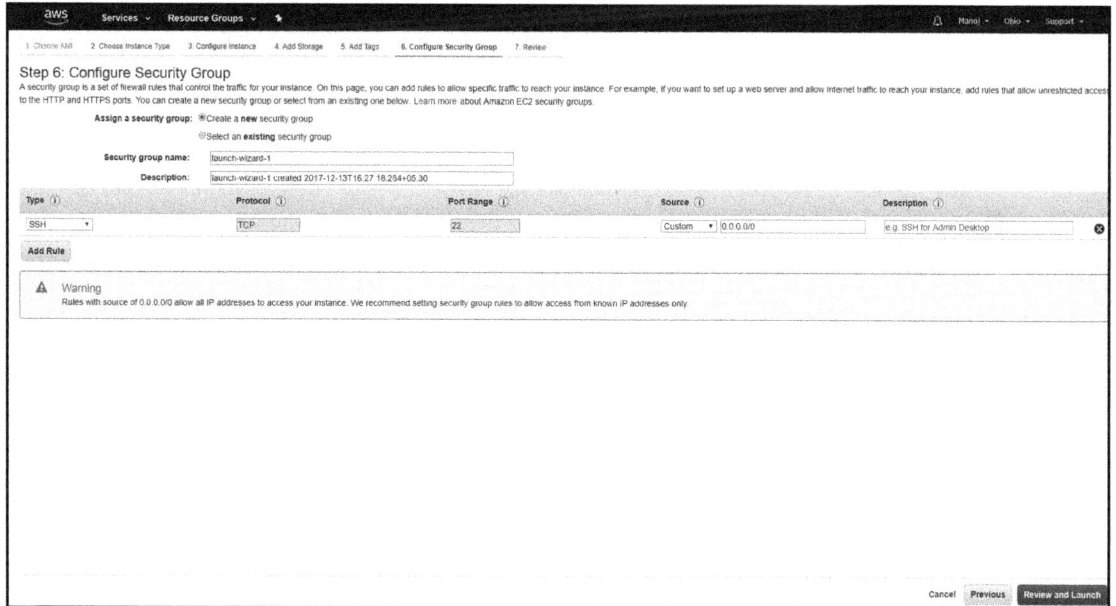

9. AWS will finally prompt for an SSH key pair to be used for accessing the instance. You can create a new key-pair or use an existing one:

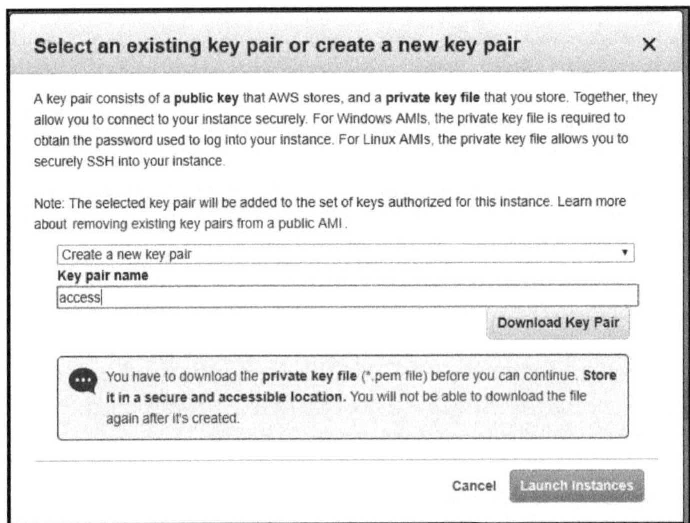

10. If everything goes well, a confirmation page is displayed indicating that the instance is now launching. You can see the status of the instance in the **Instances** page. The initial state of the instance will be shown as pending and will change to running once the instance has started running:

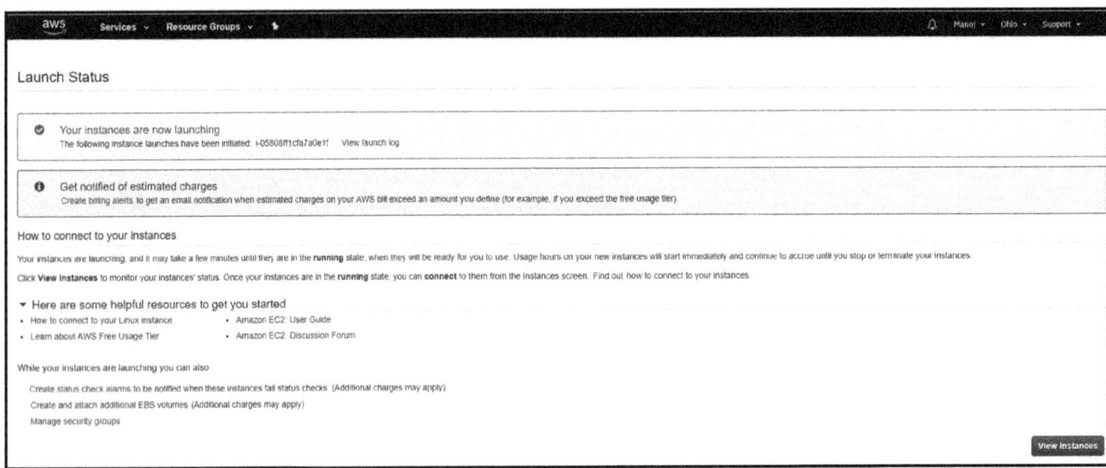

11. The instance gets a public DNS hostname and will be ready to connect to. If you click on **Connect**, you will get the DNS hostname to be used to connect to the VM:

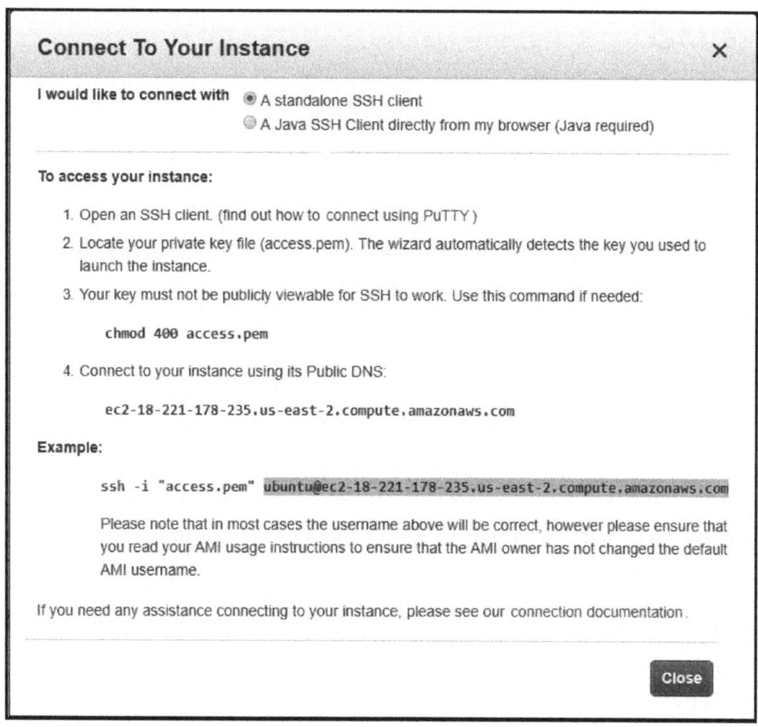

12. You can now use this hostname to connect using SSH (as this is a Linux VM):

```
[root@localhost /]# ssh -i aws.pem ubuntu@ec2-18-221-178-235.us-east-2.compute.amazonaws.com
Welcome to Ubuntu 16.04.3 LTS (GNU/Linux 4.4.0-1041-aws x86_64)

 * Documentation:  https://help.ubuntu.com
 * Management:     https://landscape.canonical.com
 * Support:        https://ubuntu.com/advantage

  Get cloud support with Ubuntu Advantage Cloud Guest:
    http://www.ubuntu.com/business/services/cloud

0 packages can be updated.
0 updates are security updates.


Last login: Wed Dec 13 11:04:36 2017 from 67.220.186.52
To run a command as administrator (user "root"), use "sudo <command>".
See "man sudo_root" for details.

ubuntu@ip-172-31-44-228:~$
```

Now that we have successfully created an EC2 instance, let's explore the storage services provided by AWS. We will now look at the block storage service called EBS.

Amazon EBS

EBS provides the ability to create storage volumes for block level access. These volumes can be created independently and attached to the EC2 instance. The EC2 instance can read and write data to this volume and stored persistently. In other words, the data stored on the EBS volume is not lost even after the instance is shut down.

In cases where the application needs to store persistent raw data for long term, EBS volume storage is best. Being block storage, the volumes are raw and unformatted. Any file system can be created on these volumes. They are also suitable for databases or other applications that require block level data accessibility. EBS works well for high throughput applications as well as ones that have random read/write operations.

AWS also provides encrypted volumes, which are very useful for storing sensitive data. The data and snapshots of these volumes are encrypted. When a first encrypted volume is created, the AWS **Key Management Service** (**KMS**) creates a default master key that can be used to access and create additional encrypted volumes. This also reduces the burden of maintaining your own key management infrastructure.

More than one EBS volume can be attached to a single EC2 instance, depending on the limits set for the AWS account. A single EBS volume cannot be attached to more than one EC2 instance at the same time.

Depending on the disk throughput required, AWS offers different types of storage that can be used for EBS volumes:

- EBS General Purpose SSD (gp2)
- Provisioned IOPS SSD (st1)
- Throughput Optimized HDD (sc1)
- Cold HDD (sc1)

The following table shows the performance statistics of these volume types. Users can choose the type of volume based on their needs:

Volume types	IOPS Rate	Throughput
General Purpose SSD	10,000	160 MB/s
Provisioned IOPS SSD	20,000	320 MB/s

Throughput Optimized HDD	-	500 MB/s
Cold HDD	-	250 MiB/s

Note that the performance of the Throughout Optimized HDD and Cloud HDD is measured in terms of throughput, rather than IOPS.

Creating an AWS EBS volume

The following steps must be followed to create an EBS volume:

1. In the web browser, go to the AWS console at: `https://console.aws.amazon.com/ec2/`.
2. Choose the **Volume** link under **ELASTIC BLOCK STORE** and click on the **Create Volume** button:

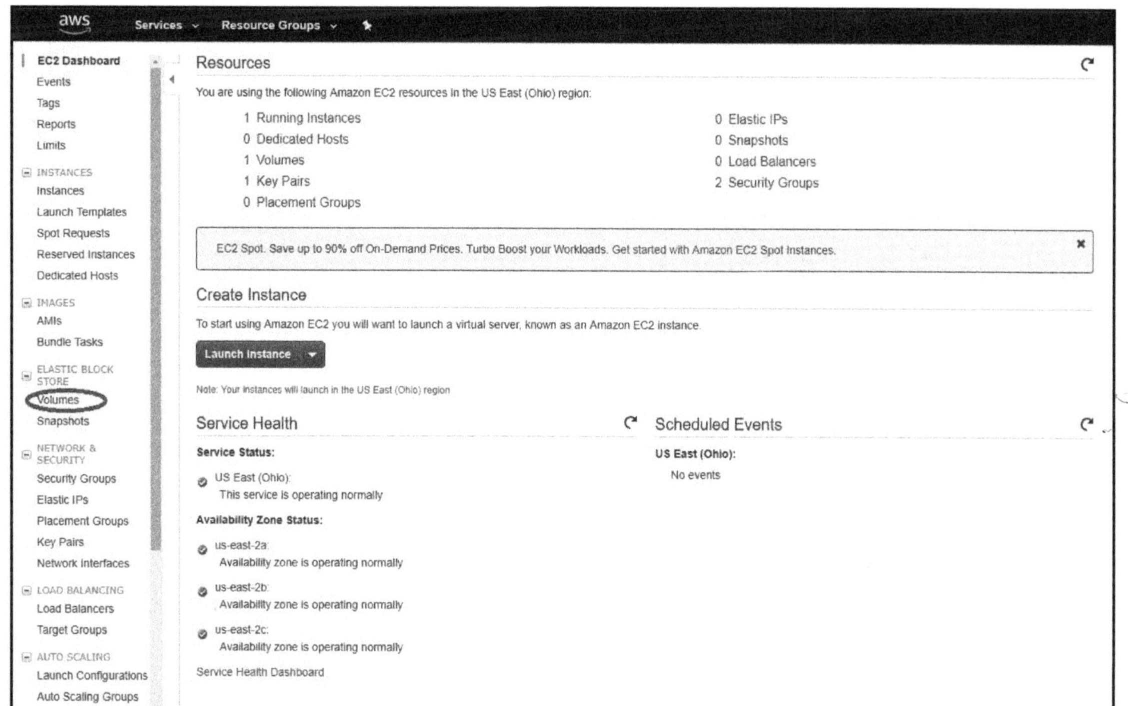

3. Choose the type of volume (GP2, IO1, SC1) and specify the size of the volume in GB. Also, select the availability zone in which you wish to create the volume:

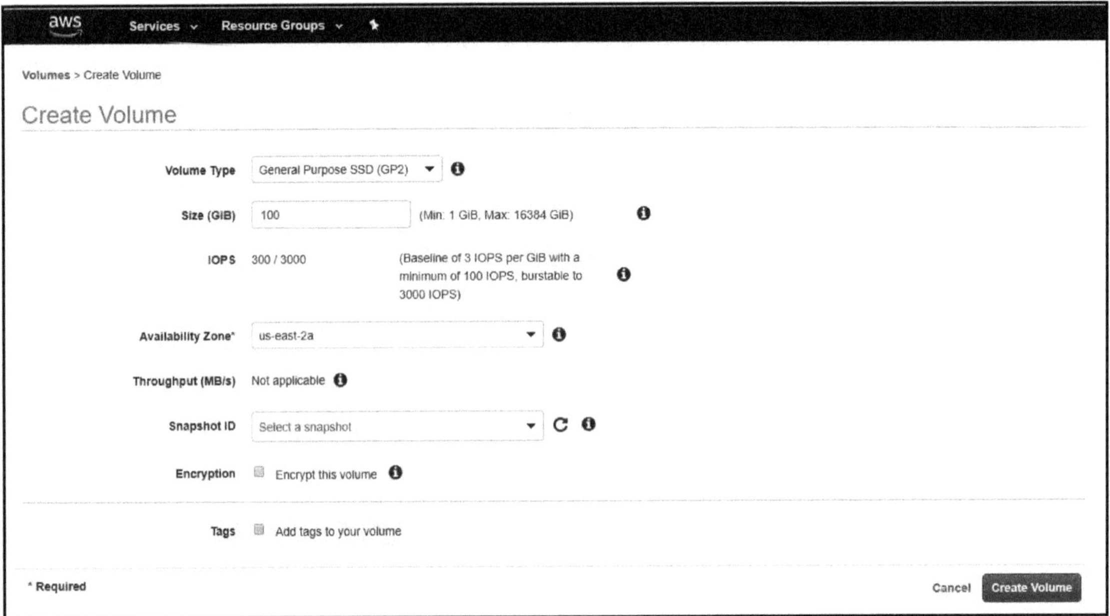

4. A volume will be created in a few seconds and a confirmation page will be displayed with the **Volume ID** of the newly created volume.

You can now use this volume and attach it to any running EC2 instance. Perform the following steps to attach a volume to a running instance:

1. Click on the **Actions** button in the volumes page.
2. Choose the instance in the drop-down menu to which you want to attach the volume.

3. Click on **Attach**:

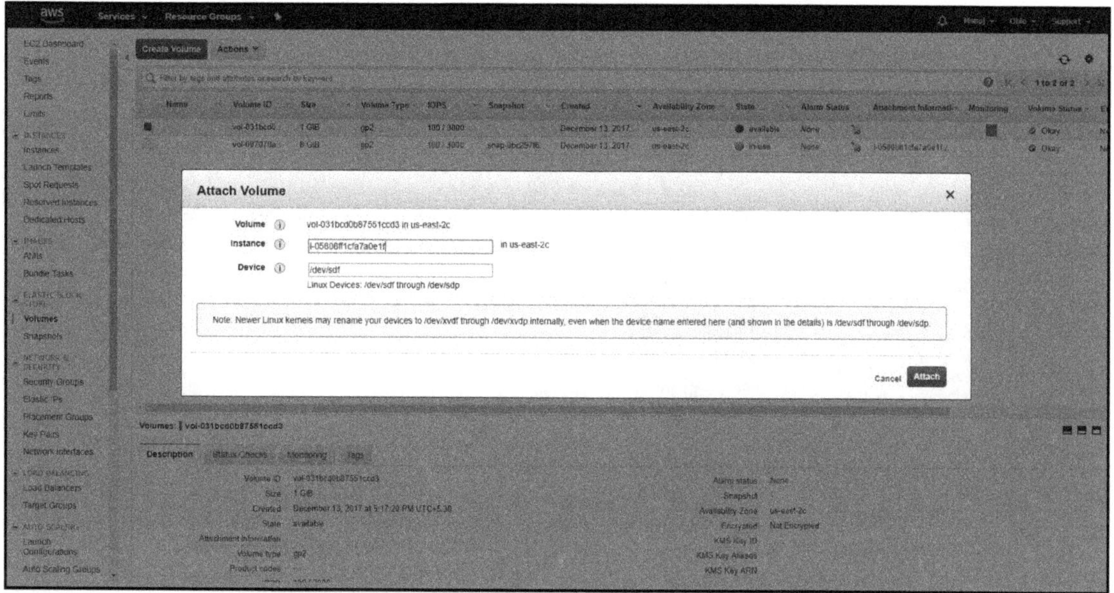

It should be noted that EBS volumes can only be attached to EC2 instances co-located in the same availability zone. For attaching volumes to an EC2 instance in a different availability zone, you must first create a snapshot of the volume and restore it to a new volume that resides in the other region or availability zone.

Snapshot of EBS volumes

To take a snapshot of a volume perform the following steps:

1. Click on the **Actions** button in the volumes page.
2. Choose the **Create Snapshot** option.
3. Specify the name to be given to the snapshot and description.

4. Click **Create** button. A snapshot creation will be initiated:

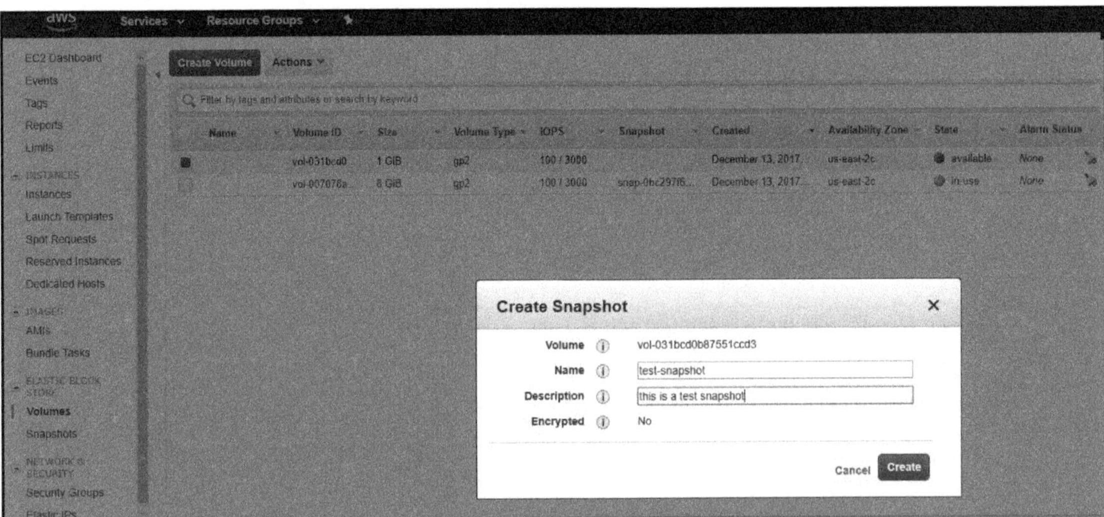

A snapshot will maintain a persistent point-in-time copy of the volume. The volume snapshot can also be used to create a new AMI.

Now that we have learned about EC2 and EBS services, let's explore one more important AWS object storage service called S3.

Amazon S3

Amazon S3 provides an object storage infrastructure that can be used by either the EC2 instance or any other software entity on the web. Objects are the fundamental storage units that can be stored in Amazon S3. All objects are stored under a logical container called a bucket. AWS allocates each bucket an internet domain name. Each object stored in the S3 bucket is also allocated a unique key value. These objects can then be retrieved using an HTTP URL address. For example, if a document is stored in the S3 bucket named `mys3bucket` and it has the key-value `/documents/resume.doc`, then users can access this document using the URL `http://mys3bucket.s3.amazonaws.com/documents/mydocument.doc`

S3 storage provides high availability as it stores redundant copies of the data at multiple locations. Thus, if any of the instances fail, users can quickly and reliably recover their data from the other copy. It also allows concurrent read/write access to this data from multiple clients or threads, thus providing performance. S3 can be used to store all kinds of files such as audio, video, and spreadsheets. EC2 instances use S3 storage to store AMIs. EBS volume snapshots are also stored in S3 storage.

S3 bucket properties

An S3 bucket has some properties that define the behavior of the bucket. Following is a description of each of these properties:

- **Versioning**: Versioning allows users to maintain multiple versions of an object in their S3 bucket. By default, this property is disabled for every new bucket that is created.
- **Server access logging**: As the name implies, when this property is enabled, AWS keeps track of detailed records about access to the bucket. By default, this property is disabled and no logs are collected.
- **Object-level logging**: Object-level logging collects information about the object-level API activity by using CloudTrail data events.
- **Tags**: Users can use tags allocated to S3 buckets to annotate billing for their use of a bucket. As discussed previously, a tag is simply a key value pair that represents a label that you assign to a bucket.
- **Default encryption**: As the name implies, this property enables encryption on the S3 bucket and all data written to the S3 bucket is encrypted.

Creating an S3 bucket using the AWS console

You can create a new S3 bucket using the console as follows:

1. Open the web browser and go to `https://s3.console.aws.amazon.com/s3`.
2. Click on the **Create bucket** button.
3. Specify the name of the bucket and the region where you want to create the bucket.

4. Select the properties you want to associate with the bucket (as described in the previous section):

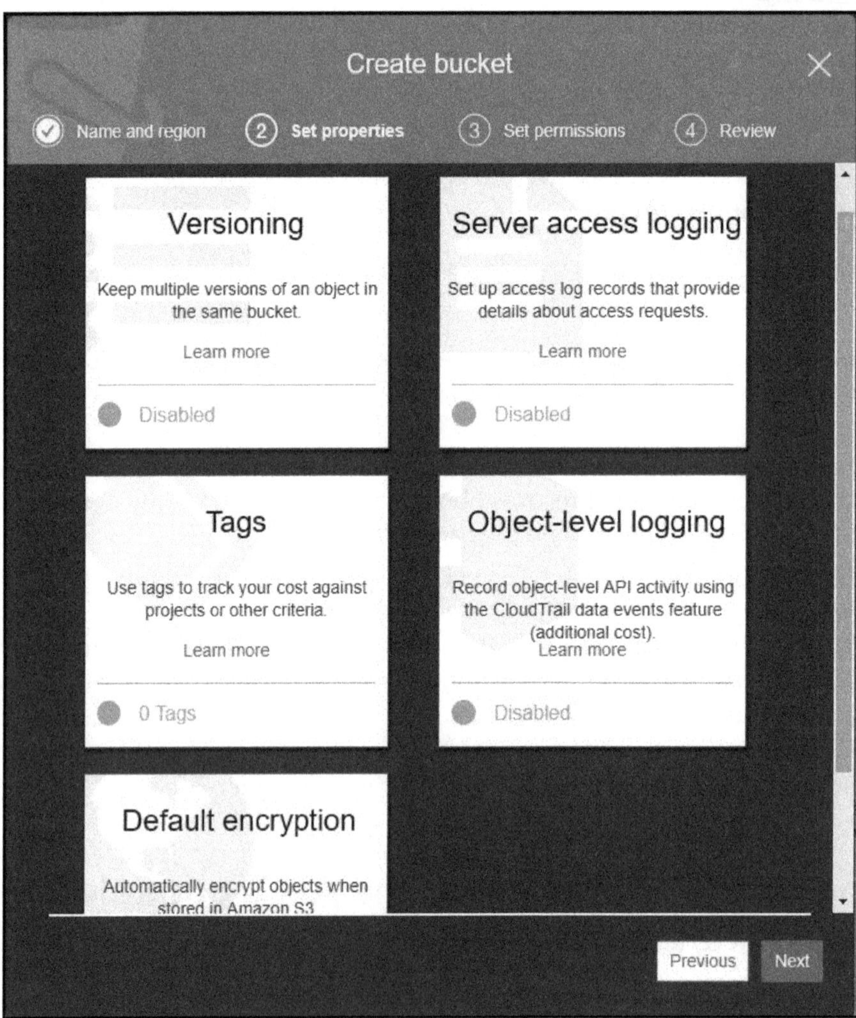

5. Set the permissions for the appropriate users:

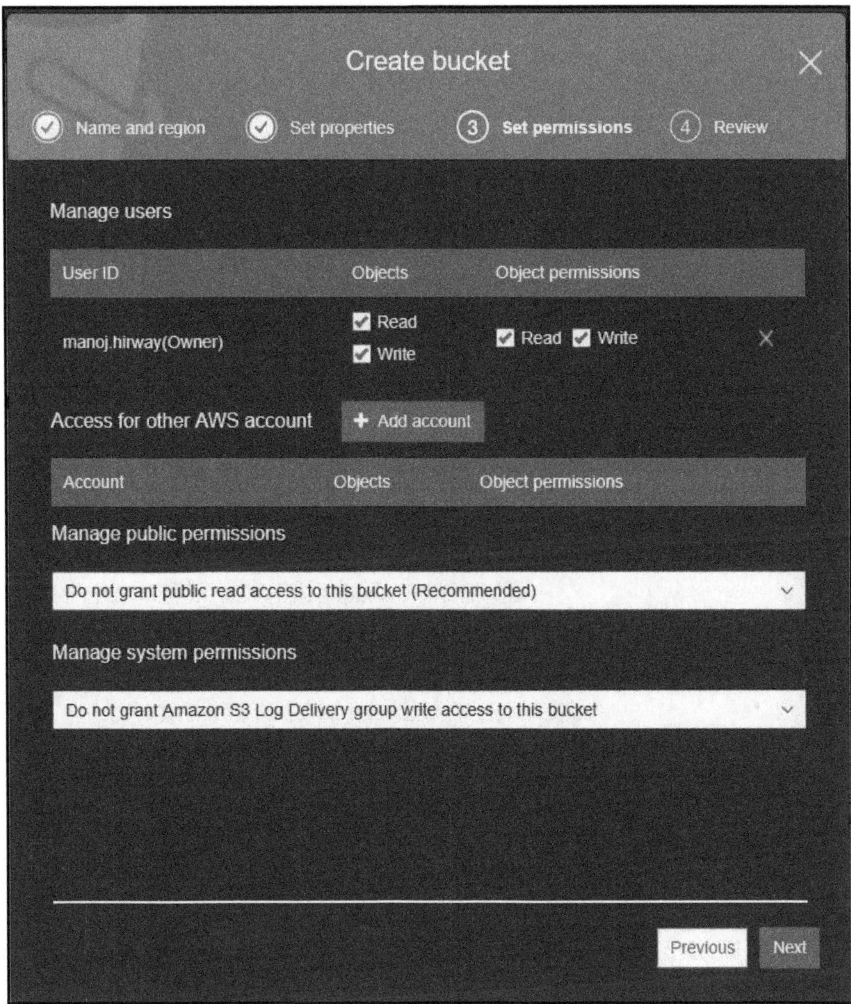

6. Confirm the settings and click on the **Create bucket** button:

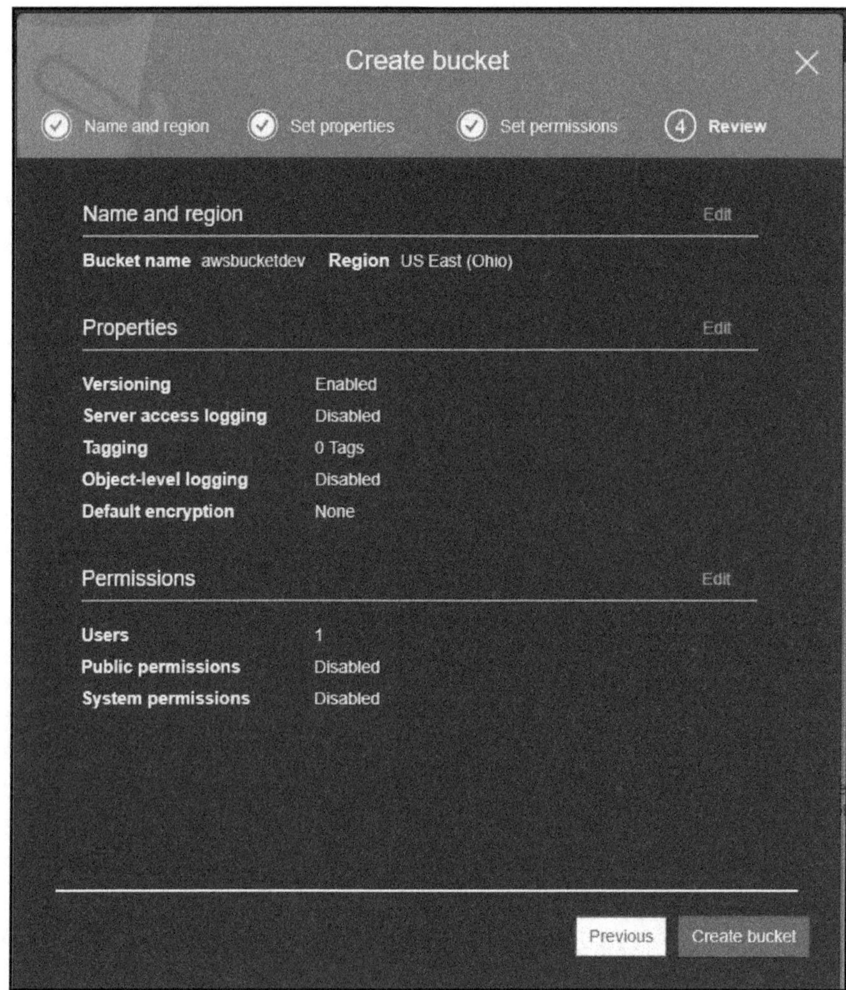

An S3 bucket will be created in a few seconds.

Uploading/downloading files to and from an S3 bucket

Files can be copied to and from an S3 bucket using the following four methods.

Using the AWS command-line interface

AWS provides a CLI for manipulating files on the S3 bucket. A simple command to copy from a S3 bucket to a local directory is as follows:

```
[ec2-user ~] # aws s3 cp s3://<bucketname>/<path to file>/<filename>
myfile.txt
```

The AWS `cp` command is very similar to the Linux `cp` command, which requires the source and destination paths of the file to be copied.

Similarly, you can use the following command to copy a file back from a local directory to the S3 bucket:

```
[ec2-user ~] # aws s3 cp  myfile.txt  s3://<bucketname>/<path to
file>/myfile.txt
```

You can also use the `sync` command to continuously sync the contents of the local directory and S3 bucket:

```
[ec2-user ~] # aws s3 sync s3://<bucket>/<path>   <local directory>
```

Using HTTP GET method or wget

You can simply download the files from the S3 bucket using the `wget` command, specifying the URL to the path of the file.

Following is an example:

```
[ec2-user] # wget https://mys3bucket.s3.amazonaws/document/resume.doc
```

Using AWS S3 API

AWS provides SDK and REST API for all kinds of operations for developers. We will discuss the S3 API in detail in `Chapter 4`, *Developing AWS Cloud Applications*.

Using the AWS console

Follow these steps for uploading a file to an S3 bucket using the AWS web console:

1. Click on the bucket that you have created.
2. Choose **Upload** and select the file that you want to upload:

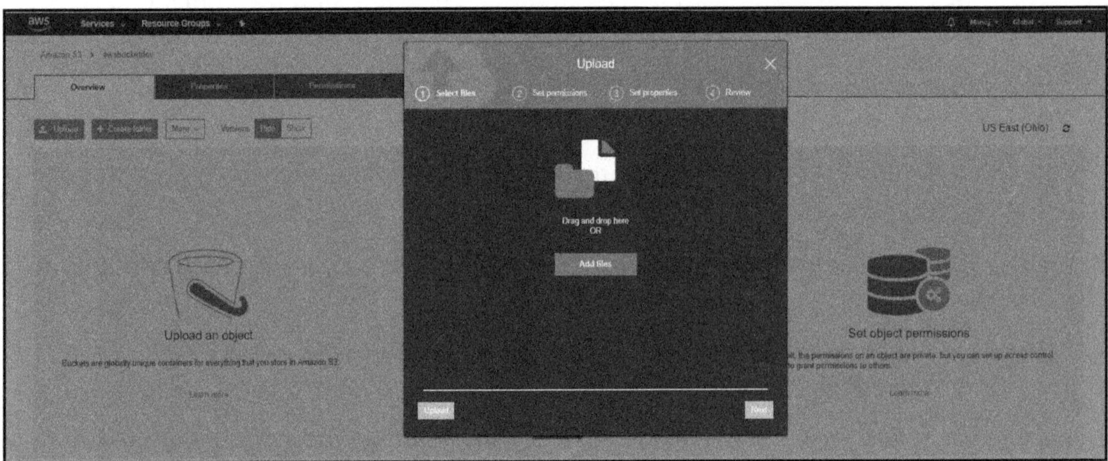

3. You can simply drag and drop any files from the local system or select the path and upload the file.

Thus, S3 storage provides a flexible way to store files in the AWS public cloud and also offers reliability and high availability.

Amazon VPC

AWS provides the ability to create a virtually isolated network and launch an EC2 instance within this isolated network. Such a virtual network is called a VPC or Virtual Private Cloud. The AWS VPC resembles a traditional network that is created in the data center but provides the benefits of the AWS cloud, such as scalability, elasticity, and so on.

A new VPC can be created by specifying the IP address range, creating subnets, and configuring network properties and firewall rules.

AWS supports two VPC platforms into which you can launch your EC2 instances:

- EC2-Classic
- EC2-VPC

When a new EC2 instance is launched, you can either choose a specific VPC or let the instance launch in a default VPC. The default VPC is a combination of both the platforms. It provides the advantages of the EC2-VPC platform as well as the ease of use of the EC2-Classic platform.

An EC2 instance launched on the default subnet in the VPC is assigned a private IP address and a public IP address. The default VPC has an internet gateway that connects the EC2 instances to the internet. The instances that are not launched in the default VPC are not assigned a public IP address, but only a private IP address. Therefore, these instances can communicate with each other, but cannot access any outside resources such as S3 storage. For enabling access to the external resources, a public IP address, also called an elastic IP address, must be explicitly assigned to the instances. An internet gateway should also be configured to allow access to the external network.

A **Network Address Translation** (**NAT**) instance can also be configured so that instances can communicate with the internet, but prevent any unsolicited inbound connections. The NAT instance maps the private IP address of the instances in the VPC with its own single public IP address. The NAT instance is connected to an internet gateway, which can thus send the packets to the external networks.

In a hybrid cloud configuration, the company's data center that hosts the private cloud is connected to the VPC using an IPSec VPN connection. In other words, the data center is extended to the public cloud.

A VPN connection consists of the **Virtual Private Gateway** (**VPG**) that is attached to the VPC. There is also a customer gateway that is attached to the data center side of the VPN connection. A virtual private gateway is a VPN concentrator on the AWS side of the connection. A customer gateway is either a software or hardware device on the consumer side of the VPN connection.

Creating an AWS VPC

Let's create a VPC:

1. Open `https://console.aws.amazon.com/vpc`.
2. Select **Start VPC Wizard**. This will start a simplified wizard to create a VPC:

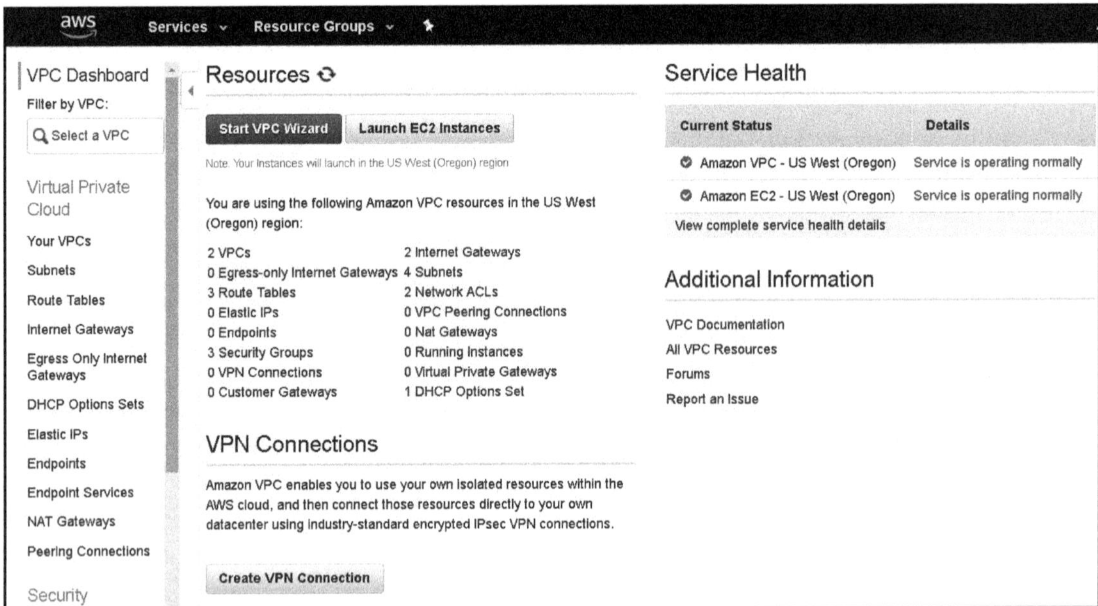

3. Specify the IP address range of the subnet. Provide a name to the VPC and also choose the AWS availability zone into which you want to create this VPC. You may also choose to have dedicated hardware for this VPC by choosing the dedicated option in the **Hardware** field:

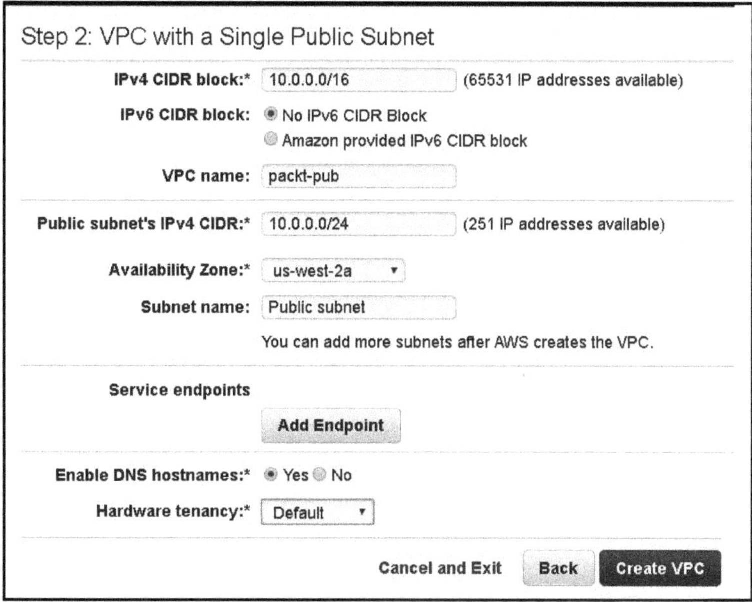

4. Finally, click the **Create VPC** button and the VPC will be created. You should be able to see it in the list of VPCs:

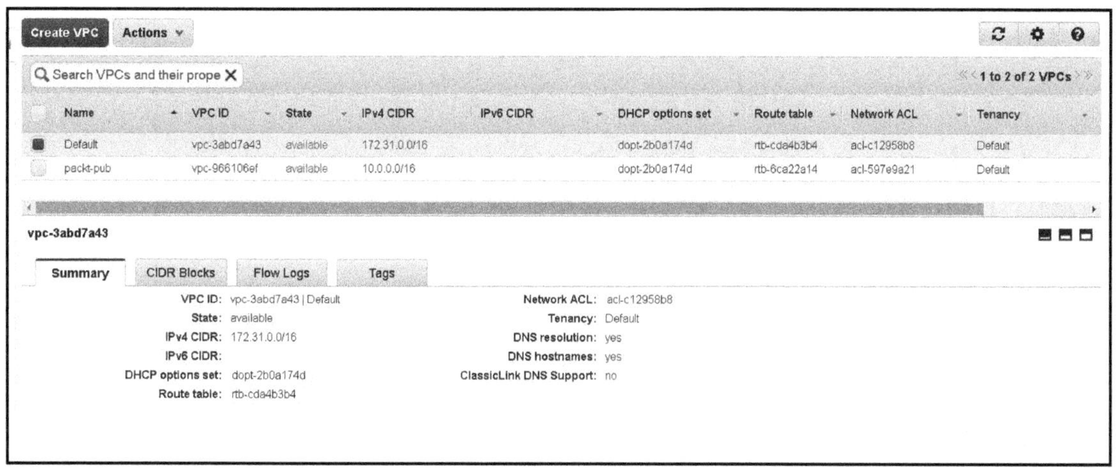

Hereafter, when you launch a new EC2 instance, you can choose to select this VPC so that the instance will be launched inside this VPC and it will get the IP address from the subnet of this VPC.

VPC configurations

Let's see a few scenarios in which VPC can be configured based on the requirements of the organization.

Scenario 1 – VPC with public subnet only

This is the simplest of the setups, where a VPC is created with a single public subnet along with an internet gateway that is configured to allow communication to the external networks or the internet. This scenario is ideal for simple applications such as a public facing website or a blog hosted on a standalone instance.

The following diagram illustrates this configuration:

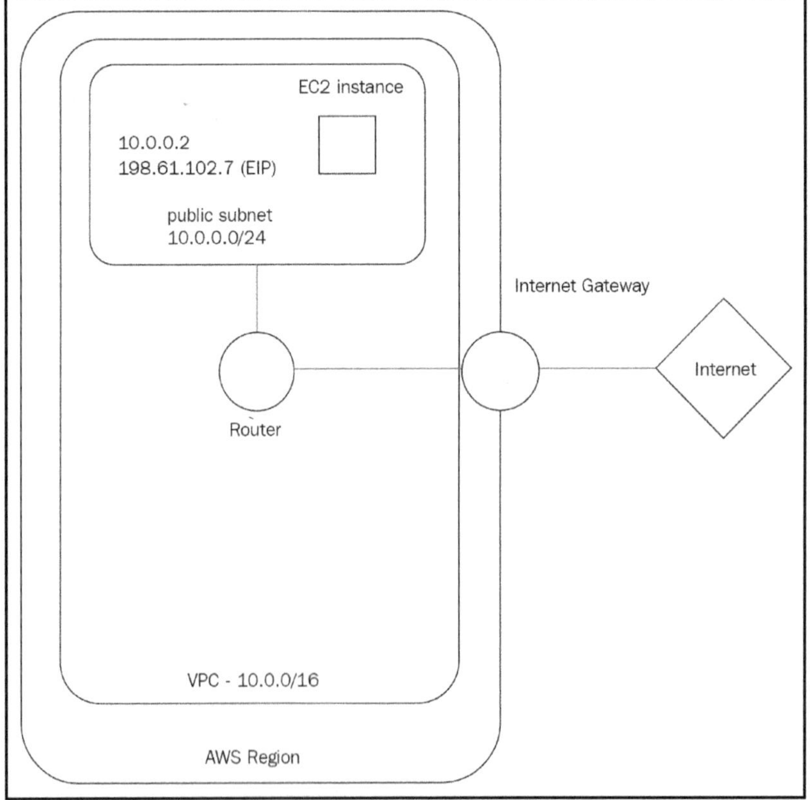

The previous setup provides a VPC with 65,536 usable private IP addresses (CIDR: **10.0.0.0/16**) along with a subnet that provides 256 usable IP addresses (**10.0.0.0/24**). An internet gateway is also attached to the VPC, which connects the instances of the VPC to the external networks, that is, the internet or other AWS products such as S3 storage and so on. The instance running the VPC is provided with a private IP address in the subnet range, that is, **10.0.0.2**, which enables the instance to communicate with other instances in the VPC. An Elastic IP address is also assigned to the instance so that it is accessible from the external networks or the internet.

A routing table should be configured to allow the instances within the VPC to be able to communicate with each other and also the external networks, that is, the internet. As discussed in the previous section, this scenario can also be configured with a NAT instance.

Scenario 2 – VPC with public and private subnet

This scenario has both a public and private subnet within the VPC. The private subnet has instances that are not made accessible to the external networks. Such a model is best suited for multi-tier applications, where the application frontend is deployed on the public subnet and the backend is deployed in the private subnet. For example, an online shopping website may use this model where it has its public-facing shopping website hosted on an instance that resides in the public subnet and the database is hosted on the instance that resides in the private subnet. The routing tables and security group rules are configured in such a way that the instances in the public subnet can communicate with the instances in the private subnet, but the private subnet is not accessible by the external networks.

A NAT instance can also be set up in the public subnet, which will allow the instances in the private subnet to access the internet using an internet gateway.

The following diagram illustrates this configuration:

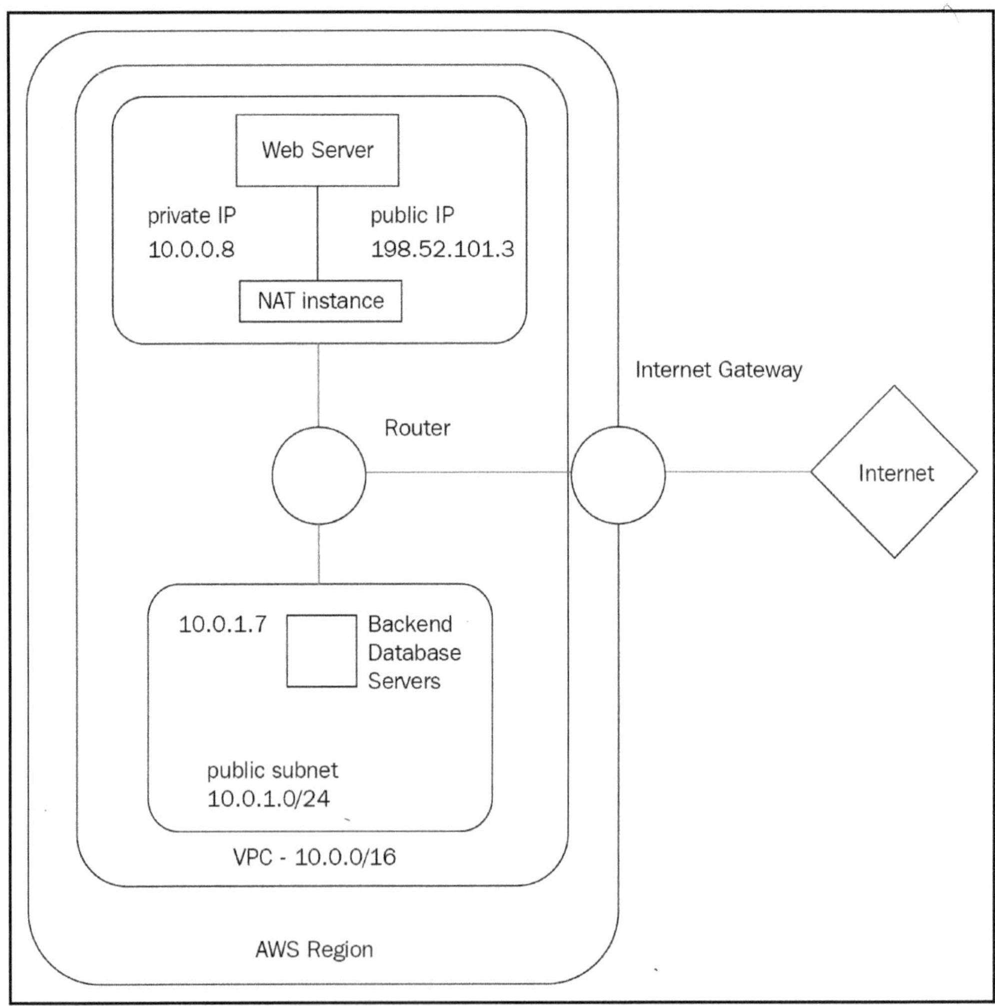

Such a scenario provides a **Virtual Private Cloud** (**VPC**) with 65,536 usable IP addresses (CIDR **10.0.0.0/ 16**) along with a public and a private subnet, each having 256 usable IP addresses, (CIDR of **10.0.0.0/ 24** for public and **10.0.1.0/24** for private subnet). An internet gateway is also connected to the VPC that allows the instances to connect to the internet and to other AWS resources, such as S3 and so on.

EC2 instances that are launched in the private subnet are assigned private IP addresses in the subnet as per the range defined (examples: **10.0.0.8**, and **10.0.1.7**). The private IP addresses only allow the instance to communicate with other instances in the VPC. In the example shown previously, the database servers are assigned private IP addresses as they do not need to accept any incoming connections directly from the internet.

A NAT instance is configured so that the instances in the private subnet are able to send requests to the external networks.

The instances that are launched on the public subnet are assigned elastic IP addresses. This enables the instances to be reachable from the external network and internet.

Routing tables are also configured for both private and public subnets to allow the instances to communicate with other instances within the VPC, and also to the internet via the internet gateway.

Scenario 3 – VPC with public and private subnet and VPN connectivity

This scenario is similar to the earlier model where there is a public and private subnet within the VPC. The only difference is that this includes a virtual private gateway that allows us to establish a VPN connection from the company's data center to the VPC. This model is suited for hybrid cloud configuration where the company's data center also hosts a private cloud.

This scenario is suitable for applications that require being scaled to the public cloud to handle the increased workload. For example, a web application can have its frontend on the public subnet in the cloud and the backend database servers in the private subnet, which is the connection to the local data center using VPN.

The following diagram illustrates this configuration:

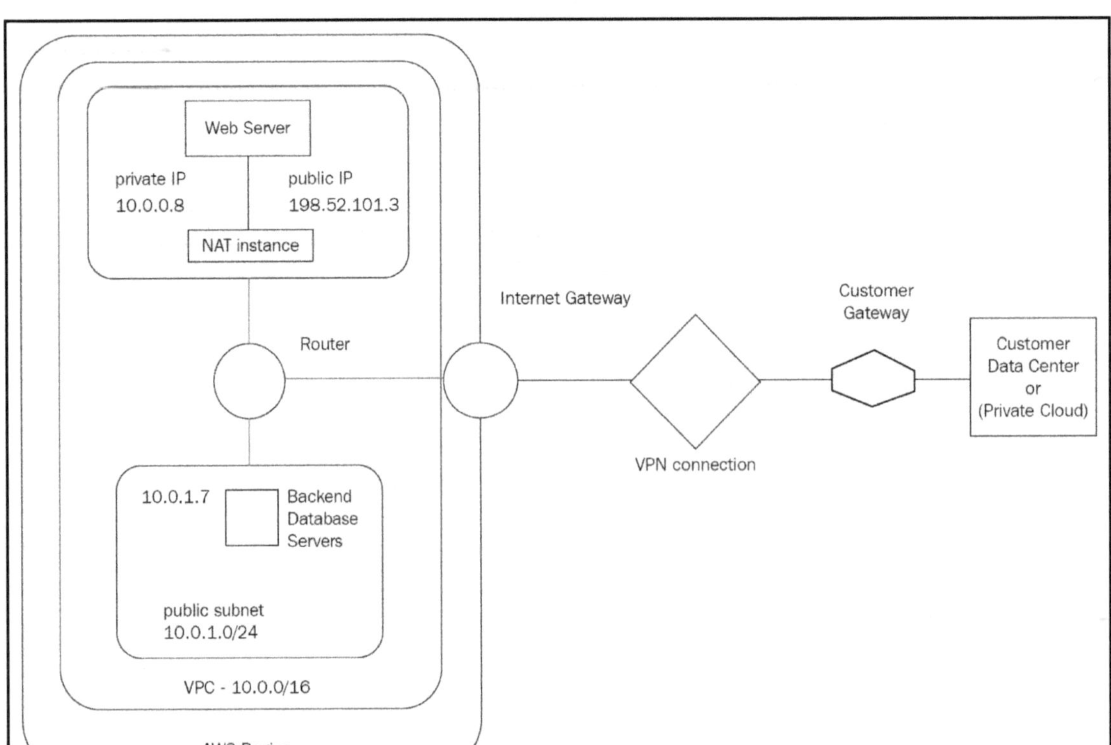

The configuration shown in the diagram has a VPC along with a public and VPN-only private subnet, each providing 256 usable IP addresses. It also has an internet gateway configured for allowing the instances in the VPC to access the internet. A VPN connection is established using the virtual private gateway, which is located on the AWS side, and a customer gateway that is located on the customer's side of the VPN connection. The instances in the private subnet are able to communicate with each other, whereas the instance in the public subnet can be accessed from the internet.

The routing table must be configured to allow the instances within the VPC to communicate with each other and also to the internet. It must also be configured such that the instances in the VPN-only private subnet should be able to communicate with the company's network via VPN.

Scenario 4 – VPC with private subnet only and VPN connectivity

This scenario is similar to the previous model, with the only difference being that there is only a private subnet in the VPC and there is no internet gateway. The public subnet is not present. The virtual private gateway connects this private subnet to the company's data center using VPN. Due to the absence of the internet gateway, the private subnet has no access to the internet.

In other words, this model is just used to extend the company's data center to the public cloud, without exposing the network to the internet. Such a model is also well suited for a hybrid cloud configuration.

The following diagram depicts this configuration:

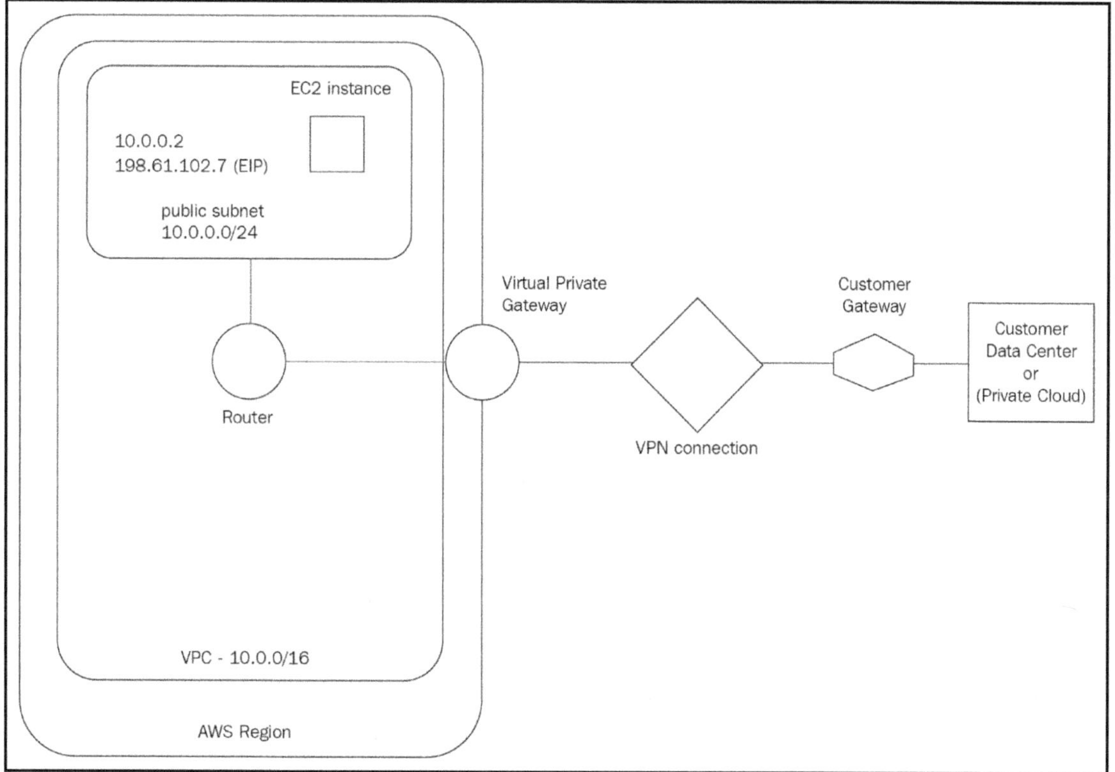

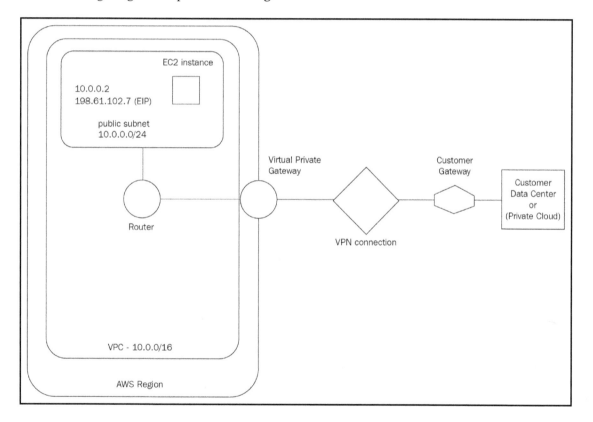

In the preceding diagram, the VPC provides 65,536 usable IP addresses along with a VPN-only subnet that provides 256 private IP addresses. The Virtual Private Gateway is configured that connects the VPC to the company's data center using the customer gateway. The instances in the VPC are assigned private IP addresses that allow them to communicate with other instances in the same VPC. A routing table is configured to allow the instances to communicate directly with the company's data center.

VPC peering

VPC peering, as the name implies, is connecting two or more VPCs to allow network traffic from one VPC to another using the private IP addresses that are assigned to the instances. The instance launched in a peered VPC can communicate with any other instance in other VPCs just as they would if they existed on the same network.

A VPC can be peered with other VPCs created by some other AWS account. However, the VPCs to be peered should be co-located in the same region. VPC peering doesn't require additional hardware. AWS uses its existing resources to peer between VPCs:

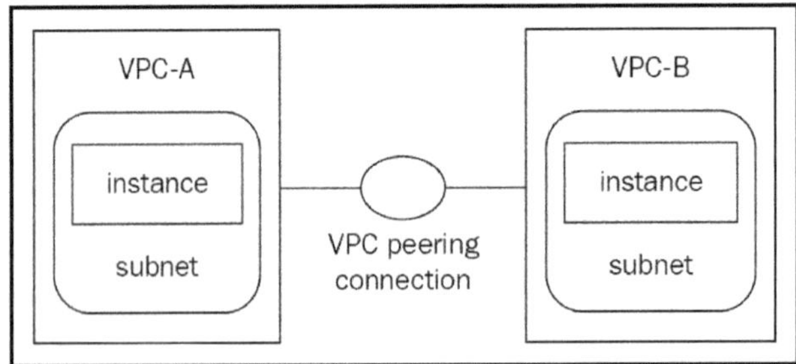

Summary

In this chapter, we introduced you to the basics of the AWS public cloud. We created an AWS account and discussed the various features of AWS. We also launched an EC2 instance, and created an EBS volume and an S3 bucket. We discussed different methods to upload and download files to and from the S3 bucket. Finally, we explored the virtual private cloud along with different scenarios in which it can be implemented.

In the next chapter, we will explore an open source private cloud platform called OpenStack.

3 Exploring OpenStack Private Cloud

In the previous chapter, we discussed the AWS Cloud and saw how organizations can leverage various features provided by Amazon such as EC2, S3, and EBS for their business needs. Amazon bills its users based on the usage of the services and as the usage increases, the costs also rise significantly. Since organizational data has to reside in the public cloud, it is prone to attacks and susceptible to security violations. It is for this reason that some organizations prefer hosting an internal private cloud within their own private data center. In this chapter, we will explore the popular open source cloud platform called OpenStack.

The following topics are covered in this chapter:

- OpenStack architecture
- Installing OpenStack
- OpenStack services - Nova, Neutron, Glance, Cinder, Keystone, Horizon, and Heat
- Launching a new virtual machine

Introducing OpenStack

OpenStack is a combination of various open source technologies glued together to create a platform that provides various cloud services. These services mainly include compute, networking, storage, imaging, identity, and user interface. It is deployed as an **Infrastructure as a Service** (**IaaS**) cloud and can be managed using either the web console, command line, or REST APIs. Users can create resources such as instances, volumes, virtual routers and switches, firewalls, load balancers, and so on using open source technologies and thus form a stack of resources, hence the name OpenStack.

The OpenStack project began in 2010 and was mainly developed by NASA and Rackspace. Later, it became an open source project and was owned by the OpenStack Foundation. The OpenStack community now includes a large number of companies, each of which contributes to the project in several different ways. The community now follows a time-based, six-monthly release cycle, based on the requirements discussed in the OpenStack summit that takes place periodically.

The following are the five recent releases of OpenStack:

Release code name	Year	Components included in the release
Liberty	October 2015	Nova, Glance, Swift, Horizon, Keystone, Neutron, Cinder, Heat, Ceilometer, Trove, Sahara, Ironic, Zaqar, Manila, Designate, Barbican, and Searchlight
Mitaka	April 2016	Nova, Glance, Swift, Horizon, Keystone, Neutron, Cinder, Heat, Ceilometer, Trove, Sahara, Ironic, Zaqar, Manila, Designate, Barbican, Searchlight, and Magnum
Newton	October 2016	Nova, Glance, Swift, Horizon, Keystone, Neutron, Cinder, Heat, Ceilometer, Trove, Sahara, Ironic, Zaqar, Manila, Designate, Barbican, Searchlight, and Magnum
Ocata	February 2017	Nova, Glance, Swift, Horizon, Keystone, Neutron, Cinder, Heat, Ceilometer, Trove, Sahara, Ironic, Zaqar, Manila, Designate, Barbican, Searchlight, and Magnum
Pike	August 2017	Nova, Glance, Swift, Horizon, Keystone, Neutron, Cinder, Heat, Ceilometer, Trove, Sahara, Ironic, Zaqar, Manila, Designate, Barbican, Searchlight, and Magnum

OpenStack architecture

The OpenStack cloud platform is a combination of various technologies interlinked together to provide cloud services. The following diagram shows the most significant components of OpenStack:

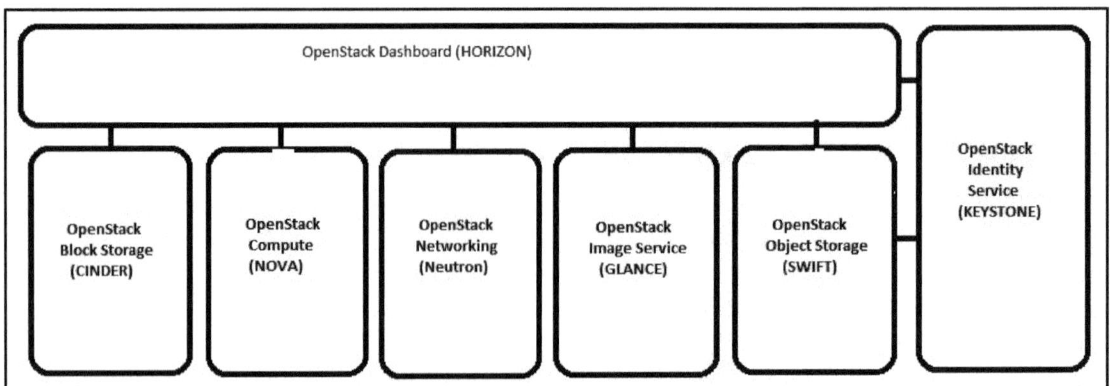

OpenStack components

The services that provide block storage, compute, networking, image, object store, and identity management are the core components of OpenStack. There are several other services provided by the OpenStack version that was released in August 2017. This release is called Pike.

The following table provides a brief description of each of the services provided by the OpenStack Pike release:

Service	Codename	Description
Compute Service	Nova	Provides a hypervisor for running virtual machines
Networking Service	Neutron	Provides networking and connectivity between various OpenStack services and virtual machines
Image Service	Glance	Provides storage for virtual machine images and snapshots
Block Storage Service	Cinder	Provides persistent block storage volumes that can be attached to virtual machines
Object Storage Service	Swift	Provides storage for files and arbitrary data
Identity Service	Keystone	Provides identity management for users, projects, and roles by performing authentication and authorization
Dashboard Service	Horizon	Provides a web-based graphical user interface for manipulating OpenStack services
Orchestration Service	Heat	Provides automation and template-based orchestration services for creating OpenStack resources
Bare Metal Provisioning Service	Ironic	Provides bare metal provisioning of various hardware vendors
Database Service	Trove	Provides relational and non-relational database services
Data Processing Service	Sahara	Provides Hadoop clusters on OpenStack for data processing

Messaging Service	Zaqar	Provides a multi-tenant cloud messaging service for web and mobile developers
Shared File System Service	Manila	Provides a shared filesystem
DNS service	Designate	Provides DNS as a service
Key Management service	Barbican	Provides secure storage, provisioning, and management of data
Search and Indexing service	Searchlight	Provides scalable indexing and searching across clouds
Container Orchestration service	Magnum	Provides container orchestration on OpenStack
Alarm service	aodh	Provides an alarming service based on events
Billing service	Cloudkitty	Provides a billing and rating service based on usage
Policy service	congress	Provides policy as a service to offer governance and compliance for dynamic infrastructures
Backup and Restore service	freezer	Provides backup and recovery as a service
Workflow service	mistral	Provides a workflow service for interconnected components
Monitoring service	monasca-api	Provides monitoring as a service
Log monitoring service	monasca-log-api	Provides monitoring of the logs
Catalog service	murano	Provides a catalog service for applications
Event storage service	panko	Provides event storage for events generated by Ceilometer
Clustering service	senlin	Provides clustering of homogenous objects.
NFV orchestration service	tacker	Provides NFV Orchestration with a VNF Manager to deploy and operate Virtual Network Functions (VNFs) and Network Services on an NFV Platform
Analysis service	vitrage	Provides a root-cause-analysis service by analyzing events and alarms

Optimization service.	watcher	Provides optimization of OpenStack resources

We can classify these components in the following categories:

Computing Services	• Nova • Glance • Ironic • Magnum • Storlets • Zun
Storage, Backup, and Recovery	• Swift • Cinder • Manila • Karbor • Freezer
Networking and Content Delivery	• Neutron • Designate • Dragonflow • Kuryr • Octavia • Tacker • Tricircle
Data Analytics	• Trove • Sahara • Searchlight
Security, Identity, and Compliance	• Keystone • Barbican • Congress • Mistral
Management Tools	• Horizon • OpenStack Client (CLI) • Rally • Senlin • Vitrage • Watcher
Deployment Tools	• Chef OpenStack • Kolla • OpenStack Charms • OpenStack Ansible • Puppet OpenStack • Tripleo
Application Services	• Heat • Zaqar • Murano • Solum
Monitoring and Metering	• Celiometer • Cloudkitty • Monasca • Aodh • Panko

Now that we have a brief understanding of the various components of OpenStack, let's get some practical experience by installing OpenStack on your computer. You will need an Ubuntu Linux 16.04 virtual machine and an internet connection to get started.

Installing OpenStack

OpenStack can be installed in a distributed environment with each component installed on a separate host. This setup is suitable for production environments. However, for application development environments, the OpenStack community provides a smaller and lighter version of OpenStack that can be quickly installed. This small version of OpenStack is called DevStack. Developers have access to all components of OpenStack and can easily make code changes or develop OpenStack applications on the DevStack environment.

An explanation of a multi-node installation of OpenStack is beyond the scope of this book. We will install DevStack on a Ubuntu 16.04 virtual machine running on the VirtualBox platform.

The following steps must be followed to install DevStack:

1. Download the Ubuntu 16.04 ISO from the Ubuntu website (`https://www.ubuntu.com/download/server`).
2. Deploy the ISO on a VirtualBox environment and provide a static IP to the virtual machine.
3. On the Ubuntu terminal, invoke `apt-get update` to update the repositories:

   ```
   root@packt-pub:/# apt-get update
   ```

4. Install git by running `apt-get install git`:

   ```
   root@packt-pub:/# apt-get install git
   ```

5. Create a user for DevStack installation; DevStack should not be installed as a root user:

   ```
   root@packt-pub:/# useradd -s /bin/bash -d /opt/stack -m stack

   root@packt-pub:/# su - stack
   ```

6. Clone the DevStack source code:
   `git clone https://git.openstack.org/openstack-dev/devstack`:

   ```
   stack@packt-pub:~$ git clone
   https://git.openstack.org/openstack-dev/devstack
   ```

7. Create a file named `local.conf` in the cloned `devstack` directory and add the following contents to it. You can set your own password in place of `mypassword`:

```
[[local|localrc]]
 ADMIN_PASSWORD=mypassword
 DATABASE_PASSWORD=$ADMIN_PASSWORD
 RABBIT_PASSWORD=$ADMIN_PASSWORD
 SERVICE_PASSWORD=$ADMIN_PASSWORD
```

8. Start the DevStack installation by invoking the `stack.sh` script in the `devstack` directory:

```
stack@packt-pub:~/devstack$ ./stack.sh
```

9. The installation will take several minutes depending on the speed of the internet connection. Once it is complete, you should see the following message on the console (the IP addresses will be different for your environment):

```
This is your host IP address: 10.0.2.81
This is your host IPv6 address: ::1
Horizon is now available at http://10.0.2.81/dashboard
Keystone is serving at http://10.0.2.81/identity/
The default users are: admin and demo
The password: mypassword
```

   DevStack creates two users by default: `admin` and `demo`. The password of these users is set to the same string as was mentioned in the `local.conf` file before starting the installation.

10. You can now open a web browser and type in the IP address of the VM where you installed DevStack.

    For example: `http://10.0.2.81`

You should see the OpenStack login screen. Specify the `admin` credentials and log in.

You should now be able to perform various administrative tasks on OpenStack such as creating a user, launching an instance, creating a volume, creating a network, and so on.

Now that you have an OpenStack instance running, let's get into a deeper understanding of the various components of OpenStack and see how they work with each other.

Each component in OpenStack is a combination of various small services. For example, the OpenStack Imaging Service (Glance) is a combination of glance-api, glance-registry, and a MariaDB database. Let's understand the most important services of OpenStack in greater detail by exploring the individual components that make up the service. We will begin by discussing the core service of OpenStack, Nova, which provides computing capabilities.

NOVA – OpenStack Compute Service

The OpenStack Compute Service (NOVA) is the core component of OpenStack. It provides the ability to run virtual machines on OpenStack nodes by providing drivers that interact with the underlying virtualization mechanism. The Nova service is capable of interacting with various hypervisors such as KVM, VMware, XEN Server, and so on. By default, the KVM hypervisor is used. The libvirt driver (`libvirtd`) is used to interact with the KVM hypervisor.

The NOVA service also interacts with the Identity Service (keystone) for authentication of instances and database access. It fetches the virtual machine images from the Imaging Service (glance) and also interfaces with the dashboard service (horizon) to provide administrative interface to the users.

The NOVA service is comprised of several components working together to provide the computing service. The following are the most important components of the computing service:

- **nova-api service:** The nova-api-service is used to accept and respond to API requests coming from the end users. It supports the OpenStack Compute API along with the Amazon EC2 API and Administrator APIs to perform administrative tasks. This service also implements policies and handles orchestration tasks such as running a virtual machine instance.
- **nova-api-metadata service**: This service is mainly used to accept metadata requests from instances. It is a server daemon that serves the Nova Metadata API.
- **nova-compute service**: The nova-compute-service is a worker daemon that creates and terminates virtual machine instances by invoking hypervisor-specific APIs. It is a simple wrapper around the hypervisor APIs. For example, it invokes the libvirt API for QEMU/KVM, the VMware API for ESX hypervisors, and the Xen API for Xenserver hypervisors. This daemon processes requests from the queue and invokes system commands to launch instances and updates the states in the database.

- **nova-placement-api service**: The nova-placement-api is a REST API stack and data model used to track resource provider inventories and their usage. A compute node, a shared storage pool, or an IP allocation pool are examples for resource providers. This service tracks the inventory and usage of such providers. For example, a virtual machine running on a compute node consumes memory and CPU from a compute node resource provider, disk storage from an external shared storage pool resource provider, and also an IP address from an external IP pool resource provider. This is tracked by the nova-placement-api service.
- **nova-scheduler service**: The nova-scheduler-service fetches the instance launch request from the queue and decides on which node to run the virtual machine by analyzing the available resources on the nodes.
- **nova-conductor module**: The nova-conductor module acts as a communication interface between the nova-compute service and the database. It prevents direct access to the database by the nova-compute service.
- **nova-consoleauth daemon**: The nova-consoleauth daemon authorizes the user tokens provided by the console proxies. This service is required for console proxies to work.
- **nova-novncproxy daemon**: This service provides the ability to connect to the consoles of the virtual machines using the VNC protocol using a VNC client or web browser.

The following screenshot shows the a single virtual machine instance running on OpenStack:

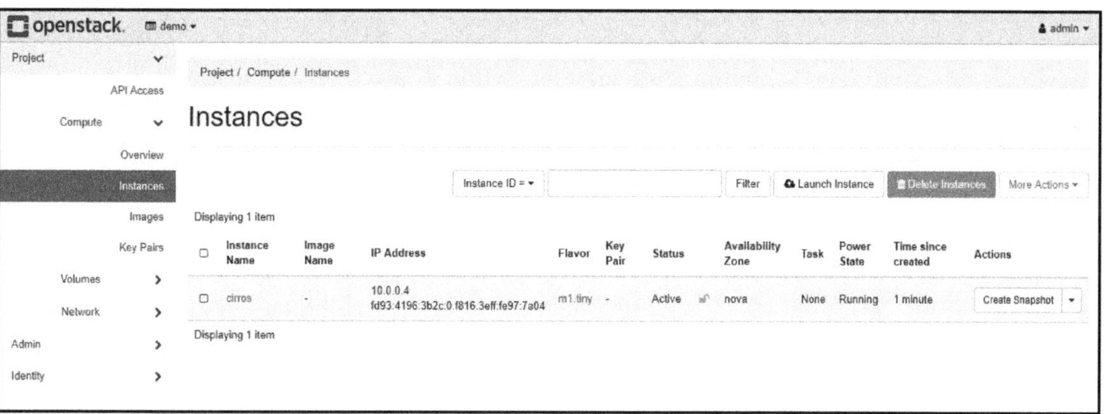

A running VM instance on OpenStack

Neutron – OpenStack Networking Service

OpenStack Neutron provides networking-as-a-service to other OpenStack components and virtual machines. It allows OpenStack users to create and manipulate networking entities such as networks, subnets, ports, DHCP configurations, and so on. Different plugins can be implemented to leverage different networking equipment and software. This makes the OpenStack network deployment flexible.

The OpenStack Neutron Service also provides APIs to define network connections and IP addressing in the cloud environment, along with managing several network services such as L3 forwarding, **Network Address Translation** (**NAT**), load balancing, and **Virtual Private Networks** (**VPN**).

The Neutron Service is comprised of two main components :

- **The Networking API server**: The OpenStack Networking provides APIs for Layer 2 networking and **IP address management** (**IPAM**). It also provides an extension for a Layer 3 router construct that enables routing between Layer 2 networks and gateways to external networks.
- **OpenStack Networking plugin and agents**: Several plugins and agents specific to hardware and software vendors that work with the OpenStack Networking Service. These plugins are used to plug and unplug ports, create network/subnets, assign IP addresses, and so on on the vendor-specific software or hardware.

The number of available vendor plugins for OpenStack Networking is growing continuously. This facilitates the interoperability with several commercial and open source networking technologies which include switches, routes, and SDN controllers.

When you install OpenStack, it creates two networks by default:

- Public network
- Private network

The following screenshot shows the OpenStack Neutron User Interface and the two default networks:

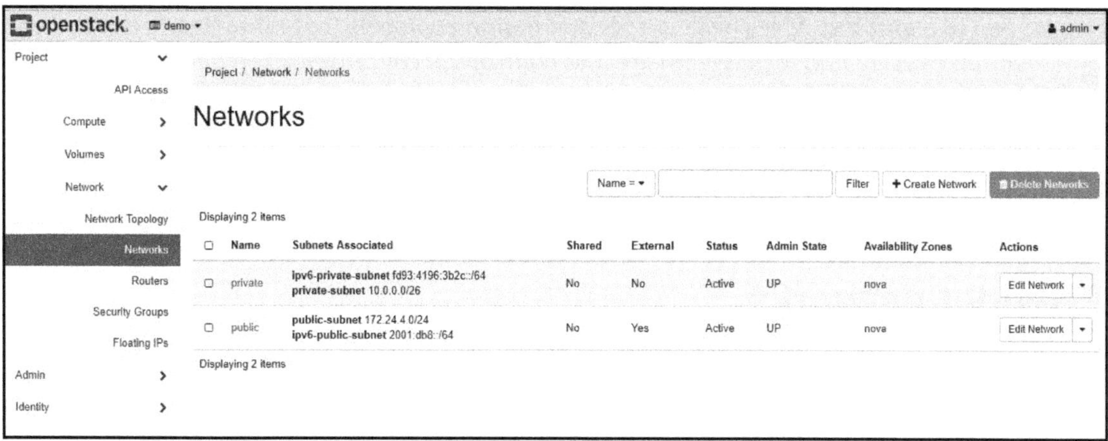

The OpenStack Compute Service (NOVA) consumes the OpenStack Networking Service to provide connectivity for its instances. It allows each tenant to have multiple private networks and also allows each tenant to choose their own IP addressing scheme. These IP addresses can overlap the other IP addresses used by other tenants.

OpenStack Neutron basically offers two types of networks:

- Tenant networks
- Provider networks

These networks can be shared among tenants.

Tenant networks

A **tenant network** is created for establishing networking connections between instances that are within a project. This network is completely isolated and is not shared with other projects. This isolation is achieved using the overlay technologies. The following network isolation and overlay technologies are used:

- **FlatAll**: In this type, all NOVA instances that is, virtual machines are on the same network which is also shared with the host. There is no VLAN tagging done.
- **VLAN tagging**: This type allows users to create virtually isolated networking called VLANs by assigning VLAN IDs (802.1Q) to individual networks. These VLANs correspond to VLANs in the physical network. This type of networking allows instances to communicate with each other and also to other Layer 2 devices such as firewalls, load balancers, and other servers.

- **GRE and VxLAN**: These are encapsulation protocols that allow the user to create an overlay network to activate and control the communication between OpenStack instances. A router is required to allow the network traffic to pass outside the GRE or VxLAN tenant network. The router is also needed to connect the tenant network to the external network. Instances can use the floating IP address so that they can be reached from an external network.

Provider networks

Provider networks usually map to the existing physical networks of the data center in which the NOVA host is present. The flat (untagged) and VLAN types of networks are used in this category.

Let's understand some networking terminology that OpenStack Networking uses:

- **Subnet**: A subnet is a technique for dividing an IP network into two or more smaller networks. This is done by splitting the IP address into network ID and host ID. The subnet mask decides how the IP address is split to represent the network ID and host ID. Subnetting is provided by the OpenStack Networking Service for tenant networks as well as provider networks.
- **Ports:** A port is a connection endpoint of attaching a networking device. For example, a virtual networking adapter can be attached to the virtual network using a port. The port also indicates the associated network configuration such as the MAC address and IP address used.
- **Routers**: A router is a logical component that forwards network packets between different networks. It also provides Network Address Translation for external network access.
- **Security Groups**: A security group is like a virtual firewall that determines what networking rules apply to the traffic that travels in and out of the instances. The security groups are defined at the port level and hence each port in the subnet can be assigned different security groups. A default security group is applied to the instance if it is not explicitly selected when an instance is launched. The default security group allows all outgoing traffic, but blocks all incoming traffic on all ports. You can explicitly define a new security group and allow the relevant ports. For example, a security group rule may be defined to allow the inbound traffic on port 22 which is used by SSH connection. This will enable SSH connections to the instance that uses this security group.
- **Extensions**: The OpenStack Networking Service allows vendor-specific plugins. This allows the introduction of new functionalities and also allows adding new features without changing the version of the Neutron service.

Networking in itself is a complex topic and may easily fill up several books. Discussing each networking term in detail is out of the scope of this book. Let's go further and discuss the Imaging Service.

Glance – OpenStack Imaging Service

OpenStack Glance is an image repository that stores virtual disk images. Users can upload new images and also take a snapshot of a running virtual machine and store it as an image. The snapshot can then be used as a template to launch new virtual machines. Glance uses a database to store the images and its metadata.

Glance supports the following image formats:

- AMI (Amazon Machine Image)
- AKI (Amazon Kernel Image)
- ARI (Amazon Ram Disk)
- ISO (archive format for CDs)
- qcow2 (QEMU/KVM image format)
- raw (raw unstructured format)
- vhd (Hyper-V format)
- vhdx (enhanced vhd format)
- vdi (QEMU/VirtualBox format)
- vmdk (VMware format)

Glance also supports the following container formats:

- bare (no metadata)
- ova (OVA tar archive)
- ovf
- aki/ami/ari (Amazon Machine Image/Amazon Kernel Image/Amazon Ramdisk Image)
- docker (docker tar archive)

For developers, OpenStack Glance provides a RESTful API that allows querying of virtual disk images and their metadata. A Glance domain controller manages tasks that are divided into separate layers.

The glance-store library interacts with the storage backends or local filesystem. It also uses a central database called Glance DB which is shared between all other components.

The following diagram shows the various components of the OpenStack Glance service:

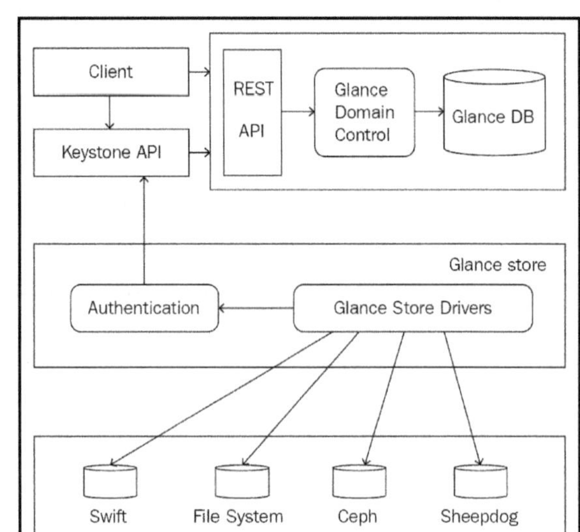

As shown in the diagram, the client invokes REST APIs that get authenticated from Keystone. The image can be fetched either from the GlanceDB or from an external storage using the Glance Store Drivers.

The default installation of OpenStack provides a tiny Linux image called Cirros in the Glance database. The following screenshot shows the OpenStack Glance user interface and the default Cirros image provided.

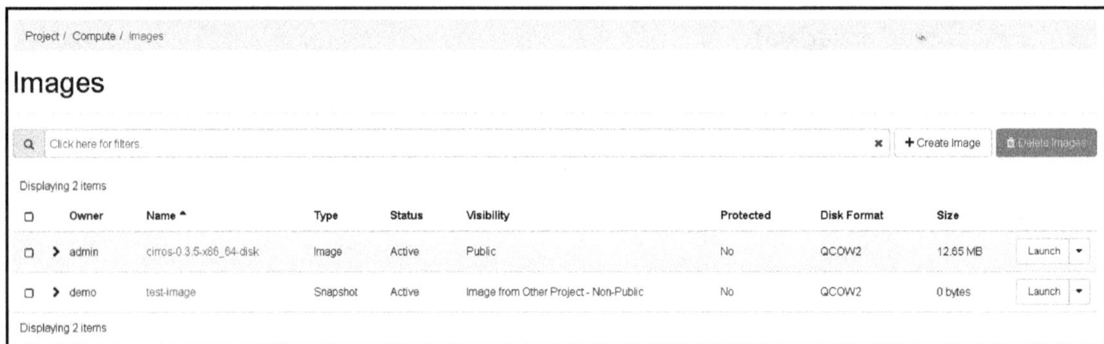

Lets now move on to the OpenStack block storage service.

Cinder – OpenStack Block Storage Service

The OpenStack Block Storage Service is code named **Cinder**. It provides persistent block storage volumes that can be attached to virtual machines running on OpenStack. This service is slightly similar to Amazon EBS where a volume can be carved out of the underlying disk and attached to the instance. It should be noted that one volume can be attached to only one virtual machine instance.

The OpenStack Block Storage Service has the following components:

- **cinder-api**: This provides a WSGI interface that authenticates and routes the requests to the Cinder service
- **cinder-scheduler**: This component schedules and routes requests to the appropriate volume service based certain parameters
- **cinder-volume**: This component manages block storage devices
- **cinder-backup**: Provides a backup and restore mechanism for the block storage to OpenStack Swift
- **cinder-db**: Cinder stores all volume information in the Cinder database

The following diagram indicates the interaction of Cinder services:

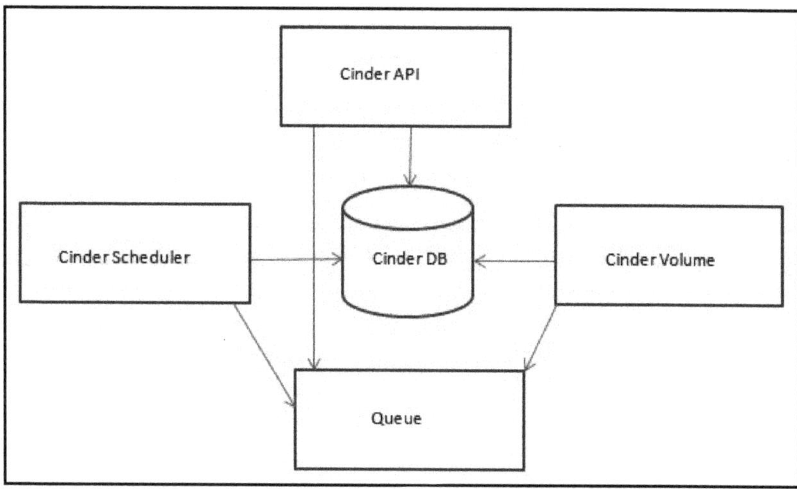

The cinder-volume service can interact with several hardware providers such as Dell EMC, IBM, and so on by enabling the appropriate driver in the Cinder configuration. By default, Cinder uses the LVM driver.

The following screenshot shows the OpenStack Cinder user interface. It shows that a single disk volume is created and is in the **In-use** state. Note the **Type** column shows the driver as `lvmdriver-1` which indicates that the LVM driver is used to create the volume. In other words, when a Cinder volume is created, an LVM volume gets created underneath on the Cinder node:

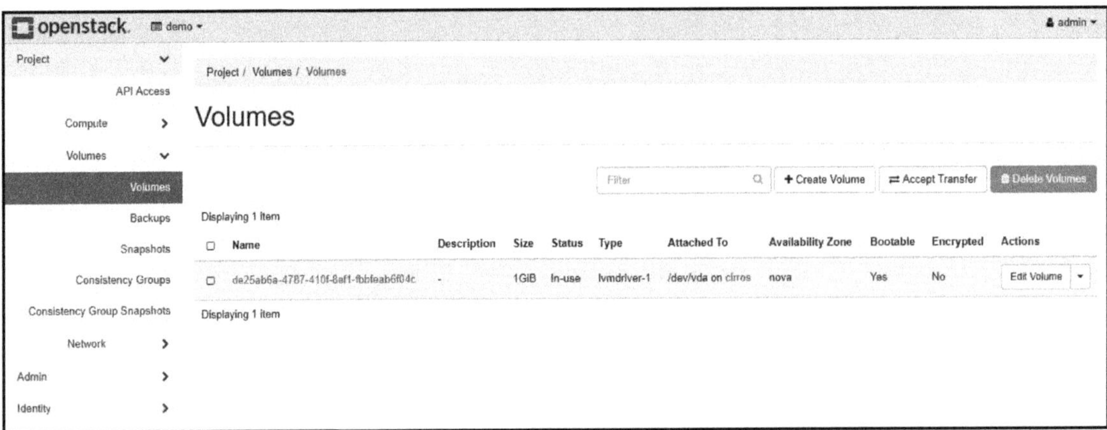

Keystone – OpenStack Identity Service

The OpenStack Keystone service is an identity service that provides authentication, service discovery, and distributed multi-tenant authorization via APIs to its consumers. It supports multiple authentication mechanisms such as username/password credentials and token-based systems. The Keystone service uses a MariaDB database in the backend for storing and retrieving tokens, catalogs, policies, and other identity information. Other authentication systems such as LDAP and SQL can also be used.

The following are the main benefits of using the Keystone Identity Service:

- **User account management**: It provides management of users' credentials and its associated accessible resources.
- **Tenant and project management**: A tenant can either be a user group, a project, or an entire organization which can be grouped and managed as a single entity.
- **Role management**: The permissions of users can be managed.
- **Domain management**: Boundaries can be set to establish isolation of resources. Domains can represent a set of users, groups, or tenants.

The OpenStack Keystone Service consists of two main components :

- **openstack-keystone API**: Provides identity services by exposing public and administrative APIs to the consumers
- **keystone**: A command-line interface to access the identity APIs

The following diagram indicates a typical authentication workflow when a user is authenticated:

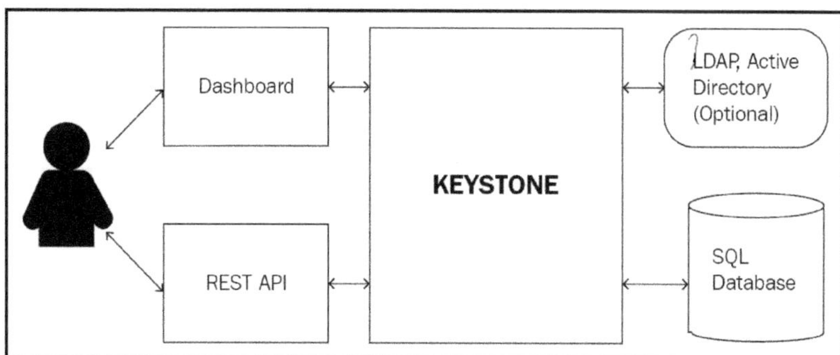

The following are the OpenStack entities that can be manipulated using the Keystone Identity Service:

- **OpenStack project**: A *project* in OpenStack terminology is an organizational unit in the cloud which is used to isolate resources. Projects are also known as accounts. A user can be a member of one or more projects. The OpenStack administrator can create and manage projects, users, and roles.

The following screenshot shows the projects in OpenStack.

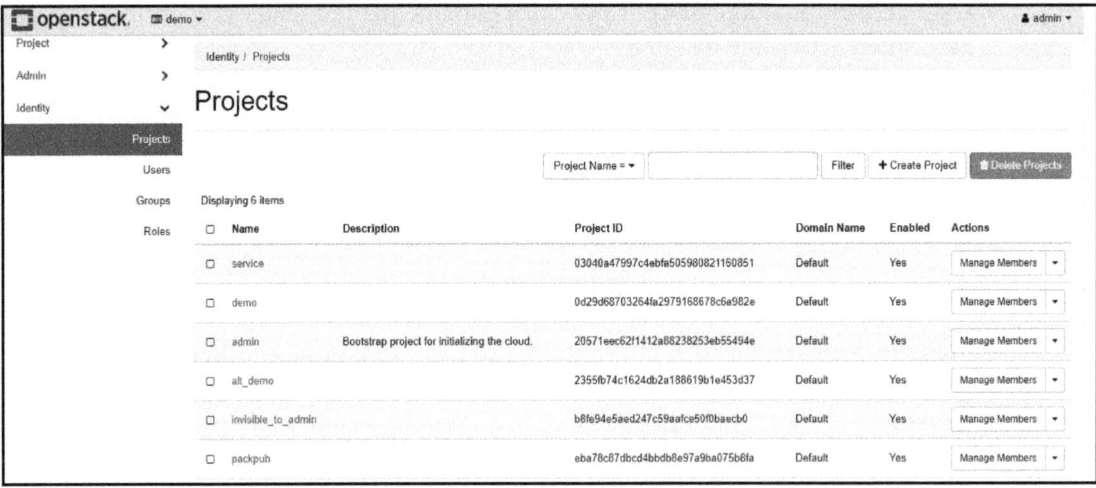

Name	Description	Project ID	Domain Name	Enabled	Actions
service		03040a47997c4ebfa505980821160851	Default	Yes	Manage Members
demo		0d29d68703264fa2979168678c6a982e	Default	Yes	Manage Members
admin	Bootstrap project for initializing the cloud.	20571eec62f1412a88238253eb55494e	Default	Yes	Manage Members
alt_demo		2355fb74c1624db2a188619b1e453d37	Default	Yes	Manage Members
invisible_to_admin		b8fe94e5aed247c59aafce50f0baecb0	Default	Yes	Manage Members
packpub		eba78c87dbcd4bbdb8e97a9ba075b8fa	Default	Yes	Manage Members

- **User or Tenant**: An OpenStack user can be any person who has an OpenStack account and can perform activities. An end user is also known as a *tenant* in OpenStack.

The following screenshot shows the users in OpenStack.

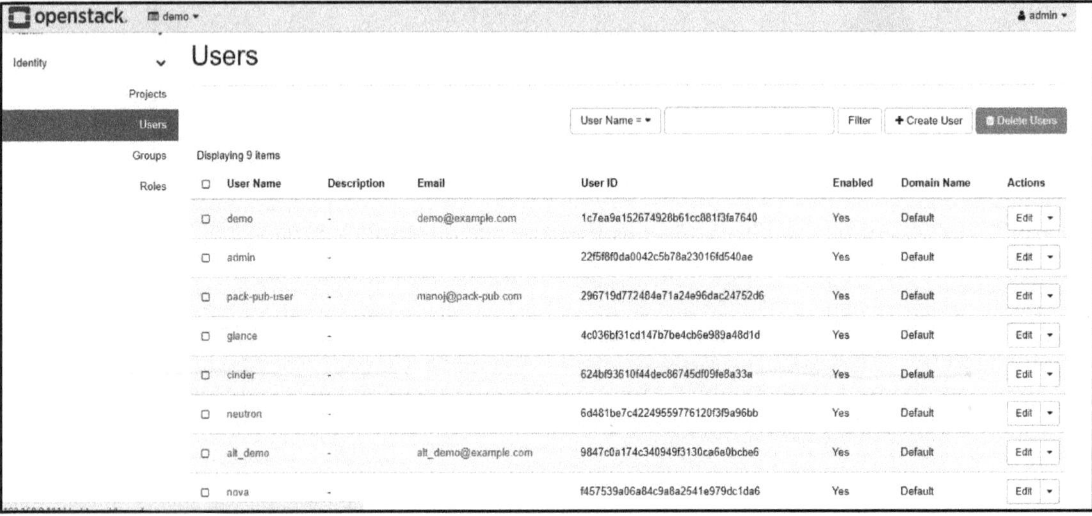

User Name	Description	Email	User ID	Enabled	Domain Name	Actions
demo	-	demo@example.com	1c7ea9a152674928b61cc881f3fa7640	Yes	Default	Edit
admin	-		22f5f8f0da0042c5b78a23016fd540ae	Yes	Default	Edit
pack-pub-user	-	manoj@pack-pub.com	296719d772484e71a24e96dac24752d6	Yes	Default	Edit
glance	-		4c036bf31cd147b7be4cb6e989a48d1d	Yes	Default	Edit
cinder	-		624bf93610f44dec86745df09fe8a33a	Yes	Default	Edit
neutron	-		6d481be7c42249559776120f3f9a96bb	Yes	Default	Edit
alt_demo	-	alt_demo@example.com	9847c0a174c340949f3130ca6e0bcbe6	Yes	Default	Edit
nova	-		f457539a06a84c9a8a2541e979dc1da6	Yes	Default	Edit

- **Group**: A group is a collection of users with similar characteristic. For example, a group can be a set of all *developers*.

The following screenshot shows the default groups in OpenStack.

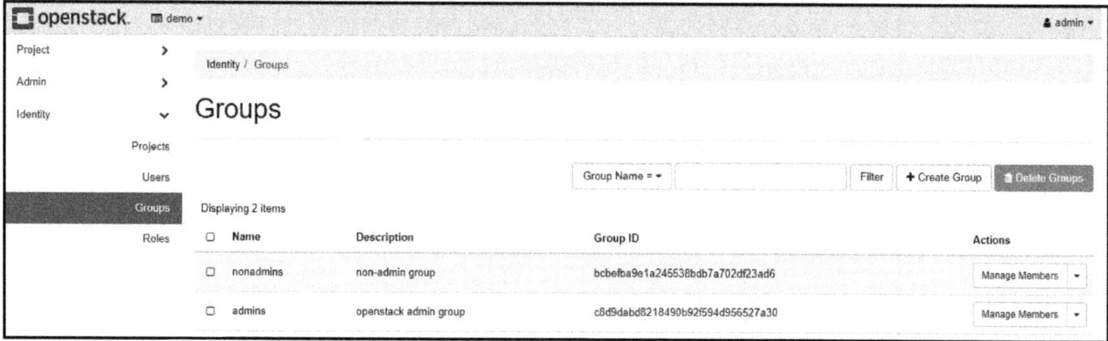

- **Role**: A role is set of certain privileges that are allotted to a particular user.

The following screenshot shows the default roles in OpenStack.

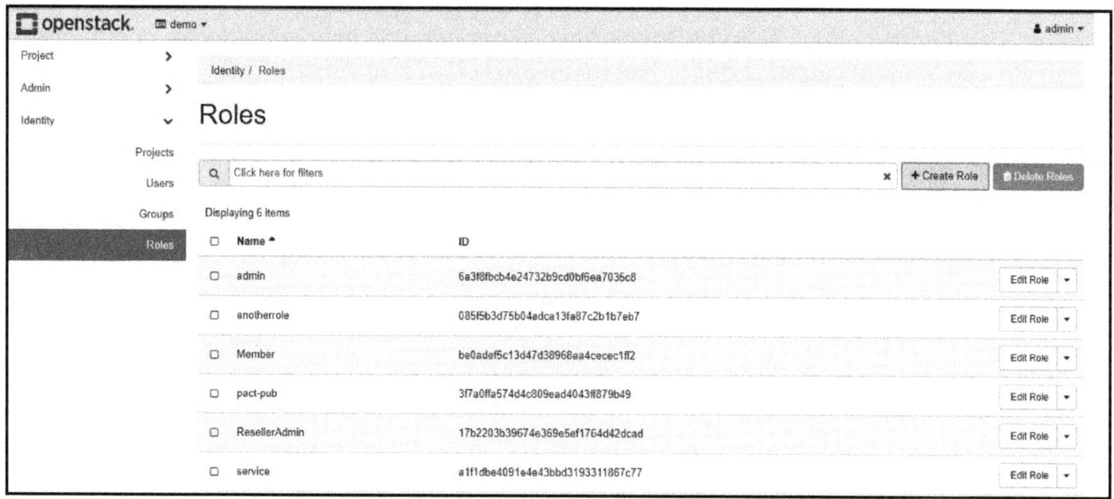

The following diagram shows the relationship between projects, users, groups, and roles:

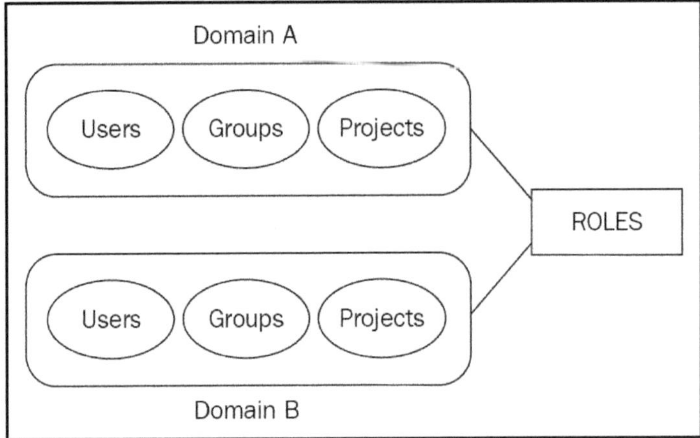

- **Token:** When a user is created in OpenStack, it has certain rights and privileges to perform certain activities. When the users performs these activities using an API call, he must be represented using a token. A token allows a user to prove his or her identity. The Keystone Service generates and provides tokens to users once the authentication is done. The token also carries authorization information that the user has on the OpenStack environment.

A token has an ID and a payload. The ID is unique in every cloud environment. The payload contains data about the user.

The following is an example of a token:

```
{
    "token": {
        "issued_at":  "2018-01-10T20:55:16.806027Z",
        "expires_at": "2018-01-10T2:55:16.806001Z",
        "roles": [{
                "id": "c23df347b23487209jsdf61ce9awlkejr87",
                "name": "admin"}
        ],
        "project": {
            "domain": { "id": "default",
                        "name": "Default" },
            "id": "sdf2342kl3h4989wjfhsj0923840wfdk",
            "name": "admin"
        },
        "user": {
```

```
            "domain": { "id": "default",
                        "name": "Default" },
            "id": "3khsdfilk3459lksjdlfj0345",
            "name": "admin"
        },
        "catalog": [
            {
                "endpoints": [...],
                "type": "identity",
                "id": "mksdf7345kjsdlkf09345345",
                "name": "keystone"
            }
        ]
    }
}
```

As you may observe, a token has information about when it was issued, when it will expire, the roles, project, user, and catalog information.

Horizon – OpenStack Dashboard Service

Although OpenStack services can be accessed using the command-line interface or REST API, using the web-based interface is much easier for end users. The OpenStack Horizon service provides a web-based interface for accessing the OpenStack services such as Keystone, Swift, NOVA, and so on. Users can use the web interface to perform various administrative activities such as launching an instance, creating networks, creating volumes, and so on. The web UI invokes OpenStack APIs to interact with other OpenStack services.

The following diagram shows how the OpenStack Horizon Dashboard Web Service interacts with other OpenStack components:

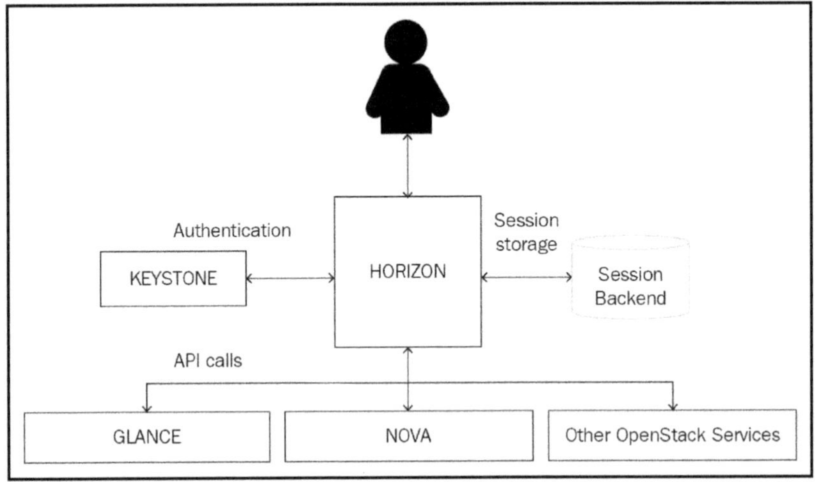

As shown in the diagram, Horizon stores the session information in the database. It also interacts with the Keystone Service for identity management. Since Horizon is the web console and provides the frontend for the user, it invokes the APIs of various different OpenStack services such as Glance, NOVA, and so on. The output returned by the APIs is processed and displayed appropriately by the Horizon Dashboard Service.

Heat – OpenStack Orchestration Service

The OpenStack Orchestration Service is code named **Heat**. It provides a template engine that executes templates to create and manage OpenStack cloud resources such as virtual machines, volumes, networks, and so on. A template creates resources one by one in the order specified, thus forming a stack of resources. The template is written in the YAML format and is called the **Heat Orchestration Template** (**HOT**).

The OpenStack Heat service is comprised of the following:

- **openstack-heat-api**: Provides a REST API to consume Heat orchestration services
- **openstack-heat-api-cfn**: Provides an AWS query API that is compatible with AWS Cloud Formation that processes API requests by sending the request to Heat
- **openstack-heat-engine**: Executes the Heat templates and generates events for API consumers

- **openstack-heat-cfntools**: Provides CloudFormation tools that handle updates to metadata
- **heat**: Provides a command-line interface that interacts with the Heat Orchestration API to execute AWS CloudFormation APIs

A simple Heat Orchestration Template that deploys a single virtual machine looks like this:

```
heat_template_version: 2015-04-30

description: A basic template to deploy a single compute (nova) instance

resources:
  pact_pub_instance:
    type: OS::Nova::Server
    properties:
      key_nam+e: pact_pub_key
      image: cirros
      flavor: m1.small
```

Let's understand the fields in this template:

- `heat_template_version`: This defines the version of the template. The template engine determines how to parse the template based on the version.
- `description`: This indicates the explanation of the template, its purpose, and other details.
- `resources`: The resources section indicates the OpenStack resources that the template will create. Underneath this section, we can define various resources such as NOVA instance, neutron network, and so on. In the preceding example, we have created a resource of type **OS::Nova::Server** which indicates a NOVA virtual machine instance using the `cirros` Glance image and `m1.small` flavor. The SSH key used to access this VM is `pact_pub_key`. The resource will be named `pact_pub_instance`.

The preceding HOT template will give you an idea of how we could write a template to create OpenStack resources for automation. Complex HOT templates can thus be written to create several NOVA instances along with multiple networks and volumes.

Now that we have covered the most important components of OpenStack, let's talk about the how these components interact with each other. We will take the use case of launching a new NOVA instance (virtual machine) on OpenStack.

Ironic – OpenStack bare metal provisioning

When a raw hardware system needs to be provisioned by deploying an operating system over it along with optional software installations and configurations, this process is called **bare metal provisioning**. OpenStack Ironic is a bare metal provisioning service. It consists of a bare metal hypervisor API and a collection of plugins that can interact with the bare metal hypervisor. Typically, a bare metal provisioning process involves the standard IPMI protocol along with PXE. These protocols are also used as default by the Ironic service. However, it also supports various vendor-specific plugins that can be used to implement more vendor-specific features and functionalities.

The OpenStack bare metal provisioning service interacts with several other OpenStack services. The following services are consumed by the Ironic service :

- **OpenStack Compute Service (NOVA)**: The NOVA service provides scheduling capabilities, tenant configuration such as resource quotas, IP address assignment, and other services. These services are used by Ironic. The bare metal service provides an API for hardware management, while the NOVA service provides an API for instance management.
- **OpenStack Image Service (GLANCE)**: The bare metal service uses the imaging service to retrieve images of image metadata.
- **OpenStack Identity Service (KEYSTONE)**: Ironic uses the Keystone service for identity management and authentication.
- **OpenStack Networking Service (NEUTRON)**: The networking service is used for network configuration.
- **OpenStack Telemetry Service (CEILOMETER)**: Ironic uses the telemetry service for consuming the IPMI metrics.
- **OpenStack Object Store Service (SWIFT)**: Ironic uses the object storage for temporarily storing user images, deployment logs, inspection data, and config drive.

The bare metal service includes the following components:

- **ironic-API**: This component provides a set of REST APIs that processes user application requests by passing them to the ironic-conductor over an RPC mechanism.
- **ironic-conductor**: This component allows addition, editing, and deletion of nodes. It also allows the powering off and powering on of nodes using the IPMI protocol or any other vendor-specific protocol depending on the plugin used. It also allows provisioning, deployment, and cleaning up of the bare metal nodes.

- **ironic-python-agent**: This component provides a Python service that provides remote access to the ironic-conductor and ironic-inspector services, in-band hardware control, and hardware introspection. This service runs in a temporary ramdisk.

The bare metal service also has some external dependencies:

- It requires a database to store hardware information and state. The administrator can choose to use the same database as the NOVA service, or can create a separate database for the bare metal service.
- A message queue engine may also be required. By default, other components of OpenStack use RabbitMQ for message queuing. Administrators can choose to use the same messaging service for the bare metal service.

The following are some optional projects that can be used along with the Ironic service:

- `python-ironicclient`: This is a Python-based command-line interface (CLI) for interacting with the ironic service
- `ironic-inspector`: This service provides in-band hardware introspection by performing a PXE boot of the unregistered hardware into the ironic-python-agent ramdisk
- `diskimage-builder`: This facilitates the creation of machine images
- `bitfrost`: This provides a set of Ansible playbooks that help in automating the deployment of base images onto the hardware.

OpenStack workflow – launching a new virtual machine

The following process flow takes place when a new virtual machine is launched on OpenStack from the web user interface:

1. When the user performs a login by entering his credentials via the Horizon dashboard, the UI invokes Keystone REST APIs for authentication. Keystone performs the authentication and returns back a token. This token is preserved by Keystone in its database and is used for authentication of further REST API requests.
2. The user then clicks the Launch Instance button on the dashboard which invokes a nova-api request.

3. The request is received by nova-api and is sent to Keystone for validation and access permissions.
4. Keystone validates the token and sends an acknowledgment, which includes roles and permissions.
5. After receiving the confirmation from Keystone, the nova-api service later creates a first entry for the instance in the database. It then contacts the queue by making an RPC invocation. The call request is then sent to nova-scheduler to determine the host on which the instance should run.
6. The nova-scheduler gets the new instance requests from the queue. It then performs some analysis of the hosts using some filtering algorithms and determines where to launch the instance.
7. After selecting the host, the request is then sent back to the queue to be picked up by nova-compute.
8. The nova-compute picks up the request from the queue and requests parameters of the instance such as memory size, disk size, and CPU along with the host information. The RPC call stays in the queue to be picked up by nova-conductor.
9. The nova-conductor picks the request from the queue, fetches instance-related information from the database, and populates its state in the queue.
10. The nova-compute then picks the instance information from the queue. It sends an authentication token by invoking a REST call to the glance-api to fetch the image URI.
11. The glance-api validates the authentication token with Keystone.
12. The glance-api returns the image URI along with the metadata.
13. The nova-compute then sends the authentication token to neutron-server by invoking a REST call to configure the network for the instance.
14. The neutron-server validates the token with Keystone and puts a request in the queue to be picked up by its agents, such as the neutron-dhcp-agent.
15. The agent picks the request from the queue, processes the request, and responds by sending the networking information for the instance.
16. The neutron-server then fetches all the networking details from the queue and stores it in the database. It also puts the details back in the queue to be picked up by nova-compute.
17. Nova-compute contacts the queue and grabs the instance network configuration. It also sends a REST request to the cinder-api for fetching the volume information.
18. After checking the validation token, the cinder-api puts the volume information in the queue.

19. Nova-compute fetches the block storage information from the queue and then sends a request to libvirt to start the virtual machine.
20. Nova-compute then sends an RPC request to nova-conductor to get the state of the instance.
21. Nova-conductor replies back with the state information of the instance.
22. Nova-api keeps polling the database to get the instance state and reports the same on the UI.

This concludes our brief discussion about OpenStack and its services.

Summary

In this chapter, we discussed the different components that make up the OpenStack private cloud. We explored the compute, networking, block storage, object store, dashboard, and orchestration modules of OpenStack. Overall, in this chapter we created the foundation required for beginning our journey of developing cloud applications on AWS and OpenStack.

In the next chapter, we will start exploring the development tools available for the AWS and OpenStack clouds and begin by developing some simple AWS and OpenStack applications.

4
Developing AWS Cloud Applications

In the last section, we discussed the AWS and OpenStack cloud platforms and their features. It's now time to explore these clouds from the developer's perspective. We will begin by setting up our own development environment and then start building applications on the AWS Cloud. We assume that the reader is familiar with basic object-oriented programming in C# and Python, as this knowledge will make it easy to understand the code examples written in this chapter.

The following topics are covered in this chapter:

- Setting up a development environment using Visual Studio on a Windows platform
- Setting up a development environment for Python on a Unix platform
- Developing Amazon S3 applications
- Developing Amazon EC2 applications
- Developing Amazon RDS applications
- Developing Amazon SNS applications
- Developing Amazon SQS applications
- AWS CloudFormation Templates

Technical requirements

The code files for this chapter are available on GitHub:

`https://github.com/PacktPublishing/Hybrid-Cloud-for-Developers/tree/master/chapter4-AWS`

Check out this video to see the code in action:

`https://goo.gl/aX8rZH`

AWS – Software Development Kit (SDK)

In the last chapter, we performed many operations with different AWS services using the web console. Most of the operations that can be done using the AWS web console can also be done using the AWS command-line interface, AWS SDKs, and also the REST API. AWS provides SDKs for many popular programming languages, such as C++, Go, Java, JavaScript, .NET, PHP, Python, and Ruby. For the purpose of demonstrating the SDKs, we have chosen the C# programming language for Windows platforms and the Python language for Linux platforms, as these languages are widely used across the industry.

Let's begin by setting up development environments on the Windows and Unix platforms.

Setting up an AWS development environment on Visual Studio

The following software prerequisites must be available for setting up a development environment on the Windows platform:

- An operating system with Windows 2008 or above
- Visual Studio 2010 or above
- An AWS account (access key and secret access key)
- An internet connection

AWS provides tools for Visual Studio that make it easier to develop, debug, and deploy AWS applications written using the .NET framework. A .NET SDK is made available, which can be used to consume the AWS services such as S3, EC2, SNS, SQS, and so on.

Let's install these tools and set up the development environment. The following steps must be followed:

1. Download the AWS tools and SDK for the Visual Studio .NET platform from `http://sdk-for-net.amazonwebservices.com/latest/AWSToolsAndSDKForNet.msi`.

2. After the download is complete, double-click on the downloaded file (msi) to install the tools and the AWS .NET SDK.
3. Once the installation is complete, start Visual Studio.
4. In the Visual Studio IDE, go to **View** | **AWS Explorer**.
5. On the left side, you should see an AWS explorer window. Click on the "add profile" icon on the top to add your AWS account.
6. Provide a name to your profile and enter your AWS secret key and AWS secret access key. Once that is done, this will connect Visual Studio to your AWS account:

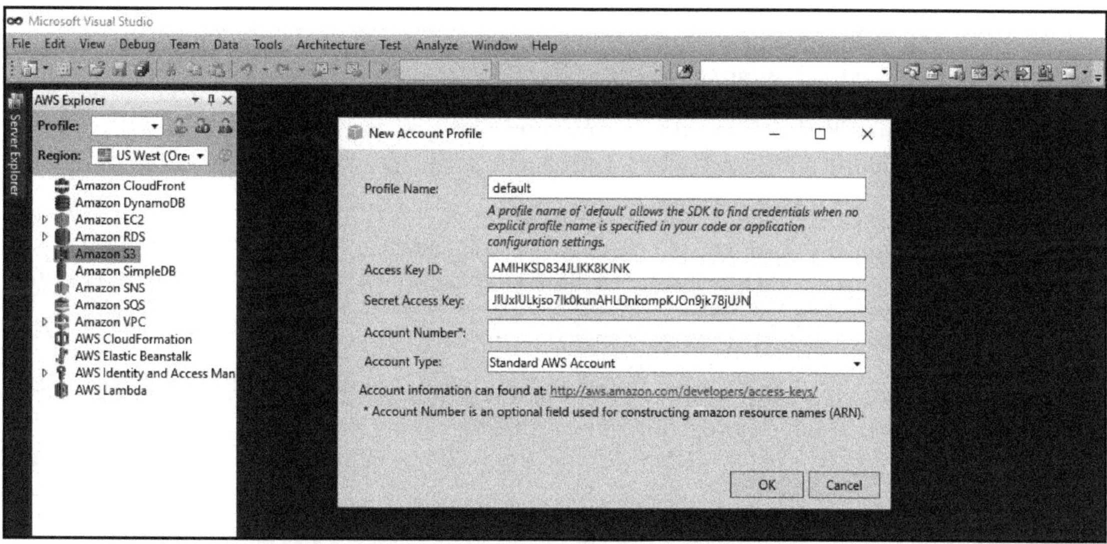

Your Visual Studio environment is now ready to use the AWS SDK APIs. Let's see how we can set up a similar development environment on Unix platforms.

Setting up a Unix development environment for Python

For Unix developers, the following prerequisites must be available for setting up the development environment:

- Any Linux distribution
- Python 2.7 or above installed

- An AWS account (access key and secret access key)
- An internet connection

AWS provides Python packages for accessing various services. For example, a Python package called boto3 is provided by AWS for accessing all AWS services.

Execute the following steps to set up your development environment on a Unix system:

1. Install Python 2.7 or above
2. Install Python package manager (pip)
3. Using `pip`, install the Python packages `boto3` and `awscli`:

```
pip install boto3
pip install awscli
```

4. Configure the AWS account by invoking the `aws configure` command and provide your AWS access key and secret access key. Also specify the region:

```
[root@packt-pub]# aws configure
AWS Access Key ID []: AJDUPOET79345LJNMSKL
AWS Secret Access Key []: KSHDF9081kjLKLLDFGlkjld9435NKLJLDlkslLKJ
Default region name [us-east-1]: us-east-1
Default output format [None]:
```

You are now ready to use your Unix environment to build AWS applications. Let's get some hands-on experience of developing AWS applications.

Developing Amazon S3 applications – Windows

We will begin by writing S3 applications that create an S3 bucket and upload/download files to it.

Creating an S3 bucket

Let's follow the tradition of building a Hello World application on AWS. We will write a simple C# .NET application that creates a new S3 bucket on your AWS account.

The following are the steps to create an S3 bucket:

1. Open Visual Studio.
2. Go to **File** | **New** | **Project** and under Visual C#, select the **AWS Sample Projects** and choose **AWS Empty Project**:

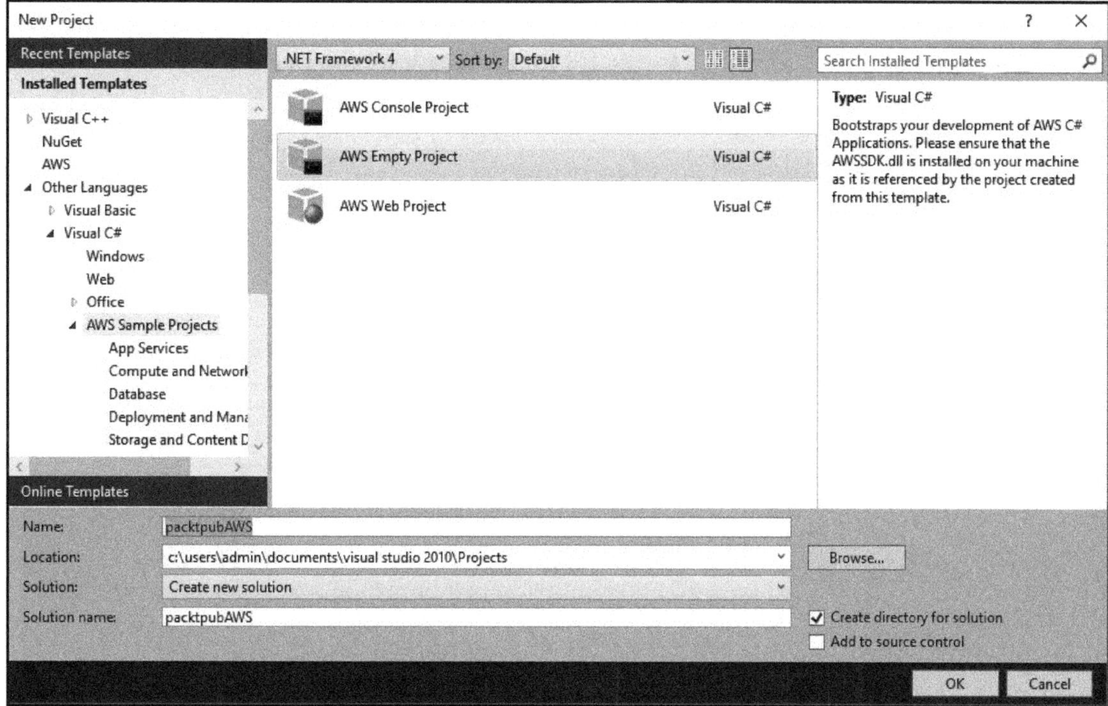

3. Provide a name for the project and click **OK**.
4. You will be prompted to provide the *AWS secret key* and *AWS secret access key*. If you already have a profile created, you can select the existing profile or create a new one by entering the credentials. Click **OK** when done.

   You will now see two files open: `App.config` and `Program.cs` . The `app.config` file is the configuration file for the application, we won't be using this file for now. The `Program.cs` file is the actual source code of your program.

5. In the `Program.cs` file, add the following lines of code:

```
using System;
using System.Collections.Generic;
using System.IO;
using System.Linq;
using System.Text;
using System.Collections.Specialized;
using System.Configuration;

using Amazon;
using Amazon.S3;
using Amazon.S3.Model;

namespace pactpubAWS
{
    class S3Demo
    {
        public static void Main(string[] args)
        {
            createS3Bucket(); // invoke the method to create an S3
bucket

            Console.ReadKey();
        }

        static void createS3Bucket()
        {
            try
            {
                IAmazonS3 s3Client = new AmazonS3Client();
                PutBucketRequest bucket_request = new
PutBucketRequest();
                bucket_request.BucketName = "packt-pub";
                s3Client.PutBucket(bucket_request);
            }
            catch (AmazonS3Exception s3exception)
            {
                Console.WriteLine("Error!!");
                Console.WriteLine(s3exception.ErrorCode);
            }

        }
    }
}
```

6. Execute the program and it will create a new S3 bucket named `packt-pub` under your AWS account.
7. If there are any errors encountered during the creation of the bucket, the error code will be displayed on the console.

In this small console application, we first included the necessary libraries from the AWS SDK. We wrote a function named `createS3Bucket` and created an S3 client object using the `IAmazonS3` and `AmazonS3Client` classes. Next, we created an S3 put-request object using the `PutBucketRequest` class and set its object property called `BucketName` to packt-pub. The request is then invoked using the `PutBucket()` method which creates a bucket on AWS. Errors are caught in the `AmazonS3Exception` object and the error code is displayed on the console.

Now that we know how to create an S3 bucket programmatically, let's try to list the available buckets.

Listing S3 buckets

We will extend our console application to list all the S3 buckets. We will add another function named `listS3Buckets` to the program and invoke that function after the `createS3Bucket()` function.

Add the following function to your application:

```
static void listS3Buckets()
{
   try
   {
       IAmazonS3 s3Client = new AmazonS3Client();
       ListBucketsResponse list_bucket_response = s3Client.ListBuckets();
       foreach (S3Bucket bucket_object in list_bucket_response.Buckets)
       {
           Console.WriteLine("Bucket Name: {0}",
bucket_object.BucketName);
       }
   }
   catch (AmazonS3Exception s3Exception)
   {
       Console.WriteLine("Error!!");
       Console.WriteLine(s3Exception.ErrorCode);
   }
}
```

Invoke this function by calling it from the `main()` function:

```
public static void Main(string[] args)
{
    createS3Bucket(); // invoke the method to create an S3 bucket
    listS3Buckets(); // invoke the method to list all S3 buckets
    Console.ReadKey();
}
```

Execute the program again. You will notice that the creation of the S3 buckets raises an exception this time. This is because there is already a bucket with the same name packt-pub present, which got created during the first execution of the program. The invocation to the `listS3Buckets()` function lists the buckets in your AWS account.

In this new function, we invoked the `ListBuckets()` method of the `s3Client` object and captured the response in the object of type `ListBucketsResponse`. We then iterated over the `Buckets` property of the response object and printed all the buckets on the console.

Uploading files to the S3 bucket

The real use case of the S3 storage is the ability to upload and download files. Each S3 object or file has the important attributes: data, a key, and metadata. The key (or key name) is a unique identification of the object in the bucket. Object metadata is a set of name-value pairs that can be set at the time of uploading the file and can be used for several purposes. This metadata cannot be modified after the object is uploaded.

Let's understand how we can upload a file object programmatically. We will write another function that uploads a file to the packt-pub S3 bucket.

Add the following function to your program and invoke it from the main function:

```
static void uploadfile()
{
   try
   {
       IAmazonS3 s3Client = new AmazonS3Client();
       PutObjectRequest request_obj = new PutObjectRequest()
       {
           BucketName = "packt-pub",
           Key = "myfile",
           FilePath = "D:\\test.txt",
       };
       // Add some metadata to the object to be uploaded and send the PUT
request
```

```
        request_obj.Metadata.Add("title", "This is the first uploaded
file");
        s3Client.PutObject(request_obj);
    }
    catch (AmazonS3Exception s3Exception)
    {
        Console.WriteLine("Error !!");
        Console.WriteLine(s3Exception.ErrorCode);
    }
}
```

The `uploadfile()` function creates a request object of the type `PutObjectRequest`. The `PutObjectRequest` object is used to upload a file or an input stream to the S3 bucket. It requires three parameter : bucket name, key, and file path to be uploaded. This object also allows uploading metadata to the file or input stream being uploaded. The request is sent using the `PutObject()` function.

It should be noted that:

- When a file is uploaded, the program automatically generates a checksum of the file and S3 uses this checksum for validation. This ensures that the all the data in the file is correctly uploaded to S3.
- AWS S3 tries to determine the content type of the file by using the extension of the file.
- When an input stream is uploaded, the program should also specify the content length before uploading the stream, otherwise the library buffers the contents of the stream to calculate the length. AWS S3 mandates that the content length be specified in the request headers.
- Since AWS S3 is a distributed system, if multiple write requests are generated simultaneously, all the objects might be stored. However, only one object will obtain the key.
- S3 doesn't provide a locking mechanism and it should be implemented by developers in their applications.
- All objects/files uploaded to the bucket are stored in the same region as the bucket.
- In order to upload a file to a bucket that already exists, the requesting account must have permission. Write permission to the bucket.

Downloading files from the S3 bucket

Let's add a function to download the file from the S3 bucket:

```
static void downloadfile()
{
    try
    {
        IAmazonS3 s3Client = new AmazonS3Client();      /* create an S3
client object */
        GetObjectRequest request = new GetObjectRequest()  /* create a
request object */
        {
            BucketName = "packt-pub",                      /* parameters to
the constructor */
            Key = "myfile"
        };

        using (GetObjectResponse response = s3Client.GetObject(request)) */
capture the response*/
        {
            string title = response.Metadata["x-amz-meta-title"];
            Console.WriteLine("The title of the file is : {0}", title);
            /* set the location of the destination file */
            string destination_file = "D:\\download\\downloaded_file";
            if (!File.Exists(destination_file))
            {
                response.WriteResponseStreamToFile(dest);   /* write the
downloaded file*/
            }
        }
    }
    catch (AmazonS3Exception s3Exception)
    {
        Console.WriteLine("Error!!");
        Console.WriteLine(s3Exception.ErrorCode);
    }
}
```

The `downloadfile()` function should now be self-explanatory. It is creating a request object and fetching the response stream using the `WriteResponseStreamToFile()` function to write the downloaded file to a specified path.

Listing files in an S3 bucket

The contents of the bucket can be listed using the following code. You can add this to a new function inside a try-catch block, similar to the previous examples:

```
IAmazonS3 s3Client = new AmazonS3Client();    /* create an S3 client object
*/
ListObjectsRequest list_request = new ListObjectsRequest(); /* create a
request object */
list_request.BucketName = "packt-pub";         /* specify the bucket name in
the object */

ListObjectsResponse list_response = s3Client.ListObjects(list_request);  /*
invoke the request */

foreach (S3Object entry in list_response.S3Objects)     /* iterate through
the response list */
{
    Console.WriteLine("key = {0} size = {1}", entry.Key, entry.Size);  /*
print keys and sizes */
}
```

Deleting a file in an S3 bucket

Finally, you can delete a file in a bucket by simply invoking the `DeleteObject()` function, as follows:

```
IAmazonS3 s3Client = new AmazonS3Client();
DeleteObjectRequest request = new DeleteObjectRequest()
{
    BucketName = "packt-pub",
    Key = "myfile"
};

s3Client.DeleteObject(request);
```

By now, you must have an idea of using the AWS SDK for accessing the S3 services on the Windows platform. Let's see how we can do the same operations using the Python programming language on Unix platforms. Note that the Python examples can also be performed on a Windows system.

Developing AWS S3 applications – Unix

Python provides a package called boto3 that can be used to access the AWS services. We will perform the same operations on the S3 service as we did using the Windows C3 SDK. Let's begin by creating an S3 bucket using Python.

Creating a bucket

A simple example of creating an S3 bucket using Python is as follows. We first import the boto3 Python library in our application and then create an object of type S3. Then, using this object, we simply invoke the `create_bucket()` function and pass the name of the bucket to be created. The `Bucket` parameter of the `create_bucket()` function is mandatory. There are other parameters that are used to set the properties of the bucket such as permissions, region, and so on.

The following is the simplest implementation of the `boto3` library, which will create a bucket named `packt-pub-bucket`:

```
import boto3

s3 = boto3.resource('s3')

s3.create_bucket(Bucket='packt-pub')
```

Notice that we created an S3 bucket by writing only three lines of code; that's the beauty of Python.

Let's now see how we can upload files to the bucket.

Uploading files to S3

Once we create a bucket, we can the upload files to it using the `put_object()` function of the S3 object. It accepts the file handle of the file to be uploaded. The following code demonstrates how we can upload a file to the S3 bucket:

```
import boto3

s3 = boto3.resource('s3')

file_handle = open('/home/packt-pub/test.txt', 'r')

s3.Bucket('packt-pub').put_object(Key='test.txt', Body=file_handle)
```

There is also another function to upload a file to S3 called `upload_file()`. It requires two parameters - the location of the file to be uploaded and the name to be given to the file when it is uploaded to the bucket.

It can be used as follows:

```
import boto3
s3 = boto3.resource('s3')
s3.Bucket('mybucket').upload_file('/tmp/test.txt', 's3.txt')
```

In the preceding code, the `/tmp/test.txt` file is uploaded to the bucket named `mybucket` and is named `s3.txt`.

Listing S3 buckets

Your application may create several buckets to hold different files. Sometimes it is necessary to list all the S3 buckets. This cane be done simply by invoking the `s3.buckets.all()` function.

The following Python code will list all the S3 buckets:

```
import boto3

s3 = boto3.resource('s3')

for each in s3.buckets.all():
   print (each)
```

Downloading files from the S3 bucket

The following code shows how we can download a file from the specified S3 bucket. Here, packt-pub is the bucket name and `test.txt` is the file that we intend to download. The downloaded file is saved as `/tmp/hello.txt`:

```
import boto3

s3 = boto3.resource('s3')
s3.Bucket('packt-pub').download_file('test.txt', '/tmp/hello.txt')
```

Deleting objects/files from a bucket

Objects or files inside a bucket can be deleted using the `delete_objects()` function of the `Bucket` class:

```
import boto3

s3 = boto3.resource('s3')
bucket = s3.Bucket('packt-pub')
bucket.delete_objects( Delete = {'Objects': [
            {
                'Key': 'test.txt',
            },
        ],
        'Quiet': True
    })
```

Deleting a bucket

A bucket can be deleted only if all the objects inside it are deleted. In other words, only empty buckets can be deleted:

```
import boto3

s3 = boto3.resource('s3')
bucket = s3.Bucket('packt-pub')

response = bucket.delete()
```

The preceding example gives you an idea about the Amazon S3 classes and the functions that can be used to manipulate S3 storage. You can now write more complex programs that can interact with the AWS S3 storage. For example, your application may be running on your private cloud (OpenStack) environment and may require access to S3 storage for uploading files such as website content. You can easily uses the preceding S3 classes and functions to build your hybrid cloud application.

Let's move ahead and see how we can manipulate EC2 instance using the SDKs.

Developing Amazon EC2 applications – Windows

In the second chapter, we discussed EC2 instances in brief.

Let's now start by looking at how we can launch an EC2 instance using the SDK by writing an application program. We will use the same .NET C# SDK classes and their functions to manipulate EC2 instances.

Launching an EC2 instance

To launch an EC2 instance on AWS, we need:

- Amazon Machine Image (AMI)
- Instance type or flavor of the instance
- Key Pair name

An EC2 instance can be launched using an existing AMI in the same region. There are two important classes used for this purpose. The `AmazonEC2Client` class is used to instantiate an EC2 client object. This class is used to manage the EC2 resources. Also, the `RunInstancesRequest` class is used to create a request object that consists of the instance details such as AMI identifier, instance type, key pair, and so on. The request object is then passed to the `RunInstances()` function of the `AmazonEC2Client` class. This function then sends a request to AWS to start the specified EC2 instance.

The following application program demonstrates this:

```
using System;
using System.Collections.Generic;
using System.Threading;

using Amazon;
using Amazon.EC2;
using Amazon.EC2.Model;
using Amazon.EC2.Util;

namespace EC2
{
    class EC2Operations
    {
        public static void Main()
        {
```

```
            launch();
        }

        static void launch()
        {
            try
            {
                AmazonEC2Client ec2 = new AmazonEC2Client();
                RunInstancesRequest request = new RunInstancesRequest();
                request.ImageId = "ami-bf4193c7";  /* AMI ID in your region
*/
                request.InstanceType = "t1.micro";   /* Flavor */
                request.MinCount = 1;
                request.MaxCount = 1;
                request.KeyName = "access";  /* Name of the key-pair */
                RunInstancesResponse response = ec2.RunInstances(request);
            }
            catch (AmazonEC2Exception exception)
            {
                Console.WriteLine("Error!");
                Console.WriteLine(exception.ErrorCode);
            }
            Console.ReadKey();
        }
    }
}
```

The `RunInstances()` function encounters errors; it throws an exception of the type `AmazonEC2Exception`.

Checking the state of your EC2 instance

After you launch an EC2 instance, it might be necessary to check the state of the instance to determine whether the instance is ready for use. The state of the instance can be easily determined by checking the `State` property of the `Instance` class object.

You can simply use the `RunInstancesResponse` object that you created for invoking the `RunInstances()` function, and get a list of instances by using the `Reservation.Instances` property. The list can then be iterated and checked for the `State` property to determine the state of the instance.

The following code snippet shows how this is done. You add this code in the preceding program inside the `try` block:

```
var instances = response.Reservation.Instances;
var id = instances[0].InstanceId;
var state = instances[0].State;
Console.WriteLine("State is : {0}", state.Name);
```

Connecting to the instance

Once the EC2 instance is launched and is confirmed to be in the Running state, you can now connect to the instance using either an SSH client for Linux or Remote Desktop for Windows, depending on what kind of EC2 instance you have launched. For SSH connections, you must ensure that port `22` in allowed in the security group. Remote Desktop uses port `3389` for connection.

For logging into the EC2 instance, you will need the public DNS name or IP address of the instance. You also need the private key for Unix instances and Administrator for Windows instances. The Administrator password can be easily obtained by invoking the `GetPasswordData()` function.

Terminating the EC2 instance

Since the EC2 instance is billed by AWS based on the type and usage, it is wise to terminate instances when their purpose is finished. The instances can easily be terminated by creating an object of the `TerminateInstancesRequest` class and adding the instance ID to it. The termination request object is then passed to the `TerminateInstances()` function which invokes the termination of the specified instances.

Append the following code snippet to your program to terminate the instance that you just launched:

```
var terminate_request = new TerminateInstancesRequest();
terminate_request.InstanceIds.Add(instances[0].InstanceId);

var terminate_response = ec2.TerminateInstances(terminate_request);
var terminating_instance = terminate_response.TerminatingInstances[0];

Console.WriteLine("Terminating instance : {0}",
terminating_instance.InstanceId);
Console.WriteLine("Instance state : {0}",
terminating_instance.CurrentState.Name);
```

The preceding examples give you an overview of writing EC2 applications using the C# SDK. Let's see how we can leverage Python's boto3 library to perform the same operations.

Developing Amazon EC2 applications – Unix

Let's start by launching a new EC2 instance using the boto3 library.

Launching an EC2 instance in Python

Launching an EC2 instance using the Python boto3 library hardly takes a few lines of code. You only have to create an instance of the `ec2` type using the `resource()` function of the `boto3` library and invoke its `create_instances()` function. This function takes parameters specific to the instance such as Amazon Machine Image identified, key name, instance type, and so on.

The following simple program will launch the AWS EC2 instance:

```
import boto3

ec2 = boto3.resource('ec2')

instance = ec2.create_instances(
    ImageId='ami-bf4193c7',
    MinCount=1,
    MaxCount=1,
    KeyName="access",
    InstanceType='t1.micro')
print instance[0].id
```

Note that the Amazon Machine Image that you specify in the program should be present in the same region that was configured using the `aws configure` CLI in the beginning of this chapter.

Listing EC2 instances in Python

Once your EC2 instance is launched, the state of the instance can be determined by invoking the `instances.all()` function of checking the state property of the returned objects.

The following Python program will list all the instances in your region by displaying their instance identified, state, and name:

```
import boto3

ec2 = boto3.resource('ec2')

for instance in ec2.instances.all():
    print instance.id, instance.state;
```

Terminating an EC2 instance in Python

Finally, we can terminate the EC2 instance by instantiating the object of the `Instance` class by passing the `instance-id` to its constructor and then invoking the `terminate()` function of the `Instance` object. The `terminate` function starts the termination operation of the specified instance.

The following program is an example of how this can be done using Python:

```
import boto3

ec2 = boto3.resource('ec2')

instance = ec2.Instance("i-0f85e284c87db5e70")
response = instance.terminate()
print response
```

The `terminate()` function returns a Python dictionary that has details of the instance being terminated. This data structure might be needed for reporting purposes. The following is an example of this:


```
{u'TerminatingInstances': [{u'InstanceId': 'i-0f85e284c87db5e70',
u'CurrentState': {u'Code': 32, u'Name': 'shutting-down'}, u'PreviousState':
{u'Code': 16, u'Name': 'running'}}], 'ResponseMetadata': {'RetryAttempts':
0, 'HTTPStatusCode': 200, 'RequestId': 'caae16b7-8e0d-497d-9ae5-
cee228831a04', 'HTTPHeaders': {'transfer-encoding': 'chunked', 'vary':
'Accept-Encoding', 'server': 'AmazonEC2', 'content-type':
'text/xml;charset=UTF-8', 'date': 'Sun, 31 Dec 2017 15:32:51 GMT'}}}
```


Let's move forward and explore the next AWS service that provides relational databases.

Developing Amazon RDS applications – Windows

Amazon RDS (Relational Database Service) is a web service that provides a relational database in the cloud. This service makes it easier to create, manipulate, and scale a relational database on the cloud. It provides several industry standard databases such as Oracle, Microsoft SQL Server, and so on.

DB Instance and instance classes

Amazon RDS spawns multiple processes that read and write to the database. Some processes create and maintain the transaction log files. A set of all such processes along with the database together are called a database instance. Every database instance has its own isolated set of processes that are specific only to its own database and log files. A single database instance can have more than one database associated with it. The database instance can be accessed using the AWS Command Line Interface, AWS RDS API, or the AWS Web Console.

The performance and computational capability of the database instance is determined by the type of the instance, which is called the instance class. AWS provides the following instances classes as per the computational requirements:

Standard database instances:

- `db.m1`: This class provides the first-generation general-purpose database instances.
- `db.m3`: This class provides the second-generation database instances which provide a balanced combination of memory, CPU, and disk sizes. This class is suited for most applications.
- `db.m4`: This class provides the third-generation database instances which provide slightly higher computing capacity that db.m3. It is suitable for highly-loaded, performance-centric applications that read and write to the database very frequently.

Memory-optimized database instances :

- `db.m2`: Provides first-generation, memory-optimized database instances.
- `db.r3`: Provides second-generation database instances that provide memory optimization and more computing capacity than the first-generation `db.m2` instance classes.
- `db.r4`: Provides third-generation database instances that are optimized for memory-intensive applications.

Burstable performance database instances:

- `db.t2`: This class provides database instances that burst their performance to adapt full CPU usage. It is suited for applications that have occasional high performance load.

You can change the database instance class of an already running database instance.

Let's discuss how we could create and operate a MySQL database on RDS using an application program.

Creating an RDS instance

An RDS instance can easily be created using the `Amazon.RDS` package. This package provides several classes for manipulating Amazon RDS instances. The first step in creating an RDS instance is to create an object of type `AmazonRDSClient`. You can then create a request object of type `CreateDBInstanceRequest` and pass the database instance specific parameters to its constructor. These parameters include the database instance identifier, storage size, type of database, database vendor, master user name, and master user password. Once a request object is created, it can then be passed to the `CreateDBInstance()` function, which creates the database instance. If this function fails, an exception of the type `AmazonRDSException` is thrown.

The following program demonstrates how to create a MySQL RDS instance:

```
using System;
using System.Collections.Generic;
using System.Linq;
using System.Text;
using Amazon;
using Amazon.RDS;
using Amazon.RDS.Model;
using Amazon.Runtime;
```

```
using System.Collections.Specialized;
using System.Configuration;

namespace pactpubAWS
{
    class RDSDemo
    {
        static IAmazonRDS client;
        static void Main(string[] args)
        {
            try
            {
                client = new AmazonRDSClient();
                CreateDBInstanceRequest request = new
CreateDBInstanceRequest("packtpub", 5, "db.m1.small", "mysql", "dbadmin",
"password");
                client.CreateDBInstance(request);
            }
            catch (AmazonRDSException exception)
            {
                Console.WriteLine("Error!");
                Console.WriteLine(exception.ErrorCode);
                Console.ReadKey();
            }
        }
    }
}
```

Now that the database instance is created, let's see how we can list the available instances running in your AWS profile.

Listing the RDS database instances

Listing the RDS database instances can simply be done by creating a request object of type `DescribeDBInstanceRequest`. This class can be used to fetch other details about a particular instance. This request object can then be passed to the `DescribeDbInstance()` function, which in turn returns a response object of the type `DescribeDBInstanceResponse`. The response object has the `DBInstances` property which is a list of the database instances running. You can simply iterate over this list to obtain the information about the instances.

The following code snippet fetches the list of RDS instances running and prints out the database instance identifier of each instance:

```
DescribeDBInstancesRequest request = new DescribeDBInstancesRequest();
DescribeDBInstancesResponse response = new DescribeDBInstancesResponse();
response = client.DescribeDBInstances(request);
foreach (DBInstance entry in response.DBInstances)
{
     Console.WriteLine(entry.DBInstanceIdentifier);
}
```

Connecting to the database instance

Connecting to the RDS database instance is specific to the type of database used. It is up to to the developer to use the database engine specific APIs for C# to invoke a connection to the database.

Each database vendor will provide its own SDK for connecting to the database. Covering each of the available database engines is beyond the scope of this book.

Deleting the RDS database instance

Finally, the RDS database instance can be deleted by creating a delete request object of the `DeleteDBInstanceRequest` class and passing the database instance identifier to its constructor. When a database instance is deleted from RDS, it tries to take a final snapshot of the database, before deleting the instance. The `SkipFinalSnapshot` property determines this. If you do not wish to take a final snapshot and directly delete the instance, set this property to true.

The following code snippet demonstrates how to delete an RDS instance:

```
DeleteDBInstanceRequest delete_request = new
DeleteDBInstanceRequest("packtpub");

delete_request.SkipFinalSnapshot = true;
client.DeleteDBInstance(delete_request);
```

Now that you know how to manipulate RDS instances using the C# AWS SDK on the Windows platform, let's look at how the same operations can be done on the Unix platform using the Python boto3 library.

Developing Amazon RDS applications – Unix

The boto3 Python library provides a rich set of classes and function to manipulate RDS database instances.

Creating an RDS instance

The RDS database instance can be created using the `create_db_instance()` function. It requires the parameters that define the instance such as instance identifier, master user name, master user password, instance class, type of database engine such as Oracle, MySQL, and so on, and the storage to be allocated to the instance.

The following Python code demonstrates the creation of a MySQL database instance with the name `packtpub` with 5 GB in size:

```
#!/usr/bin/env python

import boto3
rds = boto3.client('rds')
try:
        response = rds.create_db_instance(
        DBInstanceIdentifier='packtpub',
        MasterUsername='dbadmin',
        MasterUserPassword='password',
        DBInstanceClass='db.t2.micro',
        Engine='mysql',
        AllocatedStorage=5)
        print response
except Exception as error:
        print error
```

We create the object of type `rds` and invoke the `create_db_instance()` function. If the function fails, it raises an exception.

Listing the database instances

An application can have many database instances. The `describe_db_instances()` function will fetch all the database instances into a Python list. This list can then be iterated to determine the database instance information of all the available instances.

The following Python code demonstrates how this is done:

```
#!/usr/bin/env python

import boto3

rds = boto3.client('rds')

try:
        # Fetch the list of all database instances
        dbs = rds.describe_db_instances()

        for db in dbs['DBInstances']:
                print ("MasterUser : %s Endpoint : %s:%s Status:%s") % (
                db['MasterUsername'],
                db['Endpoint']['Address'],
                db['Endpoint']['Port'],
                db['DBInstanceStatus'])
except Exception as error:
                print error
```

Let's now see how we can connect to the database instance using a vendor-specific library.

Connecting to the database instance

Connecting to the MySQL database instance can be done using the standard MySQL Python library. You may use the Python library specific to your database engine. For example, an Oracle database will have its own library to connect to the Oracle instance:

```
db = MySQLdb.connect(host="mydb.cctjftgqysky.us-west-2.rds.amazonaws.com",
# the database endpoint
                     user="dbadmin",         # database username
                     passwd="password", # database password
                     db="packtpub")    # name of the database
```

Database vendor specific Python examples are beyond the scope of this book. Readers are requested to refer to the vendor-specific documentation for interacting with the databases.

Deleting the RDS database instance

Finally, a database instance can be deleted by invoking the `delete_db_instance()` function call by passing the database instance identifier to it.

The following code demonstrates how to delete a database instance:

```
#!/usr/bin/env python

import boto3

rds = boto3.client('rds')

try:
    response = rds.delete_db_instance(
        DBInstanceIdentifier="packtpub",
        SkipFinalSnapshot=True)
    print response
except Exception as error:
    print error
```

This concludes the basic operations on the Amazon RDS instance using application programming.

Developing Amazon SNS applications – Windows

Amazon SNS provides a notification service where users can subscribe to a topic and receive notifications based on the messages published on that topic.

It allows users and developers to push messages either using email or SMS to devices. Developers can use the SNS application programming interface (API) to send messages to the subscribers. Once a message is published to a service, the same messages can be sent multiple times to different subscribers.

To start using the SNS service, developers first need to create a topic. This topic serves as an access point for other users who wish to receive notifications related to the specified topic. The users interested in the topic are required to subscribe to the topic, and thus they become eligible to receive notifications for that particular topic. Developers publish a message to the respective topic using the API and this prompts the SNS service to distribute the message to the subscribers.

Let's look at how we can use the SNS service in our application program using the AWS C# SDK. We will start by creating a topic in SNS.

Creating a topic

The classes and functions related to the SNS service are available in the SimpleNotificationService library, which must be imported in the application program.

An SNS topic can be created simply by invoking the `CreateTopic()` function of the `AmazonSimpleNotificationServiceClient` class. The following code shows how to create an SNS topic and set its attributes:

```
using System;

using Amazon;
using Amazon.SimpleNotificationService;
using Amazon.SimpleNotificationService.Model;

namespace packtpubSNSDemo
{
    class SNSDemo
    {
        public static void Main(string[] args)
        {
            var sns_object = new AmazonSimpleNotificationServiceClient();

            string email_id = "manoj.hirway@packtpub.com";

            try
            {
                // Create an SNS topic called "PACKT-PUB"
                Console.WriteLine("Creating topic...");
                var Topic_Arn_id = sns_object.CreateTopic(new
CreateTopicRequest
                {
                    Name = "PACKT-PUB"
                }).TopicArn;
```

```
                    // Set attributes for the topic
                    sns_object.SetTopicAttributes(new SetTopicAttributesRequest
                    {
                        TopicArn = Topic_Arn_id,
                        AttributeName = "DisplayName",
                        AttributeValue = "PACKT-PUB"
                    });
                }
                catch (AmazonSimpleNotificationServiceException exception)
                {
                    Console.WriteLine("Error !");
                    Console.WriteLine(exception.ErrorCode);
                }
            }
        }
    }
```

Once a topic is created, users can then subscribe to the topic. Let's write code to add a user as a subscriber to the topic that we created.

Subscribing to a topic

Subscribing to a topic can be done simply by invoking the `Subcribe()` function of the SNS client object. The following code shows how this is done.

The protocol here can be either SMS or email, depending on what medium you want to use for the notification:

```
// Add an email subsciption
sns_object.Subscribe(new SubscribeRequest
{
    TopicArn = Topic_Arn_id,
    Protocol = "email",
    Endpoint = email_id
});
```

Publishing messages

Once users are subscribed to the topic, the publisher can publish messages to the topic which are automatically distributed to all the subscribers of that topic.

A message can be published by invoking the `Publish()` function of the SNS client class. The function accepts the message string, message subject, and the ARN of the topic:

```
sns_object.Publish(new PublishRequest
{
    Subject = "Test",
    Message = "Testing testing 1 2 3",
    TopicArn = Topic_Arn_id
});
```

Deleting the topic

Finally, a topic can be deleted simply by invoking the `DeleteTopic()` function as passing the topic ARN to the function.

The following code will delete the topic with the specified ARN:

```
sns_object.DeleteTopic(new DeleteTopicRequest
{
    TopicArn = Topic_Arn_id
});
```

Now that we have talked about developing SNS applications on the Windows platform, let's discuss how this is done on the Unix platforms using the Python programming language.

Developing Amazon SNS applications – Unix

We will use the same boto3 Python package, as it provides classes and functions for implementing the SNS service.

Let's start over by creating an SNS topic.

Creating a topic

An SNS topic can be created by invoking the `create_topic()` function of the `sns_client` object. The result is the Python dictionary that represents the SNS topic. Once an SNS topic is created, AWS automatically assigns a unique ARN to the topic. This ARN can be fetched using the TopicARN key of the SNS topic.

The following Python program demonstrates the creation of an SNS topic:

```
import boto3

# Create an SNS client object
sns_client = boto3.client(
    "sns",
   # You may have to set the AWS credentials of you haven't already set
using AWS CLI
   # aws_access_key_id="YOUR ACCES KEY",
   # aws_secret_access_key="YOUR SECRET KEY",
   # region_name=us-east-1
)

# Create an SNS topic
sns_topic = sns_client.create_topic(Name="packt-pub")
topic_arn = sns_topic['TopicArn']         # fetch the resource name
```

Once a topic is created, subcribers can be added to the topic using their email ID or phone number.

Subscribing to a topic

Subscribing a user to a topic can be done by invoking the `subscribe` function of the SNS client object and passing the type of protocol, email or SMS, the topic ARN, and the endpoint address of the subscriber, which could be a phone number or email address, depending on the protocol used:

```
# Add an email address subscription
sns_client.subscribe(
        TopicArn=topic_arn,
        Protocol='email',
        Endpoint='manoj.hirway@packtpub.com'       # email address of the
recipient
)
```

Publishing a message

Once users are subscribed to the topic, developers can publish messages to the topic by invoking the the `publish()` function and passing the message string and topic ARN to the function.

The following lines of code demonstrate this:

```
# Publish a message.
sns_client.publish(Message="Welcome hybrid cloud developers!",
TopicArn=topic_arn)
```

Deleting a topic

Finally, an SNS topic can be deleted simply by invoking the `delete_topic()` function and passing the topic ARN to it:

```
response = sns_client.delete_topic(
    TopicArn=topic_arn
)
```

This concludes our discussion about the Amazon SNS. You should now be able to use the SNS service in your applications.

Let's move forward and explore the Amazon queuing service known as the Simple Queue Service (SQS).

Developing Amazon SQS applications – Windows

The communication between two or more processes or two or more applications can be synchronous or asynchronous. Message queues are one of the fundamental techniques used for passing messages between applications.

Amazon SQS is a scalable messaging queue service that can be used to pass messages between different components of an application, thus helping to decouple the application components. SQS also allows developers to save messages or data that might get lost if the application or its components goes down.

Amazon SQS supports both standard queues as well as First-In-First-Out (FIFO) queues.

The following are the typical uses cases of implementing the SQS service in your application:

- **Application decoupling**: The components of an application can be decoupled and they can talk to each other using messages queues; thus, each component of the application can be managed independently without affecting other components.
- **Work queue and concurrently**: You can create a queue of work items that can be consumed by the worker application. As the load of the queue increases, you can spawn more worker applications to balance to load.
- **Transparent scaling**: The SQS service can scale to handle the load without any manual intervention, which could be caused because of occasional load spikes from the requester application.

Let's start writing some code and see how we can create and use a queue using the SQS service.

Creating an SQS queue

AWS provides the C# libraries for using the SQS service. You must start by including the AWS.SQS library into your application program. Next, you must create an SQS client object and then form a request object to create a queue. This is done by invoking the constructor of the `CreateQueueRequest` class and passing the name of the queue to it.

You can then invoke the `CreateQueue()` function of the SQS client object and fetch the response. The response object will have the URL of the queue that can then be used to send and receive messages to the queue.

The following C# code demonstrates how to create a new SQS queue and fetch its URL:

```
using System;
using Amazon;
using Amazon.SQS;
using Amazon.SQS.Model;

namespace packtpubSQS
{
    class packtpubSQSDemo
    {
        public static void Main(string[] args)
        {
            var sqs_object = new AmazonSQSClient();
```

```
            try
            {
                // Create the SQS queue request and give it a name
                var create_queue_request = new CreateQueueRequest
                {
                    QueueName = "packtpub_queue"
                };
                // create the queue and fetch the response object
                var create_queue_response =
sqs_object.CreateQueue(create_queue_request);
                string queue_url = create_queue_response.QueueUrl;
            }
            catch (AmazonSQSException exception)
            {
                Console.WriteLine("Error !");
                Console.WriteLine(exception.ErrorCode);
            }
        }
    }
}
```

Once a queue is created, you can then try listing the created queue.

Listing the available queues

Listing the available SQS queues can be done by invoking the `ListQueues()` function of the SQS client object. This function returns a response object that consists of a list of all the SQS queues available. You can iterate over the response object and list all the queues.

The following code lists the queues:

```
var listQueuesRequest = new ListQueuesRequest();
var listQueuesResponse = sqs_object.ListQueues(listQueuesRequest);

if (listQueuesResponse.QueueUrls != null)
{
    foreach (String urls in listQueuesResponse.QueueUrls)
    {
        Console.WriteLine(" Queue URL : {0}", urls);
    }
}
```

Now that you can list the queues that were created, let's send a message to the queue.

Sending a message to the queue

A message can be sent by invoking the constructor of the `SendMessageRequest` class and passing the URL of the queue and the message body.

The following code sends a message to the queue:

```
//Sending a message
Console.WriteLine("Sending a message to MyQueue.\n");
var send_message_request = new SendMessageRequest
{
    QueueUrl = queue_url, //URL from initial queue creation
    MessageBody = "Welcome, hybrid cloud developers !"
};
sqs_object.SendMessage(send_message_request);
```

When one component of the application sends a message to the queue, the other component should receive the message. Let's look at how to receive a message from the queue.

Receiving a message from the queue

The receiving application can simply invoke the `ReceiveMessageRequest` constructor and pass the URL of the message queue. This creates a request object that can then be used to invoke the `RecieveMessage()` function. This function then in turn returns a response object that consists of the messages from the queue. This response object can then be iterated to read all the messages received from the queue.

The following code creates a request object to receive the messages and invokes the `RecieveMessage()` function. It then iterates over the response object and prints out all the messages received from the queue:

```
var receive_message_request = new ReceiveMessageRequest { QueueUrl =
queue_url };
var received_message_response =
sqs_object.ReceiveMessage(receive_message_request);
if (received_message_response.Messages != null)
{
    foreach (var message in received_message_response.Messages)
    {
        if (!string.IsNullOrEmpty(message.MessageId))
        {
            Console.WriteLine("MessageId : {0}", message.MessageId);
        }
        if (!string.IsNullOrEmpty(message.ReceiptHandle))
```

```
        {
            Console.WriteLine("ReceiptHandle: {0}", message.ReceiptHandle);
        }
        if (!string.IsNullOrEmpty(message.MD5OfBody))
        {
            Console.WriteLine("MD5OfBody: {0}", message.MD5OfBody);
        }
        if (!string.IsNullOrEmpty(message.Body))
        {
            Console.WriteLine("Body: {0}", message.Body);
        }

        foreach (string key in message.Attributes.Keys)
        {
            Console.WriteLine("Attribute");
            Console.WriteLine("Name: {0}", key);
            var value = message.Attributes[key];
            Console.WriteLine("Value: {0}", string.IsNullOrEmpty(value) ?
"(no value)" : value);
        }
    }
}
```

Thus, you can create different application components that can exchange messages using the SQS service.

Finally, let's delete the queue.

Deleting a message from the queue

Deleting the SQS queue is pretty straight forward. You create the delete request object by invoking the `DeleteMessageRequest` constructor by passing the URL of the message queue and the receipt handle. Then, you can simply invoke the `DeleteMessage()` function call and pass the request object to it. The queue will then be deleted.

The following code demonstrates this:

```
var message_handle = received_message_response.Messages[0].ReceiptHandle;

var deleteRequest = new DeleteMessageRequest
{
    QueueUrl = queue_url,
    ReceiptHandle = message_handle
};
sqs_object.DeleteMessage(deleteRequest);
```

Now that we have seen how to manipulate SQS queues using the AWD C# SDK, let's also see how these operations can be done on the Unix platform using the Python programming language.

Developing Amazon SQS applications – Unix

The `boto3` library provides classes for manipulating the SQS queues. We will start by creating the SQS queue using the `boto3` library.

Creating an SQS queue

First, create an object of type sqs and then invoke the `create_queue()` function to create an SQS queue. The response object is a Python dictionary that can then be used to fetch the URL of the queue.

The following Python program creates a queue and fetches the URL of the newly created queue:

```
import boto3

# Create SQS client
sqs_object = boto3.client('sqs')

response = sqs_object.create_queue(
    QueueName='packtpub_queue',
)

queue_url = response['QueueUrl']
```

Once the queue is created, let's send a message to it.

Sending a message to the queue

Using the SQS object, invoke the `send_message()` function and pass the queue URL, delay time, message, and the message attributes to it. The message attributes hold the metadata related to the actual message.

The following code snippet sends a message to the queue:

```
# Send message to SQS queue
response = sqs_object.send_message(
    QueueUrl=queue_url,
    DelaySeconds=10,
    MessageAttributes={
        'Title': {
            'DataType': 'String',
            'StringValue': 'Hybrid Cloud for Developers'
        },
        'Author': {
            'DataType': 'String',
            'StringValue': 'Manoj Hirway'
        },
        'Publisher': {
            'DataType': 'String',
            'StringValue': 'packt publication'
        }
    },
    MessageBody=(
        'Welcome, hybrid cloud developers '
    )
)
```

When a message is successfully sent to the queue, the other side of the application should be able to receive it.

Receiving a message from the queue

Messages from the queue can be received from the queue by invoking the `receive_message()` function of the SQS client object and passing the queue URL, the name of the message attributes, the list of attributes that need to be returned along with each message, the maximum number of messages to return, the visibility timeout, and wait time.

The following code receives a message from the queue:

```
response = sqs_object.receive_message(
    QueueUrl=queue_url,
    AttributeNames=[
        'SentTimestamp'
    ],
    MaxNumberOfMessages=1,
    MessageAttributeNames=[
```

```
        'All'
    ],
    VisibilityTimeout=0,
    WaitTimeSeconds=0
)
print response
message = response['Messages']
print message
```

The message is in the form of a Python dictionary and looks as follows. You can parse this data structure to extract the relevant fields for your application:


```
{u'Body': 'Welcome, hybrid cloud developers ', u'ReceiptHandle':
'AQEBPZtagn6DC1plHb2quFP1bAl8YMvQumoH+zw88sWwcbj3gpyNAncmq+Jgi3AEXLU3e6pRw0
rqB+p2fNHo1huT3wjewwMMFKrdUPoi6u+Oms+AMTCXEcun45cdkBt/mdGcD5BwCAKRxPijvkDad
mxLhNec+wuOMQG1Re/B6Nyi8u6i16oG8/a1sQNf+ILdyzAlLlgpykNN7QXa+yvUNLE2w6TT5z+k
LQk12bKbnD1qY+u3gs9D+OQ4EF8B7tA3sQNne6JXtJBw83fRC05qwK8rS18PwXaliU//VOpa1TW
+/o50Gh6z0i6xa6DgVF/u0ql5EfcDIS9cmqBHPfo8bpyDNBUB+/JrhFWwCKpAsuCTqs1ZEjicwU
a1DY0rOg10+clgkfNIcpdaboBPsosrbP506Q==', u'MD5OfBody':
'64e5eb2af2e9db4024c8d7ba2e97cc4e', u'MD5OfMessageAttributes':
'f0b687b8199bcba750a3c0786a540198', u'MessageId':
'3cca35c6-2297-45c5-893f-6723e76576f5', u'Attributes': {'SentTimestamp':
'1515321718519'}, u'MessageAttributes': {'Publisher': {u'DataType':
'String', u'StringValue': 'packt publication'}, 'Title': {u'DataType':
'String', u'StringValue': 'Hybrid Cloud for Developers'}, 'Author':
{u'DataType': 'String', u'StringValue': 'Manoj Hirway'}}
```


Deleting messages from the queue

The queue can be deleted simply by invoking the `delete_queue()` function call and passing the queue URL to it.

The following lines of code will delete the queue:

```
response = sqs_object.delete_queue(
    QueueUrl=queue_url
)
```

Now that we have covered various AWS services and their implementation using the APIs, let's look at what automation mechanisms are provided by AWS to provision these resources.

Amazon CloudFormation service

Until now, we have seen how we can create and use different AWS services such as EC2, S3, SQS, and so on using their respective APIs. Consider that you want to create a stack of different resources like a few EC2 instances and then create EBS volumes and attach them to the instances, then create S3 buckets, then create a database, and so on. AWS provides a way to create such a set of resources by allowing users to write a template that specifies the resources to be created. This template can be written using the JSON or YAML format and is called a CloudFormation template, and the Amazon service that parses and executes this template is called as the AWS CloudFormation service.

Thus, CloudFormation is a service that helps users to model and set up their AWS resources and create their cloud environment without spending much time on managing these resources and allows them to focus on the applications that run in AWS. For example, if you want to launch two EC2 instances in a specific order, the CloudFormation template can easily be configured to implement this order. So, when the template is executed, the EC2 instance will be created in the order specified in the template.

How CloudFormation works

When a template is created and executed, AWS CloudFormation parses this template and starts invoking service calls to create the appropriate resources. It must be noted that AWS can create only those resources on which the user has permissions. For example, the user must have permissions to create EC2 instances if his or her template is trying to create EC2 instances. The Identity and Access Management (IAM) can be used to configure the permissions.

A CloudFormation template

A **CloudFormation template** is a text file that defines what resources are to be created in the AWS stack and their attributes. This template is written in either the JavaScript Object Notation (JSON) or the YAML format. You can edit them in any text editor and also manage them with your source control system such as git, svn, and so on.

The template must declare an object as a name-value pair along with the set of child objects (if any). Let's look at a simple template that creates an S3 bucket.

The following template declares a single resource of type `AWS::S3::Bucket:` with the name `PACKTPUB-BUCKET`.

The JSON format is as follows:

```
{
    "Resources" : {
        "PACKTPUB-BUCKET" : {
            "Type" : "AWS::S3::Bucket"
        }
    }
}
```

The YAML format is as follows:

```
Resources:
  PACKTPUB-BUCKET:
    Type: AWS::S3::Bucket
```

Thus, the following syntax is followed when creating an AWS resource:

```
Syntax:
AWS::ProductIdentified::ResourceType

Example:
AWS::S3::Bucket
```

The preceding template will create an S3 bucket with the name `PACKTPUB-BUCKET`. Creating a bucket does not require too many parameters as AWS uses most of the default parameters. However, other resources, such as an EC2 instance, will require other parameters such as Image ID and type of resource. Thus, the mandatory properties must be specified in the template in order to create the resource.

Let's add the `AccessControl` property to the S3 bucket that specifies the permission of the bucket. The following YAML template indicates how we can add a property of the S3 bucket in the template:

```
{
    "Resources" : {
        "PACKTPUB-BUCKET" : {
            "Type" : "AWS::S3::Bucket",
            "Properties" : {
               "AccessControl" : "PublicRead"
            }
        }
    }
}
```

The same template can be written in the YAML format, as follows:

```
PACKTPUB-BUCKET:
   Type: AWS::S3::Bucket
   Properties:
     AccessControl: PublicRead
```

Let's now create a more complete template that creates an EC2 instance.

Have a look at the following YAML template:

```
AWSTemplateFormatVersion: '2010-09-09'
Description: EC2 instance for packt publications
    Resources:
        MyEC2Instance:
            Type: AWS::EC2::Instance
            Properties:
                ImageId: ami-bf4193c7
                InstanceType: t1.micro
```

Notice that we have specified the template version in the first line, which tells the template engine how to parse to template and what to expect as key value pairs. We have also added a `Description` section that provides more information about the template. The other sections are similar. Instead of S3, we are only creating the EC2 resource and specifying the `ImageID` and `Instance Type` properties for it.

When this template is executed, AWS will create an EC2 instance using the Amazon Machine Image ID `ami-bf4193c7` with type `t1.micro`.

Now that you get an idea of how we write a template, let's look at a more complex template that defines a lot more properties for creating an EC2 instance.

The following template specifies the SSH key pair to be used by the EC2 instance. It also specifies the security group to be used, which applies the firewall rules to the instance. The template itself defines a set of rules for the security group:

```
{
  "Parameters": {
    "KeyName": {
      "Description": "SSH key pair to be used",
      "Type": "AWS::EC2::KeyPair::KeyName"
    }
  },
  "Resources": {
    "Ec2Instance": {
      "Type": "AWS::EC2::Instance",
```

```
        "Properties": {
          "SecurityGroups": [
            {
              "Ref": "InstanceSecurityGroup"
            },
            "packtpub-security-group"
          ],
          "KeyName": {
            "Ref": "KeyName"
          },
          "ImageId": "ami-bf4193c7"
        }
      },
      "InstanceSecurityGroup": {
        "Type": "AWS::EC2::SecurityGroup",
        "Properties": {
          "GroupDescription": "Enable SSH access via port 22",
          "SecurityGroupIngress": [
            {
              "IpProtocol": "tcp",
              "FromPort": "22",
              "ToPort": "22",
              "CidrIp": "0.0.0.0/0"
            }
          ]
        }
      }
    }
  }
```

Now that we know how to write templates, let's see how we can execute them programmatically.

Executing the CloudFormation template

You can execute the CloudFormation template either using the AWS Web Console, the AWS CLI, or the SDK. Since we are focusing on application development, let's write some Python code that executes a template written in the JSON format.

We will use the same `boto3` Python package to create the CloudFormation objects:

```
import boto3

with open('packtpub.json') as template_file:
    template = template_file.read()
```

```
cloud_formation_object = boto3.resource('cloudformation')

response = cloud_formation_object.create_stack(StackName =
'test',TemplateBody = template)
print(response)
print(type(response))
```

In the preceding program, we create an object of the type `cloudformation` and then invoke the `create_stack()` function by passing it the template. This function will start creating the AWS resources specified in the template.

Summary

In this chapter, we introduced you to the AWS SDKs for the Windows C# and Python programming languages. We then created development environments for both platforms and started writing simple AWS applications. We began by writing S3 applications where we created an S3 bucket, listed S3 buckets, uploaded files to the bucket, and deleted the bucket. We then moved to creating an EC2 instance programmatically using both C# and Python. We also saw how we could check the state of our EC2 instance and connect to it using SSH.

Next, we entered into the database world and created an Amazon RDS MySQL instance using both C# and Python. We saw how we could leverage the Amazon RDS for our cloud applications.

We then wrote application programs to use Amazon's SNS and demonstrated how we can create a topic, subscribe users to the topic, publish messages, and delete the topic. We also wrote cloud applications that leverage the AWS SQS service that provides message queues. We saw how to create a message queue, send and receive messages over the queue, and delete the queue.

Finally, we discussed about Amazon's CloudFormation service where we wrote CloudFormation templates in JSON and YAML to create stacks. We executed the template using a simple Python program.

This chapter has given you a fair idea about how to use the AWS APIs on both Windows and Unix platforms. In the next chapter, we will start writing applications for the OpenStack private cloud platform.

5

Developing OpenStack Applications

In the previous chapter, we got some hands-on experience of developing AWS cloud applications. Let's develop some OpenStack applications and see how we can leverage the available OpenStack SDK.

The following topics will be covered in this chapter:

- Introduction to OpenStack SDKs
- Setting up a development environment on a Unix platform
- Developing OpenStack image service applications
- Developing OpenStack compute service applications
- Developing OpenStack network service applications
- Developing OpenStack identity service applications
- Developing OpenStack block storage applications
- Developing OpenStack HOT templates

Technical requirements

The code files for this chapter are available on GitHub:

`https://github.com/PacktPublishing/Hybrid-Cloud-for-Developers/tree/master/chapter4-AWS`

Check out this video to see the code in action:

`https://goo.gl/Nw87mq`

Introduction to OpenStack SDK

There are a number of OpenStack SDKs available on the market that can be used to interact with OpenStack services. Being an open source cloud platform, different developer communities contribute and build their own SDKs specific to the requirements. The following are a few of the available OpenStack SDKs that can be used by developers specific to their programming language of choice.

Go

Gophercloud is an OpenStack SDK available for developers using the Go programming language. It provides APIs for many services of OpenStack, such as Compute, Block Storage, Object Storage, Networking, and Identity.

Java

Some of the available OpenStack SDKs for the Java programming language are as follows:

- **OpenStack4j:** This library has been broken up into several major API abstractions depending on the available OpenStack services
- **OpenStack Java SDK**: This library provides a good Java binding for the OpenStack APIs
- **Apache JClouds**: This library provides multi-cloud APIs for interacting with OpenStack services

JavaScript

Javascript is a popular language for web applications and the following OpenStack SDKs are available for it:

- **pkgcloud**: Provides a multi-cloud library for OpenStack using Node.js
- **JStack**: Provides an OpenStack client library for JavaScript

- **JS-OpenClient**: Provides a Node.js based API to interface with the REST API
- **Node-OpenStack-Wrapper**: Provides a wrapper interface for interacting with OpenStack services

.NET

We have already used .NET SDKs for AWS cloud application development. There is also a .NET SDK available for OpenStack:

- **OpenStack .NET**: This SDK is written for the Microsoft .NET platform for enabling developers to access OpenStack services using .NET-based classes and functions

PHP

For web developers, the following OpenStack SDK is available for PHP:

- **PHP-OpenCloud**: This is a PHP SDK for OpenStack that supports the latest Keystone V3 APIs for identity services

Ruby

The following libraries are provided for Ruby developers:

- **Fog**: This provides a multi-cloud API interface for OpenStack services
- **Aviator**: This is an old SDK for Ruby developers that provides an OpenStack interface

C

The SDK for the C language is available only for certain specific OpenStack services. The following C libraries are available:

- **Keystone and Swift libraries**: These provide C language interfaces for the OpenStack Identity service and also the SWIFT object store services
- **C-KeystoneClient**: This provides a C language library that can be used for authentication using the Keystone services

C++

The SDK, SWIFT_CPP_SDK, is available for C++ developers, which can only be used for accessing the OpenStack Swift object store using the REST API.

Perl

There is a Perl SDK available for accessing the OpenStack Compute services. This SDK is called Net::OpenStack::Compute and it also provides command-line tools for interacting with OpenStack deployment.

Python

The OpenStack platform itself is developed mostly by using the Python programming language. The following Python libraries are available for interacting with several OpenStack services:

- **OpenStack Shade**: This is an easy to use Python library for manipulating OpenStack services
- **OpenStackClients**: These provide native bindings for Python that can be used to implement application programs using the APIs
- **Apache libcloud**: This is the most commonly used Python library and works with multiple cloud providers
- **openstacksdk**: This SDK provides a universal API for OpenStack services

In this chapter, we will focus on using the `openstacksdk` Python library for developing our OpenStack application. Since Python is a platform independent language, the examples in this chapter will also work on Windows platforms.

Creating an application development environment for OpenStack

For creating a development environment on a Unix platform, you will need the following:

- A Linux system (preferably Ubuntu)
- Devstack or OpenStack installed (we have already seen how to install devstack in `Chapter 3`, *Exploring OpenStack Private Cloud*)

- Python 2.7 installed
- Python package managed (pip) installed

We will be using the commonly used `openstacksdk` Python library for developing OpenStack applications. Let's install the SDK using pip.

Log in to your Linux system as a root user and enter the following command:

```
pip install openstacksdk
```

This will install the OpenStack SDK on your system. You are now ready to write your first OpenStack application.

Writing your first OpenStack application

Let's begin by writing a simple application that lists the available VMs running on your OpenStack Compute service node.

We first need to import the OpenStack library into our application program. We will import the Connection class into our program to demonstrate how we can use it. The application program must establish a connection to the OpenStack cloud. This is achieved by creating an object of the connection class and passing the security information and credentials to the constructor of this class. We must pass the following information to the constructor:

- `auth_url`: The keystone authentication URL. This is the URL of your OpenStack keystone service. It is usually set to the IP address or domain name of your OpenStack Keystone node and it is appended with `/identity`.
- `project_name`: This is the name of the project that you want your program to operate in.
- `username`: The name of the user who will be logging into OpenStack via the application program.
- `password`: The password of the user.
- `user_domain`: The domain name of the user.
- `project_domain_id`: The domain identifier of the project.

This creates a connection object that is capable of performing several operations. We can use the object and refer to its subclasses to perform specific operations.

In the following program, we use the connection object to refer to the `compute` class and use its `servers()` function to get a list of running VMs. We then iterate over the list to print all the VMs running on the OpenStack compute node:

```
# Import the OpenStack connection class from the SDK
from openstack import connection

# Create a connection object by calling the constructor and pass the
security information
conn = connection.Connection(auth_url="http://192.168.0.106/identity",
project_name="demo",
username="admin",
password="secret",
user_domain_id="default",
project_domain_id="default")

# Iterate through the list of VMs and print them
for server in conn.compute.servers():
    print(server.name)
```

The previous program gives an idea of how to use the OpenStack Python SDK. We will now explore how we can use this SDK to interact with various services of OpenStack.

Developing OpenStack image service applications

As discussed in `Chapter 3`, *Exploring OpenStack Private Cloud*, the OpenStack imaging service called Glance stores all the VM images in various formats such as `qcow2`, `raw`, and so on. We saw how we could use the OpenStack dashboard to upload, download, and launch a VM image from the Glance database. Lets now see how we can perform the same operations using the Python SDK.

Listing images

We must first create the connection object as explained in the previous section. The VM images stored in the Glance database can be listed simply by iterating over the list by referring to the sub-class `compute` of the connection object and invoking the `images()` function.

This function returns a list of all the VM images present in the Glance database in your project:

```
# Import the OpenStack connection class from the SDK
from openstack import connection

# Create a connection object by calling the constructor and pass the
security information
conn = connection.Connection(auth_url="http://192.168.0.106/identity",
project_name="demo",
username="admin",
password="secret",
user_domain_id="default",
project_domain_id="default")

# Iterate through the list of glance images and print them
for images in conn.compute.images():
    print(images.name)
```

Downloading a VM image

We can download the image stored in the Glance database to your local system where the application program is running. This can be done by creating an image object by locating the image in the Glance database and then using the connection object to refer to the `image` class and invoking the `download_image()` function by passing it the image object.

The following function demonstrates this. It accepts the connection object as an input parameter and then invokes the `conn.image.find_image()` function to create an image object. This object represents the image to be downloaded. Next, it opens a local file for writing and then invokes the `download_image()` function by passing the image object to it. This function returns a response object, which contains the entire image file. The response object is then written to the local file:

```
def download_image(conn):
    # Find the image that you want to download
    image = conn.image.find_image("cirros-0.3.5-x86_64-disk")

    # Open a file to write to in the local system
    with open("local_image.qcow2", "w") as local_file:
        response = conn.image.download_image(image)

        # Write to the local file.
        local_file.write(response)
```

If the image size is very large, it may not be a wise thing to represent the entire VM image as an object in memory. We can choose to download the VM image as streamed data, rather than downloading the entire file all at once. This can be done by simply passing the `stream=True` parameter to the `download_image()` function. We can then read the response object in chunks of a few bytes at a time and then write them to the output file.

The following program demonstrates this:

```
def download_image_stream(conn):
    # Find the image you would like to download.
    image = conn.image.find_image("cirros-0.3.5-x86_64-disk")

    with open("local_image.qcow2", "wb") as local_file:
        response = conn.image.download_image(image, stream=True)

        # Read 2048 bytes per iteration until we read the entire file
        for chunk in response.iter_content(chunk_size=2048):
            local_file.write(chunk)
```

Uploading an image

In `Chapter 2`, *Exploring AWS Cloud*, we discussed different formats of image files such as `raw`, `qcow2`, and so on. The Glance image database stores these images, which can be used to launch VMs.

We can upload different formats of image files to the Glance image store. The following code uploads a `qcow2` image for an Ubuntu operating system. We use the `create_image()` function and pass the image file path to it. The `wait` parameter makes the function wait for the image to be uploaded completely before returning back to the calling program:

```
def upload_image(conn):
    print("Upload Image:")

    # Load fake image data for the example.
    data = 'This is fake image data.'

    # Build the image attributes and upload the image.
    image_attrs = {
        'name': "packtpub-image",
        'data': data,
        'disk_format': 'raw',
        'container_format': 'bare',
        'visibility': 'public',
```

```
    }
    conn.image.upload_image(**image_attrs)
```

Deleting the image

A Glance image can be deleted simply by creating an image object of the image that we want to delete. We can then use the connection object and refer to the `image` class and invoke the `delete_image()` function by passing the image object to it.

The `ignore_missing` determines whether the function will ignore the request if the file is not found or raises an exception:

```
def delete_image(conn):
    image = conn.image.find_image("cirros-0.3.5-x86_64-disk")
    conn.image.delete_image(image, ignore_missing=False)
```

Developing OpenStack compute applications

The OpenStack Compute service provides a hypervisor, which is used to host virtual machines. In `Chapter 2`, *Exploring AWS Cloud*, we have seen how to use the dashboard to launch and manipulate virtual machines in OpenStack. Lets now write some code to perform similar actions.

Listing nova networks

The OpenStack compute service (code-named NOVA) provides networks called nova networks, which can be consumed by the virtual machines. The connection object can refer the `network` class and invoke the `networks()` function to get a list of all the available nova networks.

The following function demonstrates this:

```
def list_networks(conn):
    print("List Networks:")

    for network in conn.network.networks():
        print(network)
```

Creating an SSH key-pair

When an OpenStack virtual machine is launched, you need an SSH key-pair to log in to the virtual machine.

In the following code, we first determine if there's already an existing keypair with the same name. If there isn't, we invoke the `create_keypair()` function of the `compute` class and pass the name of the `keypair` that we want to create. This function returns a `keypair` object, which can be used to extract the private key. We then write this private key to a local file. You may choose to write this file in your `.ssh` folder in your home directory:

```
def create_keypair(conn):
    keypair_name = "packtpub-keypair"     # The name of the keypair to be
created
    private_key_file = "private.key"     # The name of the file that stores
the private key
    keypair = conn.compute.find_keypair(keypair_name)

    if not keypair:
        keypair = conn.compute.create_keypair(name=keypair_name)   # Create
a keypair

        with open(private_key_file, 'w') as filehandle:
            filehandle.write("%s" % keypair.private_key)      # Write the
private key to a file
            os.chmod(private_key_file, 0o400)                 # Change the
permission of the key file

    return keypair
```

Launching a VM

One of the most important operations that our application might have to perform is launching a new virtual machine on OpenStack. Launching a VM requires the VM name, Glance image name, the network name to connect this VM to, and the keypair to be used. Once these parameters are available, we can easily launch a virtual machine using the `create_server()` function call.

The following program creates `image`, `flavor`, `network`, and `keypair` objects and launches a virtual machine. Note that we are using the `create_keypair()` function that we wrote in the last section. The `wait_for_server()` function will ensure that the program waits for the VM to launch and then proceeds:

```
def create_vm(conn):
    server_name = "packt-pub-vm"                  # The name to be given to the
launched VM
    image_name = "cirros-0.3.5-x86_64-disk"       # The glance image name to be
used
    flavor_name = "m1.small"                      # The flavor to be used
    network_name = "private"                      # The network to be used to
connect to

    image = conn.compute.find_image(image_name)          # Locate the image
    flavor = conn.compute.find_flavor(flavor_name)       # Locate the flavor
    network = conn.network.find_network(network_name)    # Locate the network
    keypair = create_keypair(conn)                       # Create a keypair

    # Launch the virtual machine
    server = conn.compute.create_server(
        name=server_name, image_id=image.id, flavor_id=flavor.id,
        networks=[{"uuid": network.id}], key_name=keypair.name)

    # Wait for the virtual machine to launch
    server = conn.compute.wait_for_server(server)
```

Starting a VM

A virtual machine may be in a stopped state and your application program may require to start it. The VM can be powered by invoking the `start_server()` function by passing it the ID of the VM or an object of the Server class.

The following code invokes `start_server()` by passing the ID of the VM:

```
def start_server(conn):
    server_id="7cdaa375-f1b5-40ab-81bd-7e3d052f370d"
    conn.compute.start_server(server_id)
```

Stopping a VM

You can stop a running VM by invoking the `stop_server()` function call. This is very similar to the `start_server()` function call:

```
def stop_server(conn):
    server_id="7cdaa375-f1b5-40ab-81bd-7e3d052f370d"
    conn.compute.stop_server(server_id)
```

Rebooting a VM

A virtual machine may have to be rebooted in certain situations such as after installing specific software packages and so on. We can either perform a `HARD` reboot, which is similar to pressing the `reset` button, or we could perform a `SOFT` reboot, which ensures a graceful shutdown of all running applications before the VM is rebooted.

The function `reboot_server()` accepts two parameters, the `Server` class object or ID of the instance and the type of reboot (`SOFT` or `HARD`). The following program demonstrates a `HARD` reboot of a VM:

```
def reboot_server(conn):
    server_id="7cdaa375-f1b5-40ab-81bd-7e3d052f370d"
    conn.compute.reboot_server(server_id, "HARD")
```

Pausing a VM

A VM can be paused when you do not want it to consume resources when not in need. A paused VM does not consume the resources it requires when it is running. VMs may have to be paused to free up resources so that other VMs can perform better in situations of high workload. This can be done by simply invoking the `pause_server()` function call and passing the server ID or Server object instance:

```
def pause_server(conn):
    server_id="7cdaa375-f1b5-40ab-81bd-7e3d052f370d"
    conn.compute.pause_server(server_id)
```

Unpausing a VM

Similarly, a VM can be unpaused by invoking the `unpause_server()` function call:

```
def unpause_server(conn):
    server_id="7cdaa375-f1b5-40ab-81bd-7e3d052f370d"
    conn.compute.unpause_server(server_id)
```

Creating an image from a VM

Sometimes, you may want to create a persistent image of a running VM so that you can launch more VMs with similar operating systems and applications. You can create a Glance image from a VM programmatically by invoking the `create_server_image()` function call. It accepts the ID of the VM or Server instance object, the name to be given to the image, and the metadata to be associated to the image. The metadata can be set to `None`:

```
def create_image_from_vm(conn):
    server_id="7cdaa375-f1b5-40ab-81bd-7e3d052f370d"
    conn.compute.create_server_image(server_id,"vm_image", metadata=None)
```

IP address

Once a VM is launched, we need to associate it with a network so that other VMs or external users can connect to it. You can assign a fixed or floating IP address to the VM. A fixed IP address is a private IP address that is used for communication between internal OpenStack VMs residing on the same network. A floating IP address is a public IP address that can be used by external hosts or VMs to communicate with OpenStack VMs.

A pool of floating IP addresses must be allocated to a project so that VMs running on that project can claim these IP addresses:

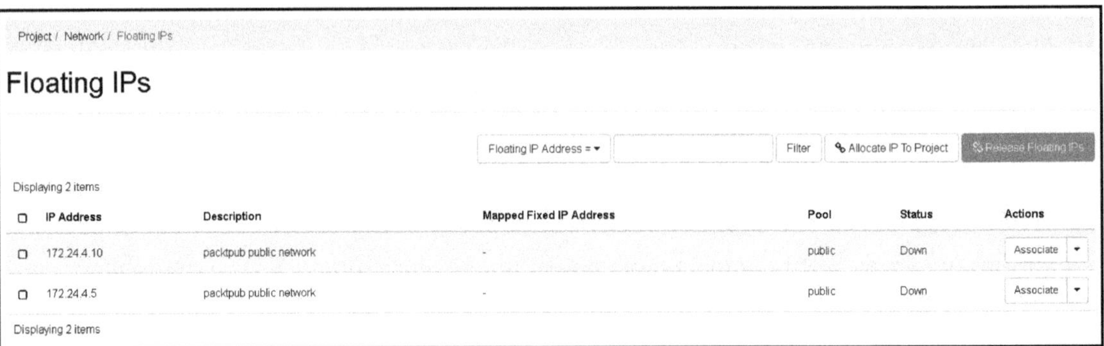

The figure shows two floating IP addresses allocated to the project.

Let's see how we can allocate or deallocate fixed and floating IP addresses using the Python APIs.

Adding a fixed IP address

A fixed or private IP address can be allocated to a VM by associating that VM to a private network. We need a network ID and the server ID to be passed to the `add_fixed_ip_to_server()` function, which assigns the private IP address to the VM:

```
def add_fixed_ip(conn):
    server_id="7cdaa375-f1b5-40ab-81bd-7e3d052f370d"
    network_id="60bf3c33-dc83-4251-8024-f2781e34321d"
    conn.compute.add_fixed_ip_to_server(server_id,network_id)
```

Removing a fixed IP address

A private IP address may also be released by explicitly specifying the IP address to the `remove_fixed_ip_from_server()` function call:

```
def remove_fixed_ip(conn):
    server_id="7cdaa375-f1b5-40ab-81bd-7e3d052f370d"
        conn.compute.remove_fixed_ip_from_server(server_id,"10.0.0.5")
```

Adding a floating IP address

As discussed, a floating IP address can be allocated to the VM by explicitly specifying the IP address from the pool of floating IP addresses available. The function `add_floating_ip_to_server()` accepts the VM instance ID, floating IP address to be assigned, and the optional fixed IP address as its parameters. The `fixed_address` can be set to `None`:

```
def add_floating_ip(conn):
    server_id="7cdaa375-f1b5-40ab-81bd-7e3d052f370d"
conn.compute.add_floating_ip_to_server(server_id,"172.24.4.10",fixed_addres
s=None)
```

Removing a floating IP address

Since floating IP addresses are limited and must be used sparingly, it's necessary to deallocate that IP address when not required.

A floating IP can be deallocated by invoking the `remove_floating_ip_from_server()` function call:

```
def remove_floating_ip(conn):
    server_id="7cdaa375-f1b5-40ab-81bd-7e3d052f370d"
    conn.compute.remove_floating_ip_from_server(server_id,"172.24.4.10")
```

Security groups

We discussed security groups in `Chapter 2`, *Exploring AWS Cloud*, but just to recap, a security group is a set of firewall rules that can be associated to a virtual machine. The ports and protocols allowed in the firewall rules are implemented in the network of the virtual machine.

The following figure shows the firewall rules configured in a security group having the ID, **44c975e3-eeb9-47ec-9f76-2245b2cb59e1**:

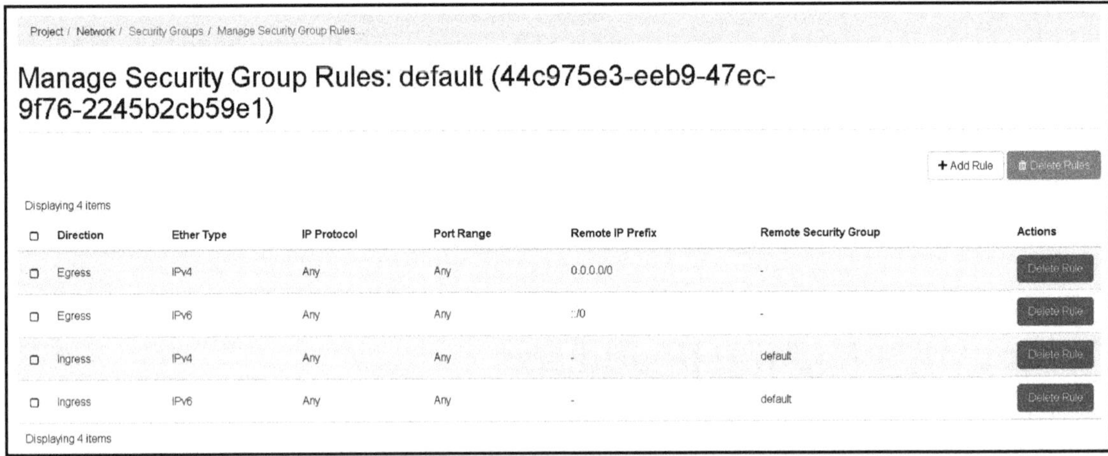

Let's see how we add and remove security groups programmatically.

Adding a security group to a VM

A security group can be assigned to a VM by invoking the `add_security_group_to_server()` function call and passing the VM instance ID and security group ID to it as parameters:

```
def assign_security_group_to_vm(conn):
    server_id="7cdaa375-f1b5-40ab-81bd-7e3d052f370d"
    security_group_id="4bffd353-78ec-4868-8e9b-35e2edc45cdd"
    conn.compute.add_security_group_to_server(server_id, security_group_id)
```

Removing a security group from a VM

Similarly, a security group can be deallocated from the VM simply by invoking the `remove_security_group_from_server()` function call:

```
def remove_security_group_from_vm(conn):
    server_id="7cdaa375-f1b5-40ab-81bd-7e3d052f370d"
    security_group_id="4bffd353-78ec-4868-8e9b-35e2edc45cdd"
    conn.compute.remove_security_group_from_server(server_id,
security_group_id)
```

Listing security groups

The available security groups can be listed by iterating the list returned by the `security_groups()` function call of the network class:

```
def security_groups(conn):
    for port in conn.network.security_groups():
        print(port)
```

Flavors

OpenStack defines a set of templates for virtual machine configurations called **flavors**. A flavor determines the characteristics of the VM such as memory size, disk size, number of CPU cores, and so on.

Listing flavors

The following Python function lists the flavors available:

```
def list_flavors(conn):
    for flavor in conn.compute.flavors():
        print(flavor)
```

Creating a flavor

You may want to define a customized flavor by choosing the amount of RAM, CPU cores, and so on. A custom flavor can be defined by creating a Python dictionary and specifying the flavor properties. The following properties can be specified:

- `links`: [Optional] Links pertaining to this flavor. This is a list of dictionaries, each including keys `href` and `rel`.
- `name`: The name of this flavor.
- `disk`: Size of the disk this flavor offers. Type: `int`
- `is_public`: [Optional] True if this is a publicly visible flavor. False if this is a private image. Type: `bool`
- `ram`: The amount of RAM (in MB) this flavor offers. Type: `int`
- `vcpus`: The number of virtual CPUs this flavor offers. Type: `int`

- `swap`: [Optional] Size of the swap partitions.
- `ephemeral`: [Optional] Size of the ephemeral data disk attached to this server. Type: `int`
- `is_disabled`: [Optional] True if this flavor is disabled, False if not. Type: `bool`
- `rxtx_factor`: [Optional] The bandwidth scaling factor this flavor receives on the network.

The following Python function is used to create a customized flavor:

```
def create_flavor(conn):
    flavor_properties = {'name':'packtpub-flavor', 'disk':'1',
'ram':'2048', 'vcpus':'2'}
    conn.compute.create_flavor(**flavor_properties)
```

Deleting a flavor

A flavor can be removed by invoking the `delete_flavor()` function call and passing the ID of the flavor:

```
def create_flavor(conn):
    flavor_id = "0f97d443-93c9-474c-91a2-6b6e58e44e1a"
    conn.compute.delete_flavor(flavor_id)
```

Developing OpenStack networking applications

We briefly discussed the OpenStack Networking service (Neutron) in `Chapter 2`, *Exploring AWS Cloud*. This service allows the creation and manipulation of virtual networks within the OpenStack environment. When a virtual machine instance is launched, it uses the networks governed by the networking service.

By default, an OpenStack installation provides two networks: public and private. However, your cloud application may require you to create several different networks for different virtual machine instances belonging to different groups. Let's see how we can manipulate networking functionalities using the Python SDK.

Networks

We will look at how we can create and configure OpenStack networking components programmatically.

Creating a network/subnet

A new virtual network can be created by invoking the `create_network()` function call and specifying the name of the network. Once a network is created, we must create a subnet that defines the IP version (IPv4 or IPv6), the subnet CIDR, the gateway, and the name of the subnet.

The following code snippet demonstrates the creation of a virtual network called `packtpub-network` and then creates a subnet called `packtpub-subnet`:

```
def create_network(conn):
    network = conn.network.create_network(name='packtpub-network')
    print(network)

    subnet = conn.network.create_subnet(
          name='packtpub-subnet',
          network_id=network.id,
          ip_version='4',
          cidr='192.168.0.0/24',
          gateway_ip='192.168.0.1')

    print(subnet)
```

Once a network is created, you can assign a network to the virtual machine, as we saw in the previous sections.

Listing networks

The available neutron networks can be listed by iterating over the list returned by the `networks()` function call:

```
def list_networks(conn):
    for network in conn.network.networks():
        print(network)
```

Listing subnets

Similarly, the available subnets can be returned by iterating over the list returned by the `subnets()` function call:

```
def list_subnets(conn):
    for subnet in conn.network.subnets():
        print(subnet)
```

Listing ports

A port defines an endpoint for attaching a networking device such as a Network Interface Card. It also describes the associated networking configuration such as MAC address and IP address that is used on the port.

The following code snippet lists the available ports:

```
def list_ports(conn):
    for port in conn.network.ports():
        print(port)
```

Listing routers

The OpenStack networking service may define routers for defining how we can route network traffic. The following program lists the available routers:

```
def routers(conn):
    for router in conn.network.routers():
        print(router)
```

Listing network agents

The networking service can be configured with different agents. A list of all the configured agents can be obtained as follows:

```
def network_agents(conn):
    for agent in conn.network.agents():
        print(agent)
```

Deleting a network

A network can be deleted by first locating it using the `find_network()` function. This will return a network object that represents the network to be deleted. We can then delete all the subnets associated with that network and then delete the whole network definition.

The following code snippet deletes the subnets, followed by the network:

```
def delete_network(conn):
    network = conn.network.find_network('packtpub-network')

    # Delete all subnets in the network
    for subnet in network.subnet_ids:
        conn.network.delete_subnet(subnet, ignore_missing=False)

    # Delete the network
    conn.network.delete_network(network, ignore_missing=False)
```

Creating a security group

We saw how we can associate a security group to a virtual machine. We can also create a new security group or modify an existing security group to change a firewall rule. For example, we might want to open port `443` on the security group.

The following program demonstrates how we can create a new security group and modify its rules. We first create a security group by invoking the `create_security_group()` function call and providing a name. This function returns an object of the security group, which can then be passed to the `create_security_group_rule()` function along with the parameters that define the rule.

The rule opens the port `443` for the HTTPs protocol for all the incoming network traffic:

```
def open_port(conn):
    security_group = conn.network.create_security_group(name='packtpub-
security-group')

    rule = conn.network.create_security_group_rule(
        security_group_id=security_group.id,
        direction='ingress',
        remote_ip_prefix='0.0.0.0/0',
        protocol='HTTPS',
        port_range_max='443',
        port_range_min='443',
        ethertype='IPv4')
```

Developing OpenStack Identity Service applications

In `Chapter 2`, *Exploring AWS Cloud,* we discussed the OpenStack Identity Service. The OpenStack Identity Service (Keystone) provides identity management and also manages and maintains the creation of users, projects, roles, and so on. This is one of the most important services that all OpenStack applications consume.

User management

An OpenStack user is simply an entity that has an associated username and password along with certain roles that allow the user to perform certain actions on the OpenStack platform. An OpenStack user with administrative privileges is allowed to manipulate users.

Creating a user

To create a new OpenStack user using the Python SDK, we first need to define the properties of the user. A Python dictionary is used to define the properties of the user.

A new OpenStack user can be created by simply invoking the `create_user()` and passing the Python dictionary to the function:

```
def create_user(conn):
    user_parameters = {
                "default_project_id":"demo",
                "email":"manoj.hirway@gmail.com",
                "is_enabled":True,
                "name":"packtpub1",
                "pasword":"secret",
    }

    conn.identity.create_user(**user_parameters)
```

Deleting a user

A user can be deleted by invoking the `delete_user()` function call as passing the ID of the user:

```
def delete_user(conn):
    userid="dc042a1877404151944d4acef30cb702"
    conn.identity.delete_user(userid,ignore_missing=True)
```

Updating a user

Sometimes, a user may update his email or password. The user properties can be updated by invoking the `update_user()` function call and passing the Python dictionary that has the updated user properties:

```
def update_user(conn):
    userid="3fcde77916894498a1d8753d2bafd8ee"
    user_parameters = {
                "default_project_id":"demo",
                "email":"manoj.hirway@packtpub.com",
                "is_enabled":True,
                "name":"packtpub",
                "pasword":"new_password",
    }

    conn.identity.update_user(userid,**user_parameters)
```

Finding a user

We determine if a user exists by finding the user using the `find_user()` function call and passing the username. This function returns an object that represents the user:

```
def find_user(conn):
    username="packtpub"
    user = conn.identity.find_user(username,ignore_missing=True)
    print (user)
```

Roles

A role is a set of privileges that can be assigned to an OpenStack user. For example, we can define a role that provides all administrative access to the OpenStack components. When this role is assigned to a user, the user can perform all administrative tasks.

Creating a role

A new role can be created by invoking the `create_role()` function and passing the Python dictionary that defines the role parameters:

```
def create_role(conn):
    role_desc = {
                 "description":"This is a test role",
                 "isenabled" : True,
                 "name":"packtpub"
    }
    conn.identity.create_role(**role_desc)
```

Updating a role

Updating an existing role is very similar. The `update_role()` function call accepts the role ID and the role parameters, which are used to update the existing role represented by the role ID:

```
def update_role(conn):
    role_id = "ce5156690f4c48bda5b5b9041325e493"
    role_desc = {
                 "description":"This is a test role",
                 "isenabled" : False,
                 "name":"packtpub"
    }
    conn.identity.update_role(role_id, **role_desc)
```

Deleting a role

Finally, a role can be deleted by simply calling the `delete_role()` function and passing the role ID:

```
def delete_role(conn):
    role_id = "ce5156690f4c48bda5b5b9041325e493"
    conn.identity.delete_role(role_id, ignore_missing=True)
```

Projects

As discussed in `Chapter 2`, *Exploring AWS Cloud,* a project is a logical entity that isolates resources from other entities. This makes segregation of OpenStack resources easier.

Creating a project

An OpenStack project can be created by invoking the `create_project()` function call and passing the project descriptor in the form of a Python dictionary:

```
def create_project(conn):
    project_desc = {
                "description":"This project is for packtpub readers",
                "isenabled" : True,
                "name":"packtpub_readers"
    }
    project = conn.identity.create_project(**project_desc)
```

Updating a project

Similarly, an existing project can be updated by passing the project ID and project descriptor Python dictionary to the `update_project()` function call:

```
def update_project(conn):
    project_id = "ce5156690f4c48bda5b5x9041325e493"
    project_desc = {
                "description":"This project is for packtpub authors",
                "isenabled" : True,
                "name":"packtpub_authors"
    }
    conn.identity.update_project(project_id, **project_desc)
```

Deleting a project

A project can be deleted simply by invoking the `delete_project()` function call and passing the project ID to it:

```
def delete_project(conn):
    project_id = "ce5156690f4c48bda5b5b2341325e493"
    conn.identity.delete_project(project_id, ignore_missing=True)
```

Developing block storage applications

The OpenStack block storage service (Cinder) provides the ability to create raw volumes on the underlying disk. The block storage service provides a pluggable architecture wherein you can attach vendor-specific plugins for creation and manipulation of volumes. By default, the block storage service uses Linux's native Logical Volume Manager driver. In other words, when a volume is created using the block storage service, an LVM volume is created underneath.

Let's see what the Python SDK offers for interacting with the block storage service.

Volumes

Let's write application programs to create and delete OpenStack volumes.

Creating a volume

An OpenStack volume can be created by invoking the `create_volume()` function call and passing properties of the volume to be created. These properties are defined using a Python dictionary.

The following properties can be defined using the Python dictionary. Only the `size` parameter is mandatory and all others are optional:

- `id`: An ID representing this volume.
- `name`: The name of this volume.
- `links`: A list of links associated with this volume. Type: `list`
- `availability_zone`: The availability zone.
- `source_volume_id`: To create a volume from an existing volume, specify the ID of the existing volume. If specified, the volume is created with the same size of the source volume.
- `description`: The volume description.
- `snapshot_id`: To create a volume from an existing snapshot, specify the ID of the existing volume snapshot. If specified, the volume is created in the same availability zone and with the same size of snapshot.

- `size`: [Mandatory] The size of the volume, in GBs. Type: `int`
- `image_id`: The ID of the image from which you want to create the volume. Required to create a bootable volume.
- `volume_type`: The name of the associated volume type.
- `is_bootable`: Enables or disables the bootable attribute. A VM can be booted from a volume. Type: `bool`
- `metadata`: One or more metadata key and value pairs to associate with the volume.
- `status`: One of the following values: `creating`, `available`, `attaching`, `in-use deleting`, `error`, `error_deleting`, `backing-up`, `restoring-backup`, `error_restoring`. For details on these statuses, see the block storage API documentation.
- `created_at`: The timestamp of this volume creation.

The following program creates a volume with a size of 2 GB and the name `packtpub-volume`:

```
def create_volume(conn):
    volume_properties = {'size':'2', 'name':'packtpub-volume'}
    volume = conn.block_store.create_volume(**volume_properties)
```

The function returns a volume object, which can be used to retrieve the ID of the volume and other volume properties.

Deleting a volume

A volume can be deleted by invoking the `delete_volume()` function and passing it the ID of the volume:

```
def delete_volume(conn):
    volume_id = "78b54fbd-8b91-4741-9fa4-9fe5416a2e2c"
    conn.block_store.delete_volume(volume_id)
```

Volume snapshots

We can take a point in time snapshot of a volume, which can be used to restore it later.

Creating a snapshot

A volume snapshot can be created by invoking the `create_snapshot()` function and passing it the snapshot properties in the form of a Python dictionary. The following properties can be defined:

- `name`: Name of the snapshot. Default is `None`.
- `description`: Description of snapshot. Default is `None`.
- `metadata`: Metadata associated with this snapshot.
- `volume_id`: The ID of the volume from which the snapshot is to be taken
- `is_forced`: Indicates whether to create snapshot, even if the volume is attached. Default is `False`. Type: `bool`

The following program demonstrates the creation of a volume snapshot. The `volume_id` and size parameters are mandatory. The function returns a snapshot object, which can be used to monitor the status of the snapshot operation by polling the `snapshot.status` parameter:

```
def create_snapshot(conn):
    snapshot_properties =
{'volume_id':'7e9df1bb-6bbf-4d96-92a0-6cb9770ce005','size':'2'}
    snapshot = conn.block_store.create_snapshot(**snapshot_properties)
```

Deleting a snapshot

A snapshot can be deleted by invoking the `delete_snapshot()` function and passing it the ID of the snapshot:

```
def delete_snapshot(conn):
    snapshot_id = "78b54fbd-8b91-4741-9fa4-34j8sdfkh456"
    conn.block_store.delete_snapshot(snapshot_id)
```

The snapshot ID can be retrieved from the id parameter of the snapshot object returned by the `create_snapshot()` function in the last example.

Developing HEAT orchestration templates

We discussed the OpenStack orchestration engine in Chapter 2, *Exploring AWS Cloud*. To recap, OpenStack provides an orchestration engine that can process a template and deploy the specified resources. The template is written in the YAML format.

A basic template that deploys a single VM using the key-pair named `test-key` and the image `cirros` is as follows:

```
heat_template_version: 2015-04-30

description: Simple template that deploys a VM
resources:
  my_instance:
    type: OS::Nova::Server
    properties:
      key_name: test-key
      image: cirros
```

A typical HOT template has three sections: `template version`, `description`, and `resources`. The description is optional, however, it is a good practice to specify the details about a template that you write.

The set of resources that a template deploys together is called a **stack**.

Let's now discuss a complex scenario where we want to deploy two VM instances in a specific order. We want VM1 to be started and booted successfully, before VM2 attempts launch. This can be achieved by using `WaitConditions`. The idea behind using `WaitConditions` is that it is associated with a particular resource and it signals back to the HEAT engine when the resource is configured. The other resource can wait for this signal and only starts its deployment when it receives the signal.

In the following template, we create two resources, VM1 and VM2. The `user_data` section in the template specifies the actions to be taken when the VM is booted. The `bash` commands specified after the `user_data` section are executed from within the deployed VM. In this case, we are sending an `HTTP PUT` request using the `curl` utility to the wait handle. This will ensure that the template engine waits till it receives the PUT request before proceeding to deploy the second resource, that is, VM2.

The second resource, VM2, has the `depends_on` parameter that has the value `VM1`. This specifies to the template engine that the resource VM2 depends on VM1.

Thus, we can ensure that VM1 gets deployed first, and only after it is successfully booted does it send the `HTTP PUT` request back to the HEAT engine, which then proceeds to deploy VM2:

```
heat_template_version: 2015-04-30

description: This template deploys 2 VMs in order. It implements a wait
condition.
resources:
  VM1:
    type: "OS::Nova::Server"
    properties:
      flavor: m1.tiny
      image: cirros
      key_name:
        get_param: key_name
      user_data:
        str_replace:
          template: |
              #!/bin/bash
              curl -X PUT -H 'Content-Type:application/json' \
                   -d '{"Status" : "SUCCESS","Reason" : "Booted
ok","UniqueId" : "VM1","Data" : "VM1 Booted."}' \
                   "$wait_handle$"
          params:
            $wait_handle$:
              get_resource: VM1_wait_handle

  VM1_wait:
    type: "AWS::CloudFormation::WaitCondition"
    depends_on: VM1
    properties:
      Handle:
        get_resource: VM1_wait_handle
      Timeout: 1000

  VM1_wait_handle:
    type: "AWS::CloudFormation::WaitConditionHandle"

  VM2:
    type: "OS::Nova::Server"
    depends_on: VM1_wait
    properties:
      flavor:
```

```
        get_param: instance_type
      image: cirros
      key_name:
        get_param: key_name
      user_data:
        str_replace:
          template: |
              #!/bin/bash
              curl -X PUT -H 'Content-Type:application/json' \
                -d '{"Status" : "SUCCESS","Reason" : "Booted OK","UniqueId"
: "VM2","Data" : "VM2 Booted"}' \
                "$wait_handle$"
          params:
            $data$:
              get_attr:
                - VM1_wait
                - Data
            $wait_handle$:
              get_resource: VM2_wait_handle
  VM2_wait:
    type: "AWS::CloudFormation::WaitCondition"
    depends_on: VM2
    properties:
      Handle:
        get_resource: VM2_wait_handle
      Timeout: 1000

  VM2_wait_handle:
    type: "AWS::CloudFormation::WaitConditionHandle"
```

Thus, OpenStack HEAT templates can be used to automate the deployment of complex environments.

Summary

We started this chapter with a discussion about various OpenStack SDKs available on the market. We created a development environment by installing the Python SDK for OpenStack called **openstacksdk**. We then started by writing a simple OpenStack application that lists the available virtual machines running on the compute node. We wrote application programs to interact with the imaging service that uploads and downloads the images, lists images, and deletes images.

We then explored the SDK further to interact with the OpenStack compute service by writing applications to create a key-pair, launch a new virtual machine, start a VM, stop a VM, pause and unpause a VM, and reboot the VM. We also saw how to create an image from a running virtual machine, assign and unassign a security group to and from a VM, assign and unassign fixed and floating IP addresses to the VMs, and create a custom flavor.

Next, we used the SDK to interface with the networking service. We wrote programs to create and delete a new virtual network and subnet, list available networks, list subnets, and list ports, routers, and network agents. We then created a new security group and defined its firewall rules programmatically.

The Identity Service was leveraged by the SDK by writing application programs that create a new user, delete a user, update the user, and find the user. We also created, updated, and deleted roles and projects. We used the SDK for creating and deleting an OpenStack volume and also created and deleted snapshots of the volumes. Finally, we discussed the OpenStack orchestration service and saw a complex HOT template that deployed two VMs in a specific order.

The code examples shown in this chapter give you an idea of how each API can be leveraged in your applications. You can now write more complex applications that can make use of these APIs.

This concludes our discussion about developing OpenStack applications.

6
Cloud Migration

In the previous chapter, we saw how we can develop cloud applications on the AWS and OpenStack platforms. The application that you developed may use some AWS features along with some OpenStack services to work as a hybrid cloud application. In this chapter, we will look at how we can migrate virtual machines across private and public clouds.

The following topics are covered in this chapter:

- Choosing the right cloud provider
- Setting up the hybrid cloud environment
- Cloud migration
- Benefits of cloud migration
- Possible risks of cloud migration
- Cost comparison

Choosing the right cloud provider

With the cloud market expanding, there are many cloud providers available in the market today. Hence, choosing the right cloud provider that meets the business needs is vital.

The following are the factors that must be considered while choosing a cloud provider:

- **Type of service offered:** The cloud computing needs of the business determine the type of services that are expected from the cloud provider. For example, if the business needs an on-demand storage space that can expand up to several terabytes, a cloud provider that provides a low cost and reliable storage service should be chosen.
- **Pricing:** Public cloud providers charge the user based on the consumption of resources. The pricing structure of the cloud provider must be taken into consideration while choosing the services.

- **Security:** Data and infrastructure security is one of the most important aspects in cloud computing. The cloud provider must enforce sufficient security measures, such as implementation of firewalls, anti-virus detection, multi-factor user authentication, and also data encryption for data at rest. The cloud provider should also perform routine security audits to meet the compliance requirements as far as security is concerned.
- **Data center locations:** The cloud provider must have data centers located in safe locations. Natural disasters such as fires, floods, earthquakes, and storms may impact the data center, which could result in loss of data and affect business continuity. Hence, a disaster recovery site should be in place.
- **Data loss:** Sufficient provisions should be made in the provider's **service level agreement** (**SLA**) to ensure rectification of a data loss situation. The cloud provider should ensure high availability of data by using backup and replication techniques.
- **Scalability:** The cloud should be able to scale with the increasing business requirements and should not become a bottleneck.
- **Downtime history:** The cloud provider should have zero or negligible downtime history. This will give confidence to the customers.

Consideration of the aforementioned factors while choosing a cloud provider will certainly help in making the right decision.

Setting up a hybrid cloud environment

In `Chapter 1`, *Introducing Hybrid Clouds*, we discussed the concept of the hybrid cloud. To recap, a hybrid cloud is a combination of a public and a private cloud connection, using a secure network.

The following steps must be carried out to set up a hybrid cloud environment:

1. Choose the public cloud provider and set up the cloud account (for example, AWS, Azure, and so on).
2. Install and configure your private cloud environment (for example, OpenStack).
3. Establish a connection between the public and private cloud using a VPN by creating a gateway and setting up networking and routing configurations.

The fundamental idea is that you must connect your private cloud data center to a public cloud. This is typically done over a secure IPsec VPN connection (also called a **VPN tunnel**). Many organizations already have a VPN device setup within their internal network so that the network is accessible from outside. Many public cloud providers also provide a VPN service.

The service instances that you launch on the AWS cloud inside a VPC cannot communicate with the private network of your organization. To enable this communication, you must:

- Attach a virtual private gateway to the VPC
- Create custom routing tables specific to your network environment
- Modify the security group rules to allow communication ports
- Create an AWS managed VPN connection

AWS supports **Internet Protocol security** (**IPsec**) VPN connections.

The VPN connection has two main components:

- **The virtual private gateway**: The virtual private gateway is the VPN endpoint on the AWS side of the VPN connection. You must create a virtual private gateway and connect it to the **virtual private cloud** (**VPC**) from which you intend to connect using the VPN. When creating a gateway, you can specify the **autonomous system number** (**ASN**) for the AWS side of the gateway. If you do not specify it, a default value of `64,512` is used. Once an ASN is set, you cannot change it.
- **Customer gateway**: The customer gateway is the hardware device or a software application on the consumer side of the VPN connection. There are several VPN software applications available in the market. For creating the customer gateway, you must provide the gateway information to AWS.

The following table indicates the information that needs to be provided to AWS:

AWS section	Description
IP address for the customer gateway	The customer gateway should have a publicly routable static IP address. If the gateway is behind the NAT device, you can use the public IP address of the NAT device and tweak the firewall rules.
Type of routing	Whether to use static routing or dynamic routing.
Border gateway protocol (**BGP**) and ASN number of the customer gateway (for dynamic routing)	You can either use an existing ASN that is assigned to the network or use a private ASN in the range of `64,512` to `65,534`. However, if you use the VPC wizard to set up the VPC, the `65,000` ASN is used.

In order to use the Amazon VPC, you must provide the gateway configuration information to your network administrator so that he can configure the customer gateway or the software application you intend to use for the VPN. Once the configuration is done, the VPN tunnel is started up when there is network traffic generated from the consumer side of the VPN connection. The virtual private gateway does not initiate the connection.

Cloud migration

We have seen how cloud computing offers several advantages over the traditional local data center approach. Due to this, more and more companies are eager to join the cloud revolution and leverage the benefits that it offers.

Cloud migration is a strategy to migrate the existing infrastructure to the cloud. For example, an organization may decide to migrate their production VM to the AWS cloud.

Cloud migration decisions can be based on several factors. Some of the common reasons why organizations choose to migrate their data centers to the cloud are as follows:

- **Data center lease expiration**: Many organizations lease their data center from vendors. When the lease is due to expire, it is wise to migrate the data center to the cloud.

- **Hardware upgrade and its costs**: A growing organization may need to upgrade their hardware from time to time, so as to accommodate the business requirements. Instead of spending large funds on purchasing new hardware, organizations prefer to migrate their IT environment to the cloud.
- **Renewal of software licenses**: Some of the software that the organizations use have huge license costs. When these licenses are due to expire, purchasing new licenses is expensive and the IT budget may not be able to accommodate this. It is therefore wise to use the application that is hosted in the cloud, which can be used at nominal costs.
- **Location and privatization requirements for regulatory compliance**: A compliance requirement may mandate the presence of the IT infrastructure across certain geographical locations or enforce the need for a non-shareable infrastructure. For example, an HIPAA compliant hosting environment requires a non-shareable environment. The cloud provides the flexibility to have the data centers at various cloud regions where the data centers are hosted.
- **Global market expansion**: Expanding the customer base of the organization may require its servers to be present in different countries. The public cloud platform provides this flexibility to deploy the data center into various cloud servers located in different countries.

Let's now looks at some simple examples of migrating a typical VM from OpenStack to AWS and vice versa.

Application migration strategies

Application migration can be done in several different ways. The following are the most popular application migration strategies that may be used for smooth migration of applications to the cloud.

The following diagram illustrates various strategies of cloud migration:

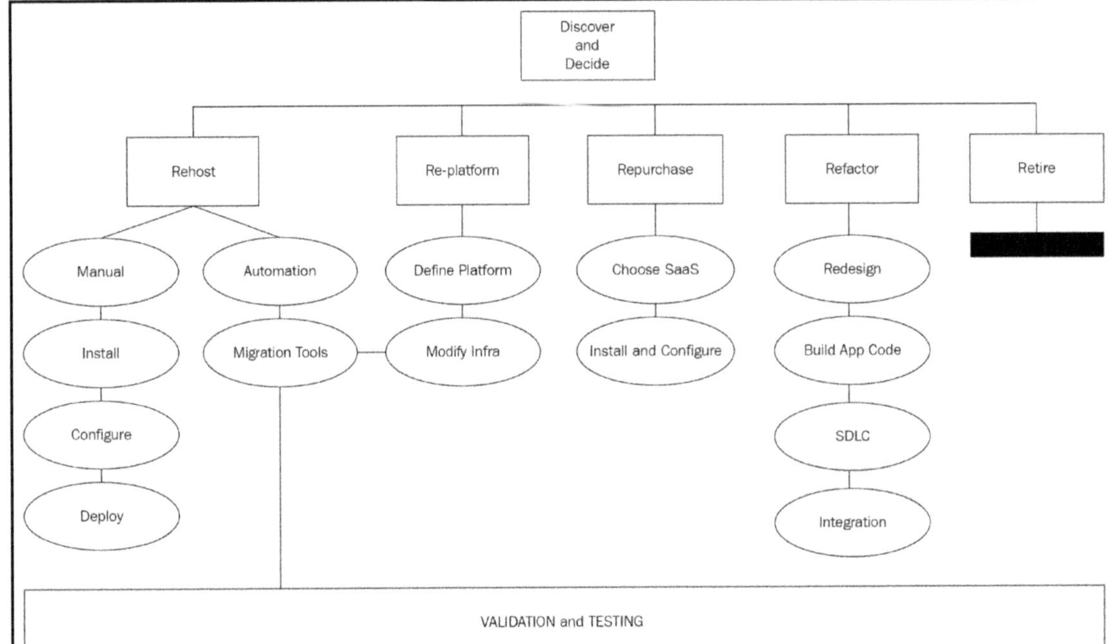

Rehosting

Rehosting is a process of migrating the entire operating system that hosts the application. For example, if you have an **Oracle E-Business Suite** application running on your Red Hat Linux operating system in the local data center, you may choose to migrate the entire operating system to the cloud. AWS provides a way to do this using the **AWS VM Import/Export** feature. (We will discuss importing and exporting a VM to and from AWS in the next section.)

Replatforming

Sometimes, it is easier to choose a different application platform than migrating the entire operating system to the cloud. For example, an organization may have a web server that uses WebLogic. Instead of migrating this entire operating system, it would be wise to choose the AWS provided Apache Tomcat server instance. This can help in saving huge license costs.

Repurchasing

Repurchasing actually means migrating to a different software product altogether. For example, an organization may find it easy to use Salesforce, which is already hosted in the cloud platform, rather than choosing to migrate their existing legacy CRM application to the cloud.

Refactoring

This approach is suitable for complex applications which have several components. It involves re-imagining how the application is architected and developed by leveraging cloud-native features. This strategy is the most expensive, but offers many benefits, as the application can be customized to utilize the cloud offerings in the most efficient manner.

For example, an organization may refactor an application with a monolithic architecture to a service-oriented architecture (serverless architecture).

Retiring

Once you have migrated your application to the cloud, many servers and appliances in your existing IT infrastructure may become idle and stay unused. Getting rid of such infrastructure will help in saving costs and thus help the business.

AWS migration tools

AWS provides several tools for making the cloud migration process smooth for its customers. The following are some of the tools that can be leveraged while migrating to the AWS cloud.

AWS Migration Hub

The **AWS Migration Hub** provides a single location to monitor and track the application migration activities across AWS and other partner solutions. It allows migration administrators to choose the AWS and partner migration tools that suit the needs of the organization's infrastructure. It also provides key metrics and processes of individual applications, irrespective of the tools used for migration.

AWS Application Discovery Service

Proper planning and application discovery are indispensable tasks that must be performed before the actual migration is done.

The AWS Application Discovery Service helps administrators to plan their migration activities by collecting information about the organization's data center. It gathers and provides reports related to configuration, usage, and data behavior from the servers of the data center. This information helps administrators to better understand the workloads and gives an idea about what will be required in the migration activity.

AWS Server Migration Service

Migration automation should be done as much as possible in the cloud migration project. The **AWS Server Migration Service** allows administrators to automate, schedule, and track incremental replications of live server volumes. This makes it easier for administrators to coordinate large-scale server migrations.

AWS Database Migration Service

Migrating databases is a complex process and must be done carefully. The AWS **Database Migration Service** (**DMS**) makes it easy and secure. It ensures that the source data remains fully online and available during the process of migration. This minimizes the downtime of the database and business critical applications that rely on the database.

The DMS supports many widely used commercial database applications as well as open source databases.

AWS S3 Transfer Acceleration

The **S3 Transfer Acceleration** service makes it faster to transfer data to the S3 buckets. It helps in maximizing the available bandwidth, regardless of the internet speed variations.

AWS Snowball

Organizations may have very large amounts of data that may have to be migrated to the cloud. **AWS Snowball** is a petabyte scale data transport solution that uses secure appliances to transfer such huge volumes of data to and from the AWS cloud. It resolves the challenges of high network costs, longer transfer times, and security concerns, which are critical problems when transferring large amounts of data.

AWS Snowmobile

The **AWS Snowmobile** is designed to transfer extremely high volumes of data to AWS. It can transfer up to 100 PB per Snowmobile, a 45-feet long rugged shipping container which is pulled by a semi-trailer truck. This makes it easier to move massive volumes of data to the cloud.

AWS Direct Connect

Sometimes it is necessary to establish a dedicated network connection between your organization's internal network and the AWS cloud. The **AWS Direct Connect** service helps you do this. It uses the industry standard 802.1q VLAN, which allows the network to be partitioned into multiple virtual networks. AWS Direct Connect improves the network speeds.

AWS Kinesis Firehouse

AWS Kinesis Firehouse provides an easy way to load streaming data into AWS. It can automatically load streaming data into S3 and Redshift by capturing it and it also allows us to use real-time analytics with the available business intelligence tools. It provides the ability to batch, compress, and also encrypt the data before loading it. This minimizes the amount of storage required to store the data and also increases security.

Let's now take a closer look at the first approach where we migrate an entire VM to and from the AWS cloud.

Migrating a VM to AWS

Consider a VM running on your local virtualized environment, be it OpenStack or any other platform. We can migrate it to AWS simply by getting its image and uploading it to an S3 bucket and then creating an AMI out of it.

The following diagram shows how this is done:

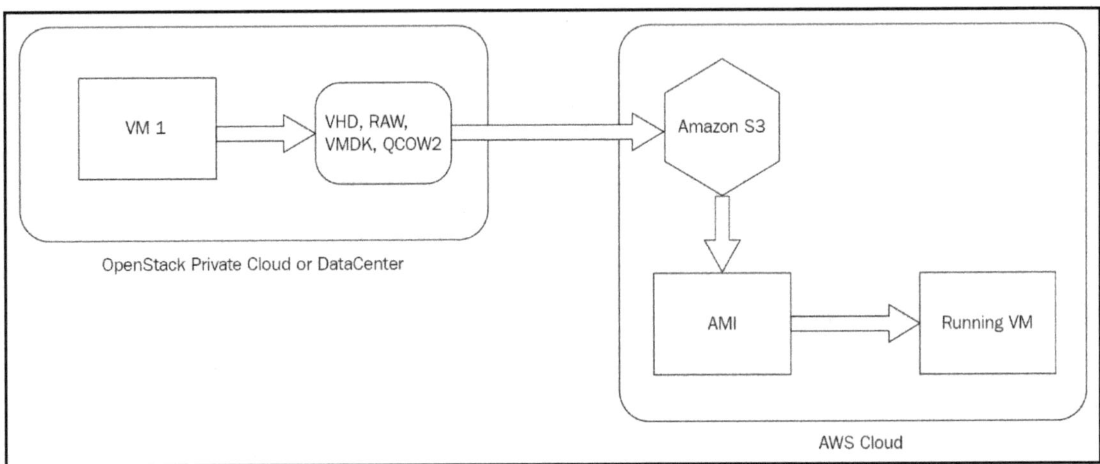

Let's see how we can migrate a VM from a local virtualized environment to the AWS cloud.

The following steps demonstrate the migration of a local VM to AWS:

1. Export the virtual machine as an image. Your virtual environment stores in VM a format such as `vmdk`, `vhd`, `qcow2`, and so on.
2. Create an AWS S3 bucket in the region where you want your AMI to be located.
3. Create a `VM-Import Service` role using the following steps (your account must have this role to be able to import a VM, download disk images from S3, and so on):
    1. Create a file named `trust-policy.json` with the following contents:

```
{
  "Version": "2012-10-17",
  "Statement": [
     {
        "Effect": "Allow",
        "Principal": { "Service": "vmie.amazonaws.com" },
        "Action": "sts:AssumeRole",
        "Condition": {
```

```
            "StringEquals": { "sts:Externalid": "vmimport" }
         }
      }
   ]
}
```

2. Create a role named `vmimport` and assign the AWS VM import/export access to it:

   ```
   aws iam create-role --role-name vmimport --assume-role-
   policy-document file://trust-policy.json
   ```

3. Create a file named `role-policy.json` with the following contents. Replace `bucket-name` with the name of your S3 bucket which you created in step 1:

```
{
   "Version":"2012-10-17",
   "Statement": [
     {
           "Effect":"Allow",
           "Action": [
                "s3:GetBucketLocation",
                "s3:GetObject",
                "s3:ListBucket"
            ],
            "Resource": ["arn:aws:s3::bucket-name",
"arn:aws:s3::bucket-name/*"]
       },
       {
            "Effect":"Allow",
            "Action": [ "ec2:ModifySnapshotAttribute",
                        "ec2:CopySnapshot",
                        "ec2:RegisterImage",
                        "ec2:Describe*" ],
            "Resource":"*"
        }
   ]
}
```

4. Attach the preceding policy to the role by invoking the following command:

   ```
   aws iam put-role-policy --role-name vmimport --policy-name
   vmimport --policy-document file://role-policy.json
   ```

4. Upload the VM image that you exported to the S3 bucket.
5. Import the image from the S3 buckets using the following command:

```
aws ec2 import-image --description "Windows 2008 OVA" --license-
type <value> --disk-containers file://containers.json
```

6. The `containers.json` file should have the bucket name and key of the image file that you uploaded:

```
[
  {
    "Description": "Windows 2008 OVA",
    "Format": "ova",
    "UserBucket": {
        "S3Bucket": "my-import-bucket",
        "S3Key": "vms/my-windows-2008-vm.ova"
    }
}]
```

7. You can now check the status of the import by invoking the following command:

```
aws ec2 describe-import-image-tasks --import-task-ids import-ami-
abcd1234
```

This command will return one of the following statuses:

- `active`: The import task is in progress
- `deleting`: The import task is being cancelled
- `deleted`: The import task is cancelled
- `updating`: The import status is updating
- `validating`: The imported image is being validated
- `converting`: The imported image is being converted into an AMI
- `completed`: The import task is completed and the AMI is ready to use

You will now have the import image as an **AMI** showing up in the selected region. You can launch an EC2 instance using this AMI.

Migrating from AWS to OpenStack

Not all of the VMs or workloads may be suitable to be run on the public cloud. Several organizations have decided to run their workloads in the local data center, so as to have more control over the resources, for better cost advantage, or for better performance. Hence, there is a need to migrate workloads from the public cloud to the private cloud.

The following diagram shows the steps involved in migrating an AWS EC2 instance to OpenStack:

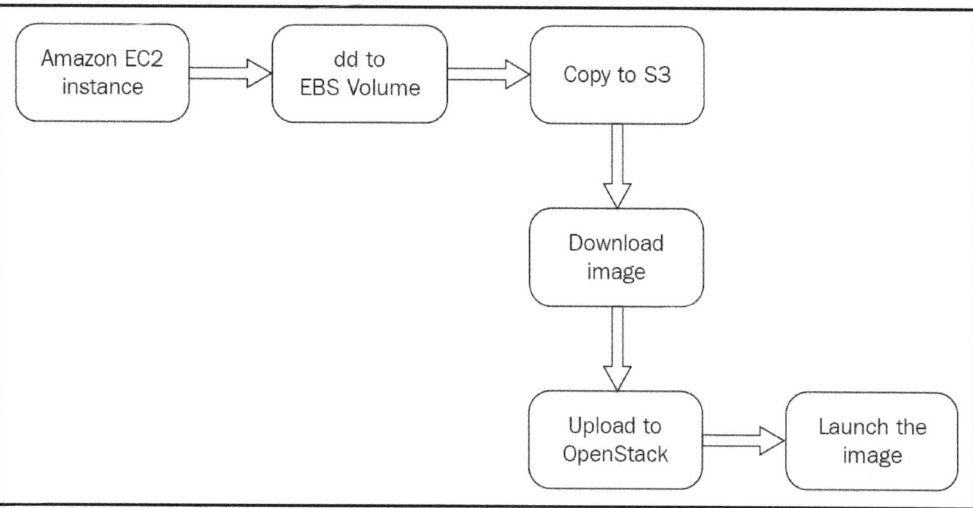

You will need the following in order to migrate an EC2 instance from AWS to your OpenStack cloud platform:

- AWS CLI installed
- AWS S3 bucket
- EC2 instance to be migrated

The following steps must be performed to migrate an EC2 instance to OpenStack:

1. Create a new AWS EBS volume with a large size as per the EC2 instance disk:

```
aws ec2 create-volume -size 16 -region us-west-1 -availability-zone
us-west-1b -volume-type gp2
```

2. Attach the volume to the EC2 instance that you intend to migrate:

```
aws ec2 attach-volume -volume-id <volume id> -instance-id
<instance id> -device /dev/sdb
```

3. Partition the newly added disk as an `ext4` filesystem:

```
mkfs.ext4 /dev/xvdf1
```

4. Mount the `disk` to a folder of your choice:

```
mount /dev/xvdf1 /mnt/disk
```

5. Using `dd`, copy the root `disk` of the EC2 instance to an image file on the new disk. This operation will take some time depending on the size of the disk:

```
dd if=/dev/xvda of=/mnt/disk/vm.img
```

6. Copy the disk file to S3 using the following command (replace the bucket name with the name that you used):

```
aws s3 cp /mnt/disk/vm.img s3://packtpub-bucket/
```

7. Copy the image from the S3 bucket to your local OpenStack image server:

```
aws s3 cp s3://packtpub-bucket/vm.img /tmp/image/
```

8. Using the OpenStack glance client, import the AMI to the OpenStack environment:

```
glance image-create -disk-format raw -container-format bare -name
packtpubAMI -file /tmp/image/vm.img -progress
```

9. Once the image is imported into the glance image server, you can now launch the OpenStack VM using the image:

```
nova boot --flavor m1.tiny --image packtpubAMI --nic net-
id=PRIVATE_NET_ID \
 --security-group default --key-name packtpubkey  testvm
```

Here `PRIVATE_NET_ID` is the ID of the network to be used for launching the instance.

Benefits of cloud migration

Migrating to the cloud offers several benefits depending on the needs of the organization.

Companies decide the migrate to the cloud due to the following benefits:

- **Scalability**: This is one of the biggest benefits of migrating to the cloud. Any future resource requirements are automatically taken care of by the cloud platform.
- **Cost**: Organizations can reduce their IT infrastructure costs by migrating to a low cost cloud platform and thus ensure efficient utilization of resources.
- **Storage**: Keeping storage devices in the local data center invokes risks as well as requiring large maintenance. It also requires periodic backups to ensure data protection. Moving to the cloud storage makes it easier to manage storage.
- **Updates to applications**: IT administrators no longer have to worry about updating their operating systems and production applications, as this is done automatically on the cloud.
- **Mobility**: The employees in the organization can access their applications anywhere from the internet.

Risks of cloud migration

Even with all the advantages that the cloud offers, there are a few drawbacks. Since cloud migration technologies are still in the nascent state, there are a few kinks that must be ironed out.

The following are a few risks arising out of cloud migration:

- **Sensitive data**: Organizations have a lot of sensitive data, which they cannot afford to get leaked or lost. Since moving this data to the cloud is a time-intensive task, migrating such data to the cloud must be done with extreme care and careful planning.
- **Security**: In today's digital world, cloud security has become one of the most indispensable needs. Special care must be taken while migrating the resources to the cloud to prevent hackers or intruders from attacking the critical data.

- **Application interoperability**: Every vendor approaches the cloud in its own way. This causes a lot of incompatibility and interoperability issues with different applications running on the cloud. Ideally, every application that runs on the cloud must be able to run across all the platforms provided by different vendors.
- **Time and cost of cloud migration**: The time required for migration to the cloud is large and organizations may have to obtain a large downtime. The costs involved in the migration process may also be high. The data transfer and bandwidth costs incurred during the first phase of migration may be very high and may also affect the productivity of the employees.

The following points should be considered in order to minimize the risks associated with cloud migration:

- **Encrypted filesystems**: When migrating data from one server to another, the data should always be stored on encrypted filesystems. This will prevent any confidential data from being discovered by unauthorized users. Technologies such as HTTPS should be used to securely transfer data across servers.
- **Regular backups**: Data protection is one of the most imported proactive measures that needs to be taken to ensure that data is not lost. In the event of a disk crash, organizations should always have a redundant copy of the data.
- **Skilled engineers**: Migrating to the cloud is a complex process and may require expertise. Getting the right people to work on the migration activity will definitely reduce the risk of failures and data loss.
- **Application identification**: Not all applications may be required to be migrated to the cloud. Organizations must decide the number of applications that will really provide value to the user once they are migrated to the cloud.
- **Costs**: A detailed costs calculation must be performed before deciding to migrate to the cloud. This will give a clear picture of the cost comparison between using the local data center versus the cloud platform.

Cost benefits of cloud migration

Migrating to the cloud offers the following cost benefits:

- **Efficient hardware utilization**: In a cloud environment, the hardware is efficiently utilized and shared among other organizations' computing needs. This optimizes the use of the hardware, which means lower costs for the organization.

- **Lower power costs**: Better hardware utilization means more efficient power usage. Idle servers waste a lot of power, which is prevented in the cloud environment. Organizations have to pay large costs when the hardware is running in their local data center.
- **Lower people costs**: In order to maintain the IT infrastructure, talented engineers are hired by the organization. Hiring such engineers is expensive, which is why the staffing budget of most organizations is much higher. The amount of money spent on staffing usually exceeds the costs of the actual hardware and software. When the data center is migrated to the cloud, these costs are saved.
- **Zero capital costs**: Running a local data center involves high initial investment to buy all the necessary hardware. Financing such hardware dents the organization's balance sheet. Using the cloud platform saves on these costs, as companies no longer have to buy, own, and maintain hardware and software.

Summary

In this chapter, we discussed setting up a hybrid cloud environment using AWS. Essentially, a hybrid cloud environment is just about connecting your data center to the public cloud, using a VPN connection. We then discussed cloud migration and saw how we could migrate the virtual machine to and from OpenStack and AWS. Later, we talked about the benefits that cloud migration offers and the risks involved with it. Lastly, we discussed the financial advantages that the cloud platform brings to the organizations.

7
Hybrid Cloud Best Practices

In the last few chapters, we discussed the AWS and OpenStack cloud platforms, along with the administration techniques involved in using the native user interface. We also saw how we could develop application programs that leverage the services offered by these cloud platforms. In this chapter, we will focus on the best practices that should be followed when using these cloud platforms.

The following topics will be covered in this chapter:

- Cloud agnostic application development
- Usage of the AWS root account
- Security group configuration
- Data backup
- High availability
- Cloud monitoring
- Cloud automation
- Cloud orchestration
- Co-location of data and applications
- Scaling
- Handling legacy applications
- Resource utilization and costs
- Centralized cloud management
- Designing for failure
- Application decoupling

Let's begin by discussing some AWS best practices that must be followed while using the AWS cloud in your hybrid cloud environment.

Hybrid cloud strategy best practices

Although there are hundreds of AWS best practices that we could discuss, the following are some of the most important ones.

Pluggable architecture

One of the most important aspects of a hybrid cloud application is that it should not be tied with a particular cloud. In other words, the application should have the ability to be easily migrated from one cloud to another. For example, if your application uses the AWS API Gateway, Lambda, S3, and Aurora DB extensively, and if in the future the application requires using object storage of some other cloud, some rewriting of the application code might be required. This will also get you locked to a particular cloud ecosystem and make it extremely difficult to move your application to any other cloud provider.

To avoid this, the hybrid cloud application must be developed using abstract APIs, which are wrappers around the actual cloud APIs. The cloud to be used underneath must be configurable. The application must be able to switch to different clouds depending on the parameters set. In other words, the hybrid cloud application should have a pluggable architecture.

Consider the application code, which has a function called **Connect()**, which actually connects to the cloud:

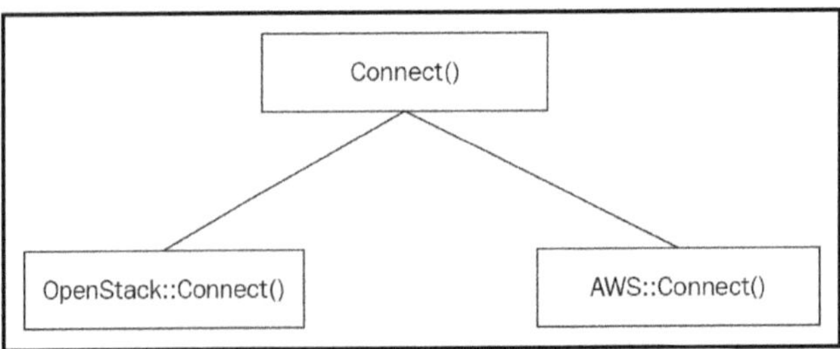

The **connect()** function is an abstract function that has concrete implementations of specific clouds. The invocation of the appropriate function must be decided upon based on the chosen cloud. When the application is configured for the OpenStack cloud, the **OpenStack::Connect()** function must be invoked. Similarly, when it is configured for the AWS cloud, the **AWS::Connect()** function should be invoked.

AWS root account

Since the usage of the AWS services is charged based on the resources used, the AWS account represents a business account between the user and the AWS Cloud. The AWS root account has the privileges to manage the services and resources. Using this account for day-to-day operations is risky. Hence, one of the most important best practices while using the AWS Cloud is to avoid creating an AWS access key for the root account. Instead, you can create separate user accounts in the **Identity Access Management** (**IAM**). The users can then be provided with the required permissions for performing their day-to-day tasks.

Security group rules

The AWS Security Group provides a firewall between the external network and the AWS Cloud. Security Groups rules should be carefully configured to allow and disallow respective protocols and network ports.

For example, consider a three-tier web application that has a database tier, an application tier, and a web server tier. Since the external users will only need access to the web server, via HTTP or HTTPS, it would be ideal to open only ports `80` for HTTP or `447` for HTTPS in the security group configured for the web server instance. This prevents the web server from being exposed to the external networks. Moreover, you may also want to allow access to the application tier only for a specific set of IP addresses. For example, you can set a rule that allows access to the application server only from IP address `192.168.2.1`. This prevents any other hosts from accessing the application server, and thus increases the security.

Data backup

Although AWS guarantees data protection, there might be instances of volume failures. It is always a good idea to regularly back up your instance data using the EBS snapshots. You can also choose to use a third-party backup tool to schedule regular backups of your critical data.

The Amazon S3 object store provides a highly secure and scalable storage facility. You may choose to use S3 to back up and restore any amount of data. The Amazon Glacier service is also another low-cost archiving service that provides secure and durable storage for data archiving.

High availability

AWS provides multiple availability zones. Each zone has its own data centers. It is wise to deploy your critical applications across multiple availability zones and keep replicating the data regularly. This provides high availability for the application. For example, when servers in one availability zone have outages, the servers in the other availability zone should still be running and can provide failover to support the application.

You must ensure that you are prepared to handle a failover. Elastic IPs and availability zones are two key resources required for creating a stable failover setup. Elastic IPs can be dynamically remapped to a different instance when needed and hence are very useful in the event of failovers.

The following diagram shows the deployment that is enabled for failovers in the AWS Cloud:

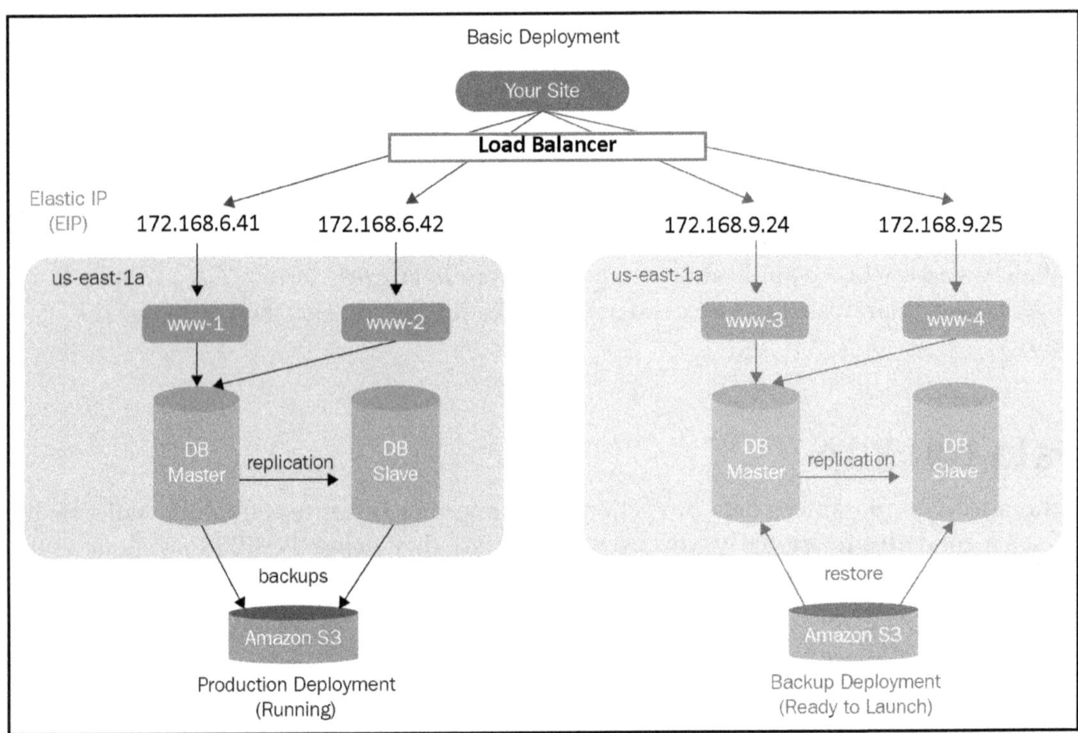

Cloud monitoring

To ensure the health of the cloud platform, it is important to keep monitoring the resources used and ensure that everything is functioning well.

The cloud monitoring platform should be able to combine the metrics from the private as well as the public cloud using the cloud-native APIs, along with traditional metrics, and present data that is essential to the business.

AWS provides the CloudWatch service, which provides a stream of events describing the changes to the AWS resources. For example, if your EC2 instance fails a system health check, the CloudWatch service generates an event and notifies the user. For developers, a suspicious API call pattern can be logged using the AWS CloudTrail service.

Such events must be attended and responded to quickly. AWS services deliver notifications in real time and hence these services should be leveraged extensively to monitor and respond to events.

In a hybrid cloud environment, it is natural to have resources distributed across private and public clouds. Monitoring both these environments separately is cumbersome. Hence it is best to have a common monitoring platform for analyzing both the environments. Uniform data gives comprehensive visibility into the hybrid cloud network and applications. There are many open source software available in the market, such as Prometheus, Sensu, Nagios, and so on, that provide a consolidated monitoring solution:

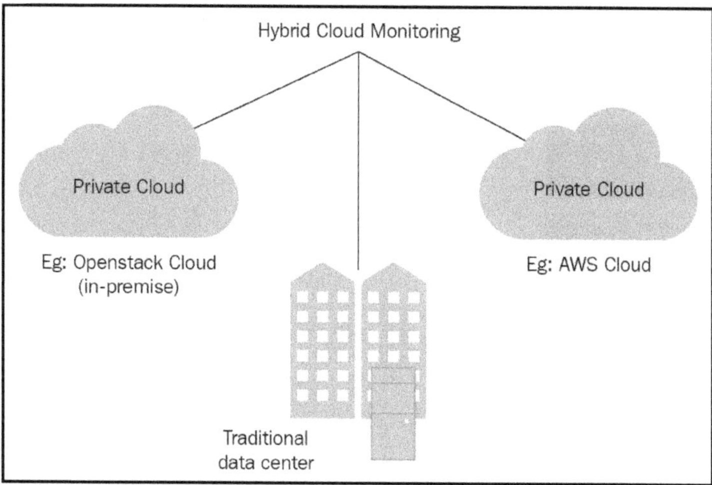

Cloud automation

Cloud automation refers to the technique of automating individual tasks, such as installing an application, restarting a service, rebooting a server, and so on. It also involves auto load balancing of servers that have a high workload and the auto-scaling of servers. AWS provides many automation tools for achieving this.

Automation tools eradicate human interference in the workflows, which therefore also reduces the risks of introducing errors. It also enables DevOps teams to request resources and provision them in the cloud environment.

Cloud orchestration

Cloud orchestration is the technique of performing automation using a specific order with certain security group rules, role assignments, and permissions. Orchestration tools leverage automation tools to create processes that perform individual tasks in a specific order.

AWS provides orchestration tools using the CloudFormation service. Similarly, OpenStack provides the HEAT orchestration service.

Both these services must be leveraged in the hybrid cloud environment and must be used by hybrid cloud applications to automate certain tasks.

There are several third-party tools available for performing cloud orchestration. The following diagram shows a few commonly used tools:

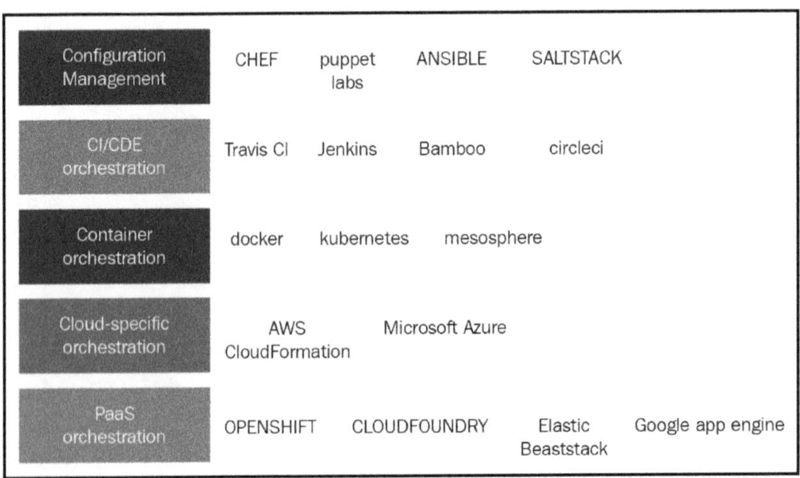

Co-locating data and application tiers

The cloud environment can be scattered across various locations and data centers. Organizations that use applications that are performance intensive should take steps to ensure that the application is co-located with the data it uses. In other words, if the application is running in a public cloud, it is a good practice to store the data it uses in the public cloud. Similarly, if the applications reside in the private cloud, it is wise to keep the data in the private data center. This improves the performance of the application.

Cloud administrators who are looking for performance benefits from their hybrid cloud platforms should consider this important point before developing and deploying hybrid cloud applications.

Scaling

One of the most significant advantages that a hybrid cloud platform provides is the ability to scale data centers. It is therefore necessary to build hybrid cloud applications considering the scalability aspects. For example, the application architecture must be designed to support growth in users, network traffic, or even data size without any impact on the application performance. The application should be able to scale linearly in such a way that adding more resources should result in the ability to service additional workloads.

The hybrid cloud application must take into account two different types of scaling: vertical scaling and horizontal scaling.

Vertical scaling

Vertical scaling happens when additional specifications are added to the individual resource, such as upgrading a server with a more powerful CPU or larger memory. OpenStack and AWS both allow resizing a virtual machine instance by stopping it and editing its properties. After a certain level, vertical scaling can reach a set limit and may not be a very cost-effective and efficient approach.

Although this approach is easy to perform, it should only be done in moderation:

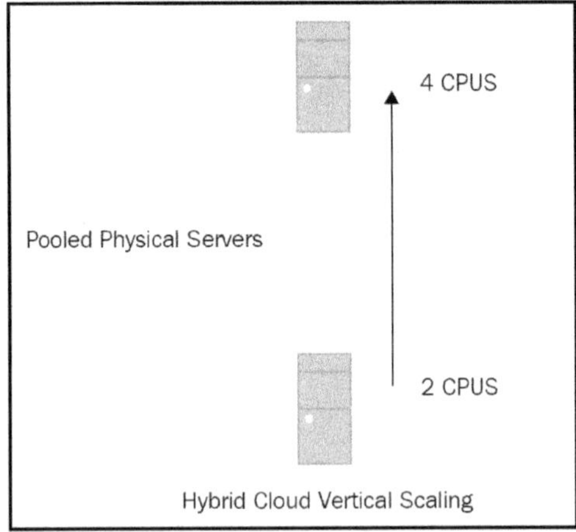

Hybrid Cloud Vertical Scaling

Horizontal scaling

Horizontal scaling is done when additional resources are added to support the application workload, such as when more servers are added to the data center to support the application. However, not all applications are designed to handle such types of scaling and hence when designing hybrid cloud applications, one must consider these factors. When a user interacts with the application, he or she usually performs activities that form a session. In other words, the activities performed by that particular user must be encapsulated in the form of a session. The application thus has to maintain a session for user activities. Such applications are stateful applications and are difficult to scale using the horizontal scaling model. However, there are stateless applications that do not maintain the state of a session. Such applications return the same output when they're given the same input even by different users. The horizontal scaling model is well suited for such stateless applications. For example, a REST API server can be scaled using this model. With no session data to store, the application can be scaled by adding more instances to the cloud and requests can be redirected to the newly added servers. When the workload is reduced, these servers can safely be turned off without affecting the applications:

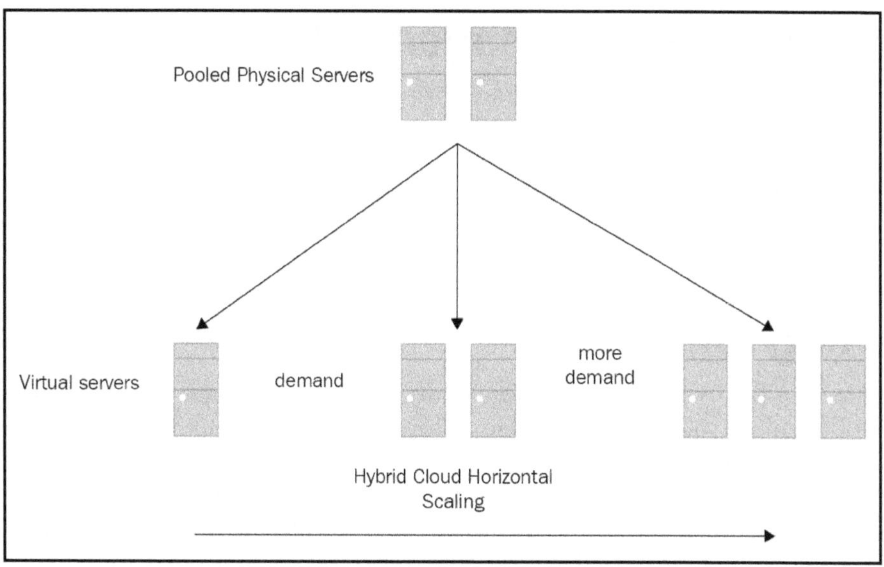

Legacy applications

A hybrid cloud application must be architected to leverage the full potential of the cloud offerings. However, organizations may have some legacy applications that are business critical and may not be suited for the hybrid cloud environment. Unless you have a highly skilled application architect who can migrate the application or redesign it, it is best to have such an application running on the legacy data center to avoid impacting the business.

Resource utilization and costs

There are many factors that impact the overall IT costs, such as amortized upfront charges, ongoing management, labor charges, facilities expenses, and, of course, the monthly bills of the cloud provider. Since public cloud provider resources are billed per usage, it is necessary to ensure that you efficiently utilize the cloud resources. Care should be taken to avoid the waste of cloud resources which are unnecessarily charged. Event monitors must be used to keep a check on such resources.

Centralized cloud management

Just as it essential to have a centralized monitoring system, it is also essential to have a centralized cloud management portal. Managing your public and private cloud enthronement using a centralized console makes hybrid cloud administration easy. It also makes it easier to identify and troubleshoot problems that may span across various components of the hybrid cloud.

Designing for failure

When architecting the hybrid cloud and developing applications for it, the administrator, architect, or developer should always keep failure in mind. In other words, the hybrid cloud application should be developed to handle failures in various cloud components and implement techniques for automated recovery from failure. Outages do occur in the cloud platform and disasters can also strike. Keeping these conditions in mind helps in developing and deploying a robust hybrid cloud application.

The following are some of the techniques used when developing hybrid cloud applications that handle failures.

Caching

Caching involves storing frequently used data in temporary faster memory or disk to improve application performance. This technique can also provide a defense when dealing with failures. Depending on the type of application and the kind of data it requires, the cached data can be made available to users in the event of disk failures.

For example, a web application may cache full HTML pages, database records, remote API calls using ElasticCache, and so on.

Retry operation

Sometimes, failures are transient in nature and just a retry operation may eliminate the problem. Application developers must incorporate the retry logic while building hybrid cloud applications. A retry operation must be done using either the exponential back off or a Fibonacci sequence for some amount of time, before throwing an exception. However, in the event of genuine failures, it is essential that the application should report the failure and fail faster, rather than trying infinitely. Hence, a reasonable amount of timeout must be determined for the retry operation.

Limiting requests

If the application accepts requests from the network, it is prone to DoS attacks. The primary defense can be established by limiting the number of requests the application can process based on the requesting user or IP address. By limiting the number of requests, you can not only avoid DoS attacks, but also improve the application performance during high workloads. When the capacity of the server peaks, it may be unable to respond to requests. Limiting requests ensures that the demand is responded to in an expected manner.

Error reporting

Your application must not fail silently. In other words, the users must not be kept waiting for the response in the event of errors. When an error occurs due to failure, after sufficient retries, the users must be sent an error message that makes sense to them. A technical error description may not make sense to the end user, which will leave him or her confused.

Application decoupling

A hybrid cloud application could be a distributed application. Various components of the applications may be deployed across various parts of the cloud. It is ideal to build components that do not have tight dependencies on each other. If one component of the application fails or has become slower in response, the other components should continue to work seamlessly. In other words, hybrid cloud application components must be loosely coupled and isolated across various layers, so that each component can asynchronously interact with the other.

For example, a web application architecture should have the web server, application server, and the database isolated from each other. The application server may not know anything about the web server and vice versa. This provides decoupling between the components and there is no dependency.

Decoupling the components of the application also makes it easier to scale the application by adding more servers.

As a hybrid cloud application developer, you can build loosely coupled application components by using **message queues**. A message queue is a buffer that is used to connect components together. The application components use the message queue to communicate and send/receive messages to each other. This approach ensures that even if one component dies or becomes temporarily unavailable, the message remains in the queue and is processed when the component comes back up online.

The following diagram shows hybrid cloud application components using a message queue:

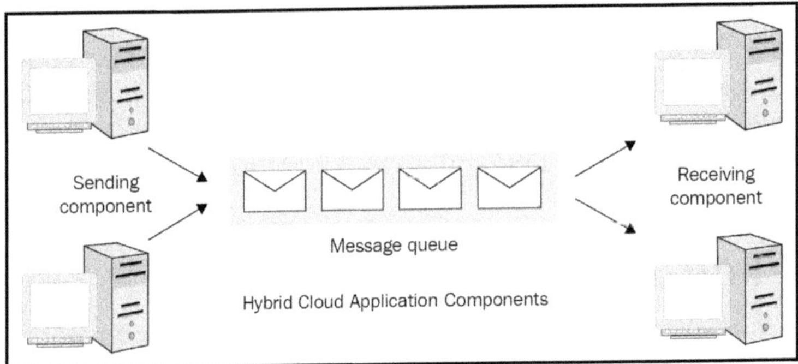

Continuous delivery and integration

The term *DevOps* is the latest buzzword and has been getting a lot of attraction in recent years. To leverage the advantages of the DevOps processes, it is necessary to start adapting this new paradigm. DevOps changes the way applications are developed, built, and deployed. Using the CI/CD approach when developing hybrid cloud applications will offer its own benefits, such as faster deployment and faster test cycles.

Continuous integration is a technique that involves frequently integrating the code changes made by various developers into the main branch of the code repository. It also involves testing this merged code frequently, which results in finding any integration errors much earlier in the release cycle. Ideally, developers should integrate their code daily into the branch, if not multiple times during the day:

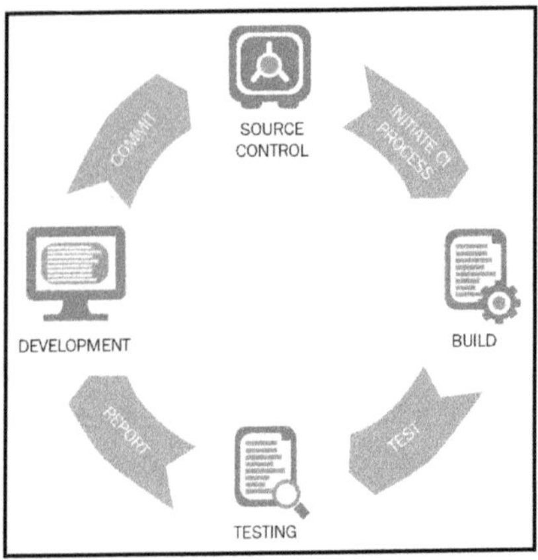

Continuous delivery involves making sure that the code base that is integrated is always deployable or ready to go to the production environment. It is recommended to deploy the built code base to the production environment as soon as possible, but organizations may choose to have slower release cycles depending on their business requirements:

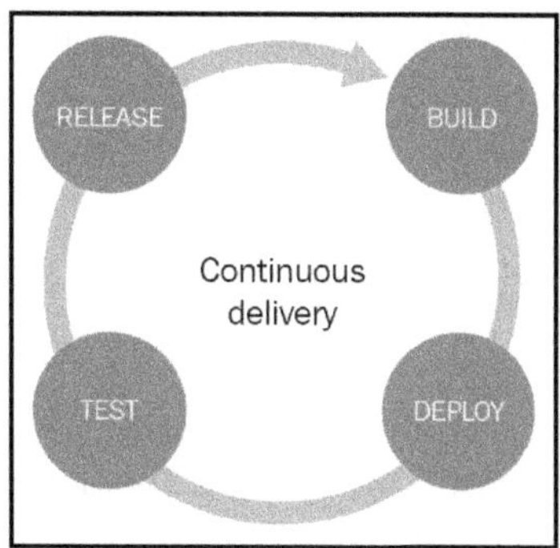

Software development organizations must implement both continuous integration and continuous deployment. When applications are deployed, you must ensure that there are workflows in place on the build systems that can deploy built code on different environments.

Deploying the application at multiple locations

One of the major advantages of a cloud application is that it can be deployed in any of the available geographical regions supported by the cloud provider. With a customer-facing hybrid cloud application, it might be ideal to deploy the application as close to the customer region as possible. For example, for a customer located in Asia, the application must be deployed in the Asian data center of the cloud, whereas for customers in North America, the application must be deployed in a data center in that region.

Having access to deploy the code in multiple locations on the cloud will definitely improve customer satisfaction, as the application will be located close to the target audience.

Developing the application locally or in the cloud

Most cloud application developers may first write their code on the local systems and then when they reach a milestone, they move the code to the team's development environment. However, hybrid cloud applications should be ideally developed with a real environment that resembles the hybrid cloud platform. With the availability of cloud technology, it is easy to build a hybrid cloud platform even for application developers. It is therefore a good practice to develop code on the hybrid cloud platform.

Summary

Pursuing a hybrid cloud platform and building hybrid cloud applications combines the computing benefits of the private cloud along with the flexibility of the public cloud. The benefits that the hybrid cloud application can derive from the hybrid cloud platform depends on the amount of time and effort put into designing, developing, deploying, and monitoring the environment.

This chapter discussed the various best practices that must be followed to derive maximum benefit from the hybrid cloud platform. In the next chapter, we will look at the security aspects of the hybrid cloud.

8 Monitoring and Troubleshooting Hybrid Cloud

Configuring a hybrid cloud may have its own challenges, and sometimes troubleshooting problems can be very daunting. In this chapter, we will focus on basic troubleshooting skills that can be very handy when handling hybrid cloud issues. Since we have been focusing on OpenStack and AWS in the hybrid cloud environment, we will discuss the troubleshooting techniques for various OpenStack services. Later, we will also shed some light on how we can approach fixing AWS problems. The issues discussed here could be the causes of the cloud APIs failing and hence developers should be aware of these issues.

The following topics will be covered in this chapter:

- Linux monitoring and troubleshooting tools
- Troubleshooting the OpenStack KeyStone service
- Troubleshooting the OpenStack Identity service
- Troubleshooting the OpenStack Image service
- Troubleshooting the OpenStack Network service
- Troubleshooting the OpenStack Compute service
- Troubleshooting the OpenStack Block Storage service
- Troubleshooting the OpenStack Object Storage service
- Troubleshooting the OpenStack Orchestration service
- Troubleshooting Amazon Web Services
- Troubleshooting OpenVPN issues

Troubleshooting OpenStack

In `Chapter 3`, *Exploring OpenStack Private Cloud*, we discussed various different services of OpenStack. Each of these services have their own log files and troubleshooting techniques. Hence, we will discuss each OpenStack service separately and explore various troubleshooting techniques for each of them. Let's first begin by discussing some Linux monitoring and troubleshooting tools that are very handy for identifying and fixing OpenStack issues.

Linux troubleshooting and monitoring tools

The Linux operating system offers several native tools that are very useful for troubleshooting problems. The following are a few tools that you must be aware of to quickly identify problems with your OpenStack environment:

- `ps`: The Linux `ps` command can be used to list the OpenStack services. The output can be piped to `grep` to filter the service that we are interested in.
- `top` and `htop`: The `top` and `htop` commands will list the running processes and also provide information about how much CPU and memory they are consuming. You also can sort the processes based on the amount of CPU and memory consumed. This command comes in handy when identifying resource contention issues.
- `df`: The Linux `df` command provides the disk space information.
- `fdisk`: This command can be used to manipulate disk partition tables. It is useful when dealing with OpenStack Block Storage issues with the underlying disk.
- `watch`: The `watch` command provides a way to keep monitoring the output of a particular command and refreshing it with a specified interval. For example, you can monitor the output of the `ps -aux | grep cinder` command simply by using the `watch ps -aux | grep cinder` command. You can also specify the `-n` option to the `watch` command to specify the time interval using which the output must be refreshed.
- `arp`: This display the ARP table. It is useful when a node is not able to find the address of other nodes.
- `iptables`: The iptables are firewall rules that can allow or disallow packets.
- `tcpdump`: This is one of the most commonly used tools to investigate networking issues. It allows you to capture packets that are sent or received on a given network interface, network, port or subnet.

Apart from the previous native Linux tools, `rabbitmqctl` may also be very useful. It is a command-line utility that gets installed along with the RabbitMQ message queuing system. Various components of OpenStack use the RabbitMQ message queuing system to transfer messages between each other. Hence, this utility is very useful for communication issues between components.

For example, the following command will provide the status of the RabbitMQ message broker:

```
# rabbitmqctl status
 Status of node rabbit@ubuntu ...
 [{pid,1841},
 {running_applications,[{rabbit,"RabbitMQ","3.5.7"},
 {os_mon,"CPO CXC 138 46","2.4"},
 {mnesia,"MNESIA CXC 138 12","4.13.3"},
 {xmerl,"XML parser","1.3.10"},
 {sasl,"SASL CXC 138 11","2.7"},
 {stdlib,"ERTS CXC 138 10","2.8"},
 {kernel,"ERTS CXC 138 10","4.2"}]},
 {os,{unix,linux}},
 {erlang_version,"Erlang/OTP 18 [erts-7.3] [source] [64-bit] [async-
threads:64] [kernel-poll:true]\n"},
  .....
  .....
  .....
 {alarms,[]},
 {listeners,[{clustering,25672,"::"},{amqp,5672,"::"}]},
 {vm_memory_high_watermark,0.4},
 {vm_memory_limit,1657490636},
 {disk_free_limit,50000000},
 {disk_free,30812069888},
 {file_descriptors,[{total_limit,65436},
 {total_used,53},
 {sockets_limit,58890},
 {sockets_used,51}]},
 {processes,[{limit,1048576},{used,862}]},
 {run_queue,0},
 {uptime,585}]
```

You can start and stop the RabbitMQ service using the following command:

```
# sudo service rabbitmq-server start
# rabbitmqctl stop
```

To list the queues in the the message broker, you can use the `list_queues` parameter to the command line:

```
# rabbitmqctl list_queues
cinder-scheduler 0
cinder-scheduler.ubuntu 0
cinder-scheduler_fanout_91143a2ceafc473f887e84d584ee543e 0
cinder-volume 0
cinder-volume.ubuntu@lvmdriver-1 0
cinder-volume.ubuntu@lvmdriver-1.ubuntu 0
cinder-volume.ubuntu@lvmdriver-1_fanout_a060ce20a78c4658905d622a00c767af 0
cinder-volume_fanout_d0775346883e406a8a54f658babbcb2f 0
....
....
q-server-resource-versions_fanout_8512feab67ea406d93181dd4207e550d 0
reply_60075b55450746d6b0c8b8cca4dc501a 0
reply_9dffe4691a3d44c091e9bdc727cc880a 0
reply_9f6e9e66e6254536828e471f00ab5b35 0
reply_c4c6251086be460a8d3166243a551110 0
scheduler 0
scheduler.ubuntu 0
scheduler_fanout_a172414abf5a40fb8510e0512f643502 0
versioned_notifications.info 2
```

Similarly, you can also list the exchanges that RabbitMQ uses by using the `list_exchanges` parameter. Exchanges are the entities responsible for delivering the messages from the producer to the appropriate queue:

```
# rabbitmqctl list_exchanges
Listing exchanges ...
amq.direct direct
amq.fanout fanout
amq.headers headers
amq.match headers
amq.rabbitmq.log topic
amq.rabbitmq.trace topic
amq.topic topic
cinder-scheduler_fanout fanout
cinder-volume.ubuntu@lvmdriver-1_fanout fanout
cinder-volume_fanout fanout
conductor_fanout fanout
......
......
......
q-l3-plugin_fanout fanout
q-plugin_fanout fanout
q-reports-plugin_fanout fanout
```

```
q-server-resource-versions_fanout fanout
reply_60075b55450746d6b0c8b8cca4dc501a direct
reply_9dffe4691a3d44c091e9bdc727cc880a direct
reply_9f6e9e66e6254536828e471f00ab5b35 direct
reply_c4c6251086be460a8d3166243a551110 direct
scheduler_fanout fanout
```

The bindings between exchanges and queues can be listed using the following command:

```
# rabbitmqctl  list_bindings
Listing bindings ...
        exchange cinder-scheduler queue cinder-scheduler []
        exchange cinder-scheduler.ubuntu queue cinder-scheduler.ubuntu []
        exchange cinder-scheduler_fanout_91143a2ceafc473f887e84d584ee543e
queue cinder-scheduler_fanout_91143a2ceafc473f887e84d584ee543e []
        exchange cinder-volume queue cinder-volume []
        exchange cinder-volume.ubuntu@lvmdriver-1 queue cinder-
volume.ubuntu@lvmdriver-1 []
        exchange cinder-volume.ubuntu@lvmdriver-1.ubuntu queue cinder-
volume.ubuntu@lvmdriver-1.ubuntu []
        exchange cinder-
volume.ubuntu@lvmdriver-1_fanout_a060ce20a78c4658905d622a00c767af queue
cinder-
......
......
l3_agent_fanout_775c77054a5547eb8602caa85ff441c7 []
        exchange neutron-vo-Network-1.0 queue neutron-vo-Network-1.0 []
        exchange neutron-vo-Network-1.0.ubuntu queue neutron-vo-
Network-1.0.ubuntu []
        exchange neutron-vo-
Network-1.0_fanout_e90e68ed89d747bbb761bdd49ba2fc79 queue neutron-vo-
Network-1.0_fanout_e90e68ed89d747bbb761bdd49ba2fc79 []
        exchange neutron-vo-Port-1.1 queue neutron-vo-Port-1.1 []
        exchange neutron-vo-Port-1.1.ubuntu queue neutron-vo-
Port-1.1.ubuntu []
```

Finally, the connections to the RabbitMQ server from the clients can be listed by using the `list_connections` command:

```
# rabbitmqctl list_connections
Listing connections ...
stackrabbit 192.168.0.106 53856 running
stackrabbit 192.168.0.106 53858 running
.....
.....
stackrabbit 192.168.0.106 53958 running
stackrabbit 192.168.0.106 53960 running
```

```
stackrabbit 192.168.0.106 53964 running
stackrabbit 192.168.0.106 53966 running
```

Thus, the `rabbitmqctl` utility can be used with several parameters to identify any issues with the message queuing service.

Let's now delve into the OpenStack services and how we can troubleshooting individual services.

Troubleshooting the OpenStack Identity service

The OpenStack identity service (Keystone) is one of the most significant services. It is responsible for providing identity, token management, authorization, and authentication. Many other OpenStack services depend on the Identity service. If there are any problems with the Identity service, it can cause other OpenStack functionalities to fail. Hence, it is vital to understand and know how to troubleshoot the Identity service.

In most OpenStack installations, the default location of the log file for the Keystone service is:

```
/var/log/keystone/keystone.log
```

A different location for storing the log files can also be configured by editing the following file:

```
/etc/keystone/logging.conf
```

Authentication issues

The most common issues that OpenStack users encounter are related to authentication. The Keystone log file shows any errors related to the authentication requests. The errors could be due to incorrect passwords, expired details, or even unexpected failures in the Keystone authentication system. Being able to identify the root cause of such problems will allow you to restore the service and have the user continue using the environment.

Before invoking any OpenStack commands, ensure that the environment variables are correctly set:

```
export OS_USERNAME=packtpub
export OS_PASSWORD=secret
export OS_AUTH_URL=https://192.168.0.10:5000/v2.0
export OS_TENANT_NAME=packtpublab
```

We can first check if the user account is listed in the registered accounts. This can be done using the following command:

```
# keystone user-list
```

Once we confirm that the relevant user account exists, we can fetch more information for the user account by invoking the following command and specifying the user ID:

```
keystone user-get 79bgh344e500c898723435aa62k782734hd
```

This output may indicate whether a user's password needs to be reset. The password can be reset by using the following command and passing in the new password string along with the user ID:

```
keystone user-password-update --pass newpassword
79bgh344e500c898723435aa62k782734hd
```

If the user is disabled, you can re-enable the user by invoking the following command and passing the user ID:

```
keystone user-update --enabled true 79bgh344e500c898723435aa62k782734hd
```

Keystone service issues

Sometimes, the Keystone service goes down, thus preventing any other OpenStack service from being able to connect to it for fetching a token or performing authentication.

You can check whether the Keystone service is running using the following command:

```
systemctl status openstack-keystone
```

If the service is not running, you can start it by invoking the following command:

```
# systemctl start openstack-keystone
```

Keystone database issues

Keystone uses its own database to store identity information and metadata. There might be situations where the Keystone database has connection errors. For example, consider a situation where your Keystone service is running, however, when any of the Keystone commands are invoked, it hangs. The Keystone log file shows error messages with `DBConnectionError`.

In such cases, make sure that the MySQL database is up and running and is accessible using the address and port specified in the `keystone.conf` file. This configuration file has a `[database]` section, which specifies the connection string:

```
[database]
connection = mysql://keystone:keystone@packtpubDBserver.com/keystone
```

You can manually test the connection to the Keystone MySQL database using the `mysql` command. This will prompt you for a password for the specified user. Once you are able to connect to the database and run a simple `show tables` command on the prompt, you can ensure that the database is up and running properly:

```
# mysql -u <username> -p -h <hostname> keystone
```

If the `show tables` command returns empty, it indicates that the Keystone database does not have any tables created. In this case, we can initialize the database using the `keystone-manage` command. This will create all the required tables in the database and the Keystone service will be able to insert new records into it:

```
# keystone-manage db_sync
```

The previous techniques cover only a handful of issues that may occur with the Keystone service. The `keystone.log` file is the key resource for identifying different failures, and appropriate tools must be used to troubleshoot the respective problems.

Lets now see how we can troubleshoot the OpenStack Image service.

Troubleshooting the OpenStack Image service

The OpenStack Image service (Glance) provides the functionality that allows OpenStack users to manipulate virtual machine images. Users can discover virtual machine images, upload new images, and also launch a VM from an existing image. Glance also provides a REST API which is consumed by the Glance command-line utility.

The Image service has an API service and a registry service. Both are required for Glance to work properly. It also uses a backend database that is either MySQL or postgres. It supports storage backends where the actual virtual machine images are stored. The backend to be used is configurable in the `glance-api.conf` file.

The Glance service doesn't often need any troubleshooting and it doesn't perform any complex operations. However, as an administrator, we should be aware of the basics.

By default, the Image service writes its log files in the following directory:

```
/var/log/glance/
```

You may have to turn on the logging level in the file, `/etc/glance/glance-api.conf` by setting the `debug` flag to `true`:

```
debug = true
```

In this directory, there are many log files. The `api.log` file likely has error messages that provide a hint to the root cause. You may also need to check the Keystone logs, as Glance uses Keystone for authentication.

Glance service issues

Lets begin by verifying whether the Image service is working properly. We can simply invoke the `glance image-list` command to list all the images present in the image store:

```
# glance image-list
```

If the preceding command returns an error, check the Glance services by using the `ps` command:

```
# ps - aux | grep glance-
stack 996 0.0 0.0 92256 3940 ? Ss 04:28 0:00 glance-apiuWSGI master
stack 1000 0.0 0.6 226756 24500 ? Ss 04:28 0:01 /usr/bin/python
/usr/local/bin/glance-registry --config-file=/etc/glance/glance-
registry.conf
stack 1582 0.1 3.2 319660 129564 ? S 04:28 0:06 glance-apiuWSGI worker 1
stack 1583 0.1 3.3 319660 133560 ? S 04:28 0:06 glance-apiuWSGI worker 2
stack 2689 0.0 0.4 226756 19836 ? S 04:29 0:00 /usr/bin/python
/usr/local/bin/glance-registry --config-file=/etc/glance/glance-
registry.conf
```

If the `glance-api` and the `glance-registry` processes are not running, you can simply start the services by using the `glance-control` command:

```
# glance-control all start
```

Glance database issues

Similar to Keystone, Glance also has its own database and sometimes there might be issues with connection to the database. In such cases, you should verify whether the database is up and running by using the `mysql` command line:

```
# mysql -u <username> -p -h <hostname> glance
```

If you can successfully connect to the Glance database, ensure that you can list the tables by invoking the `show tables` SQL command.

If the `show tables` command returns empty, you can initialize the database by invoking the `glance-manage dbsync` command:

```
# glance-manage db_sync
```

This command will recreate all the tables in the database.

You may also check the `/etc/glance/glance-api.conf` file and check the for the connection string:

```
connection = mysql::/packtpub_user:secret_password
```

The Glance service is pretty straightforward and doesn't cause major problems in the OpenStack environment. The techniques discussed previously should help the administrator to quickly identify problems and resolve them.

Let's move on further and see how we can troubleshoot the OpenStack networking service.

Troubleshooting the Networking service

The OpenStack Networking service is one of the most diverse and complex services. Troubleshooting this service requires a good understanding of networking fundamentals.

It might be necessary to understand how an IP address is allocated to an OpenStack virtual machine in order to troubleshoot networking issues better.

IP address allocation to the VM

The following series of events take place when an IP address is allocated to the VM.

1. The VM requests an IP address by sending the DHCP request packet.
2. The request reaches the firewall bridge, which has iptable configuration. The iptables rules must allow the packet to reach the integration bridge.
3. The integration bridge will tag the packet with the local VLAN ID and forward it to the tunnel bridge.
4. The tunnel bridge will translate the VLAN ID into segmentation ID and the packet will be sent out of the NOVA Compute host to the Neutron host.
5. The tunnel bridge on the Neutron host will receive the packet and de-encapsulate it and forward it to the integration bridge.
6. The integration bridge will forward the packet to the DHCP namespace.
7. The `dnsmasq` in the DHCP namespace will reply with a DHCP offer message having the IP address.

Let's now look at common issues faced by OpenStack administrators.

Unable to ping to VM

One common reason for a ping request not responding is the security group rules set in OpenStack. The default security group doesn't allow the ICMP packet. You may thus have to allow the ICMP packet in the security group configured for the virtual machine that you are trying to ping.

If the security group is correctly configured to allow the ICMP packet, the next step is to check if the virtual machine instance is up by invoking the following command:

```
# nova list
+--------------------------------------+---------------+---------+--------
----+-------------+-----------
| ID | Name | Status | Task State | Power State | Networks |
+--------------------------------------+---------------+---------+--------
----+-------------+-----------
| 7cdaa375-f1b5-40ab-81bd-7e3d052f370d | packtpub-vm | SHUTOFF | - |
Shutdown | private=fdf7:4ae1:646c:0:f816:3eff:fe66:92f2 |
+--------------------------------------+---------------+---------+--------
----+-------------+-----------
```

If the virtual machine has failed to boot, you can check if there were port binding failures in the VM, the router, or the DHCP.

If the instance is not running and is in the `FAILED` state, you must check the nova and neutron logs:

```
# grep -E -R -i "trace|error" /var/log/nova/ /var/log/neutron
```

These logs should provide clues about the root cause of the error.

If the VM is up and running and the security group also appears fine, you can check if the VM received an IP address by invoking the following command:

```
# ip a
```

If there's no IP address given to the VM, check if the DHCP agent is up:

```
# neutron agent-list
```

You can also check if `dnsmasq` is running by invoking the following command:

```
# ps -ef | grep dnsmasq | grep <network-id>
```

There is also a lease file generated that should have the MAC address of the VM. Check if this file was created using the following command:

```
# cat /var/lib/neutron/dhcp/<network_id>/host
```

Finally, check the dhcp-agent logs for any errors:

```
# less /var/log/neutron/dhcp-agent.log
```

The `dhcp-agent` logs may have errors that indicate the cause of the failure.

VM cannot reach the external network

Another common issue with virtual machines running on OpenStack is that they can connect to other VMs inside the same virtual network, but are unable to reach the external network. In order to troubleshoot such problems, let's first understand how the packet reaches the external network when the network is correctly configured:

1. The VM sends a packet destined for the external network.
2. The packet reaches the firewall bridge, which has iptable configuration. The iptables rules must allow the packet to reach the integration bridge.

3. The integration bridge will tag the packet with the local VLAN ID and forward it to the tunnel bridge.
4. The tunnel bridge will translate the VLAN id into segmentation ID and the packet will be sent out of the Nova Compute host to the Neutron host.
5. The tunnel bridge on the Neutron host will receive the packet and deencapsulate it and forward it to the integration bridge.
6. The integration bridge on the networking host will forward the packet to the router namespace, which is the default gateway.
7. The iptable rules translate the private IP into a public address using SNAT.
8. The packet then reaches the external bridge as it is set as the default gateway for the router namespace.
9. The external bridge then forwards the packet to the external network.

You must first check if the security group rules are configured correctly to allow the ssh port and ICMP protocol.
Next, confirm that you can ping the private IP address in the same network and the router in the same network. This is because any packet that intends to reach the external network must first reach the router. Once you are sure that the packet can reach the router, try to ping the VM from the router namespace using the floating IP address:

```
# sudo ip netns exec qrouter-2349df24-x3949-23934-92009182037023 ping
<floating IP>
```

It may also help to check the `l3-agent` log for any related errors:

```
sudo grep -E -i "error|trace" /var/log/neutron/l3-agent.log
```

If you are using Open vSwitch in your OpenStack Networking configuration, the following commands may be useful in troubleshooting issues:

- `ovs-vsctl show`: Displays the bridge configuration on the networking node
- `ovs-ofctl show`: Displays the available datapaths
- `ovs-ofctl dump-flows`: Dumps all the flows installed on the machine
- `ovs-ofctl dump-flows br-tun`: Dump all the flows on the tunnelling bridge
- `ovs-ofctl dump-flows br-tun table=21`: Dump all the flows on the tunnelling bridge for the given table.

Troubleshooting the Compute service

The OpenStack Compute service is one of the most significant services. It provides a hypervisor to run virtual machines.

By default, this service stores its log files for each in `/var/log/nova`. For example, `nova-compute.log` is the log for the `nova-compute` service. You can set the following options to format log strings for the `nova.log` module in the `nova.conf` file:

```
logging_context_format_string
logging_default_format_string
logging_debug_format_suffix   # if debug logging is enabled
```

For enabling logging, include the logfile option in the `nova.conf` file to enable logging. Alternatively you can set `use_syslog = 1` so that the nova daemon logs to syslog.

The first steps in ensuring that the Compute service is running fine is to check if all the required nova services are running:

```
# ps -aux | grep nova-
stack 907 0.0 0.0 92256 3680 ? Ss 04:28 0:00 nova-api-metauWSGI master
stack 919 0.0 0.1 92252 4192 ? Ss 04:28 0:00 nova-apiuWSGI master
stack 922 0.2 2.0 275992 83640 ? Ss 04:28 0:13 /usr/bin/python
/usr/local/bin/nova-scheduler --config-file /etc/nova/nova.conf
stack 925 2.9 0.9 266076 40308 ? Ss 04:28 2:22 /usr/bin/python
/usr/local/bin/nova-conductor --config-file /etc/nova/nova.conf
stack 946 2.9 1.1 266052 47872 ? Ss 04:28 2:21 /usr/bin/python
/usr/local/bin/nova-conductor --config-file /etc/nova/nova_cell1.conf
stack 981 0.3 1.6 272192 65980 ? Ss 04:28 0:17 /usr/bin/python
/usr/local/bin/nova-consoleauth --config-file /etc/nova/nova.conf
stack 1002 0.0 1.0 325360 40488 ? Ss 04:28 0:04 /usr/bin/python
/usr/local/bin/nova-novncproxy --config-file /etc/nova/nova.conf --web
/opt/stack/noVNC
stack 1038 0.7 3.0 1154820 124892 ? Ssl 04:28 0:37 /usr/bin/python
/usr/local/bin/nova-compute --config-file /etc/nova/nova-cpu.conf
stack 1579 0.0 1.1 270212 45988 ? S 04:28 0:02 nova-api-metauWSGI worker 1
stack 1580 0.0 1.1 270212 45960 ? S 04:28 0:02 nova-api-metauWSGI worker 2
stack 1581 0.0 0.0 92256 1236 ? S 04:28 0:00 nova-api-metauWSGI http 1
stack 1584 0.3 3.8 480600 156228 ? Sl 04:28 0:14 nova-apiuWSGI worker 1
stack 1585 0.3 3.8 479224 154844 ? Sl 04:28 0:14 nova-apiuWSGI worker 2
stack 2746 0.7 2.7 286692 112396 ? S 04:29 0:34 /usr/bin/python
/usr/local/bin/nova-conductor --config-file /etc/nova/nova_cell1.conf
root 2843 0.0 0.8 134940 35024 ? S 04:29 0:00 /usr/bin/python
/usr/local/bin/privsep-helper --config-file /etc/nova/nova-cpu.conf --
privsep_context vif_plug_ovs.privsep.vif_plug --privsep_sock_path
/tmp/tmpF9F4c7/privsep.sock
```

This command should list the following processes:

- nova-api
- nova-scheduler
- nova-conductor
- nova-compute

If any of these essential services are not running, you can manually start them. For example, if the nova-api service is not running, you can start it by invoking the service start nova-api command or by manually starting it as follows:

```
# sudo -u nova nova-api --config-file=/etc/nova/nova.conf
```

If the preceding command fails, it will certainly provide a meaningful error message that will help in identifying the root cause.

For example, the command may fail with the following error : Address already in use. This indicates the port on which the nova-api service listens is already consumed by some other running process. To find out which process is using this port, run the following command:

```
# lsof -i 8774
```

This command will print out the process that is using port 8774. Once you have made the necessary changes and freed up that port, you can attempt to start the nova-api service again by using the service start nova-api command.

If the command succeeds, you should now see the nova-api service running. You may confirm this by invoking:

```
# ps -aux | grep nova-api
stack 907 0.0 0.0 92256 3680 ? Ss 04:28 0:00 nova-api-metauWSGI master
stack 919 0.0 0.1 92252 4192 ? Ss 04:28 0:00 nova-apiuWSGI master
stack 1579 0.0 1.1 270212 45988 ? S 04:28 0:02 nova-api-metauWSGI worker 1
stack 1580 0.0 1.1 270212 45960 ? S 04:28 0:02 nova-api-metauWSGI worker 2
stack 1581 0.0 0.0 92256 1236 ? S 04:28 0:00 nova-api-metauWSGI http 1
stack 1584 0.3 3.8 480600 156228 ? Sl 04:28 0:15 nova-apiuWSGI worker 1
stack 1585 0.3 3.8 479224 154844 ? Sl 04:28 0:15 nova-apiuWSGI worker 2
```

A similar strategy should be used to troubleshoot the nova-scheduler service, the nova-conductor, and the nova-compute service. In addition, if you encounter errors in the nova-scheduler.log that are related to connection to the message broker, you must also check the status of the RabbitMQ server.

We have already seen how to start and stop the RabbitMQ server in the previous sections:

```
# rabbitmqctl status
```

Let's discuss some common issues encountered with the Compute service.

Database issues

The OpenStack Compute service uses its own database called the Nova database. This database must be up and running for the other Nova services to function properly.

If you happen to encounter any database-related error messages in the log files, you should first check the database by connecting to it using the MySQL command line:

```
# mysql -u nova -p -h packtpub-dbserver nova
```

If the connection is successful, you should ensure that all the tables are present in the database:

```
# show tables
```

If there are no tables present, you can initialize the database by invoking the following command:

```
# nova-manage db sync
```

This will create the required tables and the Nova services should come back online.

Instance issues

Consider a case where you have started an OpenStack instance but the state is shown `pending` or you simple cannot SSH to it.

This is a very common problem and occurs mostly due to the image not being able to fetch the IP address from the DHCP server or the image does not support interface injection. The solution is to use an image that supports this method, so that it can obtain an IP address automatically from the FlatManager network settings.

If this is not the problem, you may check the directory of that particular instance in the nova-compute host and ensure that the following files are present:

- `libvirt.xml`
- `disk`
- `disk-raw`
- `kernel`
- `ramdisk`
- `console.log`

The `console.log` is created only after the instance starts.

If any of the preceding files are absent, it indicates a problem with the nova-compute service being not able to download the virtual machine image from the Glance image store. You may also check the `nova-compute.log`, which usually provides meaningful hints about the problem.

To test whether the instance configuration was correctly created, go to the `/var/lib/nova/instances` directory for the instance and execute the following command:

```
# virsh create libvirt.xml
```

This output of this command should provide hints about the problem.

When a Linux instance is started and it doesn't show any output on the console, make sure that the following is passed to the kernel parameters:

```
console=tty0 console=ttyS0,115200n
```

Sometimes, an instance can remain in a deleting state and you may have to reset the state. The following command can be used to reset the state of the instance:

```
$ nova reset-state d83hr93-b230a-234e7-823c-eb17bdme9385
$ openstack server d83hr93-b230a-234e7-823c-eb17bdme9385
```

Sometimes, instances may boot very slowly, or do not boot at all. File injection can cause this problem. It can simply be disabled in the `nova.conf` file by adding the following entry:

```
[libvirt]
inject_partition = -2
```

Volume issues

Another problem that is commonly encountered is that when a volume is detached from an instance, it doesn't get attached again. To resolve this problem, you must change the device name on the `nova-attach` command. The VM might not clean up after a `nova-detach` command runs.

A volume may also fail to attach with the error, `systool is not installed`:

```
WARNING nova.virt.libvirt.utils [req-1139818-12je-8f39f-c0f8-
kf983nkf984kf0\
admin admin|req-1139818-12je-8f39f-c0f8-kf983nkf984kf0 admin admin] systool
is not installed
ERROR nova.compute.manager [req-1139818-12je-8f39f-c0f8-kf983nkf984kf0
admin\
admin|req-1139818-12je-8f39f-c0f8-kf983nkf984kf0 admin admin]
[instance: ksdf09834-sdf35-4er3a-d323-234lw34epwe0c|instance:
s87324hf9-8c3f-234a-be9b-47c97626555c]
Failed to attach volume 394wer23-23ra-2342-34f2a-2349ske934ser at /dev/vdk.
```

In this case, simple install the `sysfsutils` package on the compute host:

```
# apt-get install sysfsutils
```

The previous discussion gives your a brief understanding of the approach to troubleshooting the Nova Compute service. The logs usually have sufficient error messages to indicate the root cause of the problem.

Lets move on to the OpenStack Block Storage service and see how we can troubleshoot it.

Troubleshooting the Block Storage service

The OpenStack Block Storage service is the volume manager service of OpenStack. It provides storage volumes from the underlying storage provider and provides the ability to attach the volumes to the OpenStack virtual machine instances running on the compute node. By default, the Block Storage service uses the Linux native LVM provider for carving out volumes.

Cinder services store their log files in the `/var/log/cinder` directory.

To check if all the cinder services are running, invoke the following command:

```
# ps -aux | grep cinder
stack 1015 0.3 2.5 356060 104432 ? Ss 04:28 0:19 /usr/bin/python
/usr/local/bin/cinder-scheduler --config-file /etc/cinder/cinder.conf
stack 1019 0.0 0.0 92252 3980 ? Ss 04:28 0:00 cinder-apiuWSGI master
stack 1027 2.5 1.3 354572 53608 ? Ss 04:28 2:07 /usr/bin/python
/usr/local/bin/cinder-volume --config-file /etc/cinder/cinder.conf
stack 1577 0.1 2.8 448804 116956 ? Sl 04:28 0:07 cinder-apiuWSGI worker 1
stack 1578 0.0 2.9 373696 119184 ? S 04:28 0:04 cinder-apiuWSGI worker 2
stack 2712 1.9 2.6 356796 108132 ? S 04:29 1:34 /usr/bin/python
/usr/local/bin/cinder-volume --config-file /etc/cinder/cinder.conf
```

You may find several instances of each cinder process running. Essentially, the following services should be running:

- cinder-api
- cinder-scheduler
- cinder-volume

If any of the preceding services are not running, you may start them manually by invoking the respective commands:

```
sudo -u cinder cinder-api --config-file=/etc/cinder/cinder.conf --log-file=/var/log/cinder/cinder-api.log
sudo -u cinder cinder-scheduler --config-file=/etc/cinder/cinder.conf --
log-file=/var/log/cinder/cinder-scheduler.log
sudo -u cinder cinder-volume --config-file=/etc/cinder/cinder.conf --log-
file=/var/log/cinder/cinder-volume.log
```

Now, lets look at some common issues that are encountered with the cinder volume service.

Common issues

A simple volume creation can be tested by creating a volume from the OpenStack dashboard or using the cinder command line.

Invoke the following command to create a cinder volume with size 1 GB:

```
# cinder create 1
```

If the command exits silently, it typically means that the volume was created successfully. However, if you encounter an error, the first thing to check is whether the underlying LVM has a volume group named cinder-volumes. This error is clearly evident in the `/var/log/cinder/scheduler.log` file:

```
#vgdisplay
```

This should show you LVM volume groups present on the cinder host.

Another common issue encountered while creating a volume is that the volume gets stuck in the **Creating** state and doesn't respond. OpenStack doesn't even allow you to delete this volume. In such cases, you can simply reset the state of the volume by using the `reset-state` parameter on the cinder command line:

```
# cinder reset-state  d83hr93-b230a-234e7-823c-eb17bdme9385
```

If there are some issues with the volume, the previous command will change the state of the volume to an error state. You can then delete the volume. Similarly, if the volume was in a stuck state with no other problem, the previous command will move the volume to the **Available** state. The volume can then be attached to the virtual machine running on the Compute node.

Insufficient free space in the volume group also throws the following error:

```
Volume group "cinder-volumes" has insuffcient free space
```

You must ensure that the volume group has sufficient space to create new volumes.

Let's now look at the Object Storage service and its issues.

Troubleshooting the Object Storage service

The OpenStack Object Storage service, also called Swift, provides object-based storage space for storing files. Unlike the block store, the object store is accessed using the API, and not the file system directly.

The Object Storage service writes its log files in `/var/log/syslog` (or `messages` on some distros). Logging can be customized by editing the `log_name`, `log_facility`, and `log_level` parameters in the object server configuration files.

To begin troubleshooting any issues with the Object Storage service, you must first ensure that the required services are running.

The following processes should be running on the node where Swift is installed:

- Proxy server
- Account server
- Container server
- Object server
- Auth server

If any of the preceding processes are not running, you must look at the syslog to get hints about the errors. If no errors are logged to syslog, you can attempt to start the server manually from the command line as follows:

```
# swift-object-server /etc/swift/object-server/1.conf
```

The Swift proxy server is the endpoint that listens for Swift API requests. To check if this process is running properly, simply execute the `swift list` command. If this command returns an error, there is a problem with the proxy server process:

```
# swift list
```

In case of errors, you can check the syslog to get clues about the root cause.
You can then attempt to start the process manually by invoking the following command:

```
# swift-init main start
```

Swift authentication

We are already aware that OpenStack components use the Keystone service for performing authentication. The Swift service can be configured to use either one of the following for authentication:

- TempAuth
- Keystone

To determine which authentication is configured, you can check the configuration file, /etc/swift/proxy-server.conf. This file should have a section with the following title. The authentication configuration is done under this section:

```
[pipeline:main]
```

It is not recommended to use TempAuth in a production system. However, TempAuth is fully functional and can be used as a model to develop your own auth system. It has the concept of admin and non-admin users within an account. Admin are super users with full access within the account, whereas non-admin users can only perform read operations.

For configuring Swift to use Keystone, you must ensure that you have the auth_token middleware installed and you should have a service endpoint of type object-store in Keystone pointing to your Swift proxy.

For example, you should have these parameters set in your /etc/keystone/default_catalog.templates:

```
catalog.RegionOne.object_store.name = Swift Service
catalog.RegionOne.object_store.publicURL =
http://swiftproxy:8080/v1/AUTH_$(tenant_id)s
catalog.RegionOne.object_store.adminURL = http://swiftproxy:8080/
catalog.RegionOne.object_store.internalURL =
http://swiftproxy:8080/v1/AUTH_$(tenant_id)s
```

On your Swift proxy server you will want to adjust your main pipeline and add auth_token and keystoneauth in your /etc/swift/proxy-server.conf as follows:

```
[pipeline:main]
pipeline = [....] authtoken keystoneauth proxy-logging proxy-server

[filter:authtoken]
paste.filter_factory = keystonemiddleware.auth_token:filter_factory
auth_uri = http://keystonehost:5000/
auth_url = http://keystonehost:35357/
auth_plugin = password
project_domain_id = default
user_domain_id = default
project_name = service
username = swift
password = password
cache = swift.cache
include_service_catalog = False
delay_auth_decision = True
```

You must also add the `keystoneauth` configuration:

```
[filter:keystoneauth]
use = egg:swift#keystoneauth
operator_roles = admin, swiftoperator
```

The preceding configuration will set the Swift authentication to Keystone.

As discussed previously, Swift works with different authentication mechanisms and understanding them is crucial for troubleshooting the problems related to Swift.

Lets now turn our attention to the OpenStack Orchestration service.

Troubleshooting the Orchestration service

The OpenStack Orchestration service, also called HEAT makes it extremely easy to build a resource stack. It coordinates with various OpenStack services to build the requested resources. For example, a user may write his own customized template that defines what OpenStack resources he or she requires. This template can then be executed by the HEAT orchestration engine, which in turn deploys the resources with minimum or no user intervention. Such templates are called HEAT Orchestration Templates (HOT).

For the Orchestration service to be fully function, there are two processes that are required to be running:

- `heat-api`
- `heat-engine`

There is one more process that is required in case you want the Orchestration service to be compatible with the AWS Cloud Formation service:

- `heat-api-cfn`

Service errors

Before we start troubleshooting problems with the HEAT orchestration service, it's always a good idea to check if the required services are running:

```
# ps -aux | grep heat
```

If any of the preceding services are not running, commands related to HEAT will fail.

For example, if the the `heat-api` service is not running, you can start it by invoking the following command:

```
# service heat-api start
```

If the previous command doesn't start the service, you can manually start the service to figure out the error message that prevents the service from starting:

```
# sudo -u heat heat-api --config-file=/etc/heat/heat.conf
```

This command will display startup messages on the console and will also include any error messages. These messages usually provide a hint about the root cause of the problem.

Once the `heat-api` service is up and running, you can test it by invoking any `heat` command:

```
# heat stack-list
```

The preceding command should list the available stacks or return empty if none are present. If this command returns a time-out error, it indicates that the problem is with the `heat-engine` service.

To troubleshoot this further, you must look at the heat logs located in `/var/log/heat/heat.log` on the node that is hosting the HEAT services. In case the default log directory is changed, you can find the location of the log directory in the `/etc/heat/heat.conf` file for the `log_dir` parameter. The error messages in the log file should provide hints about the root cause of the problem.

You can attempt to start the heat-engine service by invoking the following command:

```
# service heat-engine start
```

If the preceding command fails, you can manually invoke the `heat-engine` command and check the output of the command:

```
# sudo -u heat heat-engine --config-file=/etc/heat/heat.conf
```

Once, you fix the root cause, you can check if the service has started successfully by invoking the following:

```
# heat service-list command
```

Stack errors

Once you have ensured that the `heat-engine` and the `heat-api` services are up and running, you can then create and execute stacks.

A stack is a set of OpenStack resources that are created in the specified sequence.

Following is an example of creating a stack using the command line:

```
$ openstack stack create -t
http://git.openstack.org/cgit/openstack/heat-templates/plain/hot/F20/WordPr
ess_Native.yaml --parameter key_name=key --parameter image_id=linux-image -
-parameter instance_type=m1.small mystack
```

The stack creation command requires the path to the template file, which defines the resources to be created as a part of the stack. This template uses the YAML format.

Once the stack creation command is invoked, you can check the status of the stack by listing the stacks:

```
# heat stack-list
```

If the stack you intend to create is in the `CREATE_FAILED` state, you can then check the events that happened while creating the stack. This will indicate where exactly the creation failed:

```
# heat event-list mystack
```

Here `mystack` is the name of the stack that you want to create. The preceding command will list down all the events during the creation of the stack.

This will provide a clue to the exact step where the failure occurred. You can then fix it and attempt to re-create the stack.

Lets now look at how we can troubleshoot the AWS cloud and explore some common issues faced by cloud administrators.

Troubleshooting AWS

The AWS public cloud provides several services and troubleshooting each of these services requires its own set of expertise. We will look at the the most commonly used services that are involved in hybrid cloud configuration, for instance, the EC2 service.

AWS Direct Connect

The AWS Direct Connect service is widely used for configuring hybrid cloud environments. Let's discuss some of the most common issues with AWS Direct Connect:

- If you are unable to ping the Amazon peer IP address, check if the IP address is correctly configured and is in the proper VLAN. Also in the ARP table, check that the router has a MAC address of the AWS endpoint.
- If there are any intermediate devices in between, check that they have VLAN trunking enabled for the 802.1Q VLAN tag.
- Its always a good idea to flush the ARP table cache before testing connectivity issues.
- If you are able to ping the AWS peer IP address, but the virtual interface seems down, check if the BGP ASN and AWS ASN are correctly configured.
- You can also check the MDG authentication keys. They should match the keys in the downloaded router configuration files.
- Check that there are no firewall or ACL rules that are blocking port `179` or any other higher ports, as these ports are required for BGP to establish a TCP connection.
- The router must also be configured to have a route for the private cloud network prefix over the BGP session. For a private virtual interface, use a private or public prefix, however, for a public virtual interface, you must use a publicly routable network prefix.

Lets now look at some common issues with the EC2 service, which is widely used by cloud applications.

EC2 instance issues

The EC2 service provides virtual machines to the cloud users. The following are some commonly encountered issues when using the EC2 service.

Instance connection issues

This is one of the most common problems faced by AWS users. If you try to connect to your EC2 instance and get the following error message, it usually indicates a problem with the security group configuration:

```
Network error : Connection timed out
```

The `ping` command may also fail because the ICMP protocol is not allowed in the inbound connections of the security group rules.

In such situations, ensure that the instance has an elastic IP address and the AWS security group that is associated with the EC2 instance has the required ports open. For example, a Linux instance may require port 22 to be open for SSH access. Similarly, a Windows instance may require port 3389 for remote desktop access. Also, enable ICMP inbound connections.

For a VPC, you must check the routing table of the subnet in which the EC2 instance is running. There must be a route that sends all traffic destined outside the VPC to the internet gateway for the VPC. Also, check the network **access control list** (**ACL**) for the subnet. The network ACLs must allow inbound and outbound traffic from your local IP address on the proper port. The default network ACL allows all inbound and outbound traffic.

Empty console output

When a Windows EC2 instance is booted up on AWS, the console of the instance displays messages that indicate the boot process. In some cases, there is no output and the user is unaware of whether the instance was booted up successfully or not.

To get the console output of the instance, go to **Actions** | **Instance Settings** | **Get System Log**:

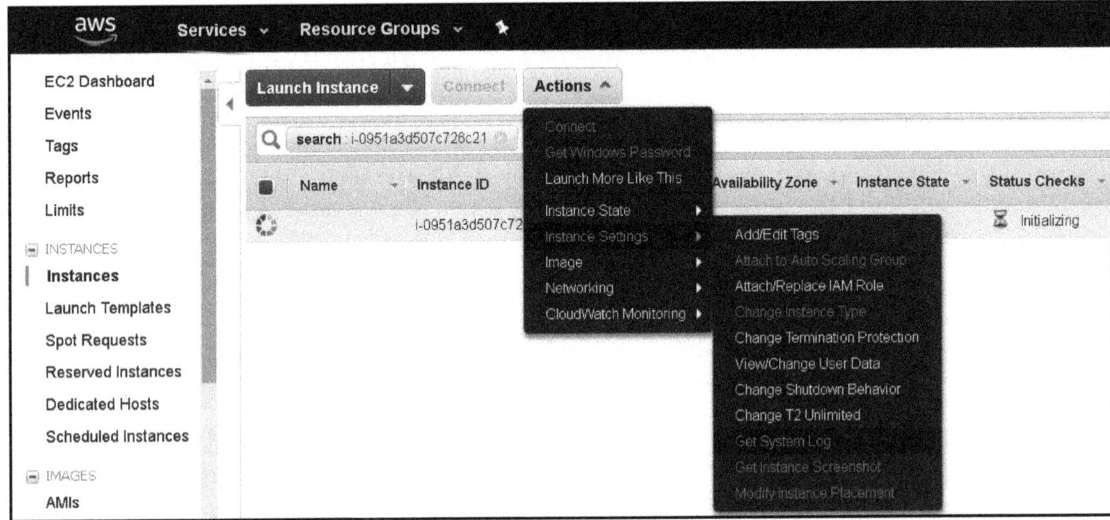

All the windows AMIs (excluding Windows 2016) have an optional service called EC2Config service, which is started when the instance is booted. It performs certain tasks when the instance is started or stopped. If the console output is empty, it usually indicates a problem with the EC2Config service. You can download the latest version of the EC2Config service and check again.

SSH key issues

For connection to Linux instance, the user must use the SSH key pair. Sometimes, the SSH key has problems and users cannot connect to their Linux instances.

In such cases, the first step is to invoke the `ssh` command using the `-vvv` parameter, which prints verbose debug messages. These messages provide a more specific message about the cause of the connection failure:

```
ssh -vvv -i [your key name].pem ec2-user@[public DNS address of your
instance].compute-1.amazonaws.com
```

Also, ensure that you use the correct username to connect to the EC2 instance. AWS has different usernames for different operating system instances.

EBS volume issues

The AWS EBS service is mostly managed on the AWS side. It hardly requires any troubleshooting from the users' perspective. However, the following are some typical problems that users should be aware of.

Volume stuck in Attaching state

When an EBS volume is created and attached to an EC2 instance, the state of the volume changes to the Attaching state, and if it is successfully attached, the state changes to **Attached**. However, in some cases, the volume may get stuck in the Attaching state.

This usually happens when the device name given to the volume is already being used by the block device driver of the EC2 instance. This can happen if the block device driver has not released the device name for reuse despite forcing a detachment of the volume.

Volume in Error state

There are cases where the EBS volume attached to an instance may go into the **Error** state. Such volumes become unusable and it is difficult to repair such problems without the help of AWS support.

Hence, it is always advised to keep a snapshot of the volume so that the snapshot can be recovered in case of volume failures.

Volume snapshot in Pending state

When taking a snapshot of the EBS volume, the snapshot can get stuck in a **Pending** state. This might indicate a problem with the gateway VM or the state of the volume might have changed to **PASS THROUGH** or **IRRECOVERABLE**. In such cases, it is advisable to delete the snapshot and wait till the volume comes back to the **AVAILABLE** state.

The snapshot operation can then be re-initiated.

S3 object store issues

The S3 object store is also a stable and well managed AWS service and hardly needs any troubleshooting. The issues faced by users are usually related to networks and accessibility. Since we have already covered the networking aspect of troubleshooting, resolving S3 issues mostly requires the same skillset and techniques.

Troubleshooting OpenVPN issues

As we already discussed, a hybrid cloud is created by connecting the private cloud and the public cloud using an encrypted network link. One of the most commonly used open source software packages for establishing a VPN connection is OpenVPN. Since this is widely used, let's discuss some common troubleshooting techniques when working with OpenVPN.

OpenVPN log files

A typical problem that administrators face is that they are unable to connect to the OpenVPN access server. For example, when the VPN client attempts to establish a connection to an OpenVPN access server, it is disconnected immediately. In such cases, it is helpful to look at the log files of the OpenVPN access server. The most important log files to look at are as follows:

- `/var/log/openvpnas.log`
- `/var/log/openvpnas.node.log` (for failover setups)

The messages in these log files provide a hint to the root cause of the problem, which can then be fixed by the administrator. It is better to add some additional debug flags in the OpenVPN configuration file to get some more verbose log messages.

Let's look at some commonly faced issues.

VPN connection issues

One of the most commonly faced errors while attempting connection to the OpenVPN access server is a TLS handshake failure.

The following message is written in the log file:

```
OpenSSL: error:140760FC:SSL routines:SSL23_GET_CLIENT_HELLO:unknown
protocol'
TLS_ERROR: BIO read tls_read_plaintext error'
TLS Error: TLS object -> incoming plaintext read error'
TLS Error: TLS handshake failed'
SIGUSR1[soft,tls-error] received, client-instance restarting'
```

This usually happens when the server expects a higher TLS version from the message, but the VPN client problem uses an older version. The solution to this problem is to upgrade the client program to support the version that the server expects.

Another common problem with connections is that there is a mismatch between the OpenVPN parameters used on either side of the connection. For example, if any of the following parameters are used to make the connection, the same parameters should be provided on both the sides of the connection:

```
--udp-mtu
--tun-mtu
--no-replay
--auth
--secret
--fragment
--tls-auth
--proto udp
--dev tun|tap
--tun-ipv6
--comp-lzo
--no-iv
--keysize
--cipher
--dev-type tun|tap
--key-method
--link-mtu
--ifconfig x y [matched with --ifconfig y x on the other end of the
connection]
--tls-server [matched with --tls-client on the other end of the connection]
--tls-client [matched with --tls-server on the other end of the connection]
```

Authentication issues

Another common issue that users face is with user authentication. To troubleshoot authentication issues, OpenVPN provides a very helpful command-line interface utility called `authcli`. This utility can be used to perform user authentication manually and fetch the output of the result.

For example, the following command can be invoked to perform user authentication:

```
./authcli --user <USER_NAME> --pass <PASSWORD>
```

The previous command displays the output of the authentication result (as shown in the following) and the properties that are applied to the user. This output can thus help in determining if any invalid properties are applied to the user:

```
API METHOD: authenticate
AUTH_RETURN
 status : SUCCEED
 session_id : AaJkamAuZgjXwsjk+N96eA==
 reason : local auth succeeded
 expire : 1505404548
 user : test
 proplist : {'pvt_password_digest':
'9f86d081884c7d659a2feaa0c55ad015a3bf4f1b2b0b822cd15d6c15b0f00a08
```

Starting and stopping OpenVPN

Sometimes the problem might be with the startup of the OpenVPN access server. The same logs can provide more information about the startup of the service. A good practice is to stop the service, move the log files to a different location, and start the service again. This creates a clean log file that has messages only for the startup of the service. It is then easier to isolate the problem.

OpenVPN access server can be stopped and started using the following commands:

```
service openvpnas stop
service openvpnas start
```

Summary

In this chapter, we discussed various techniques to troubleshoot the AWS public cloud and the OpenStack private cloud. We also touched upon a few OpenVPN troubleshooting techniques. The ability to troubleshoot both these cloud platforms is essential to successfully administrating and troubleshooting the hybrid cloud.

In the next chapter, we will explore the best practices of both the private and public cloud platforms.

9
Hybrid Cloud Security

In last few chapters, we explored the hybrid cloud platform and saw how we could implement and develop applications for it. For any organization, information security is the most important aspect that must be prioritized and looked at while configuring a hybrid cloud environment. When an organization chooses to move to a hybrid cloud platform, it should enhance the security and not diminish it. Cloud technology has matured and provides reliable security, but that does not mean that organizations should stop worrying about security considerations.

In this chapter, we will discuss the security measures that must be taken while configuring a hybrid cloud so that an organization's data stays secure in the cloud environment.

The following topics will be covered in this chapter:

- Hybrid cloud security threats
- Virtualization software security
- Virtual machine security
- Patch management
- Intrusion detection and prevention
- Identity access management
- Developing secure applications

Hybrid cloud security threats

A hybrid cloud can be implemented using various services and deployment models. Each model may address different data and application security aspects. The decision about the deployment model to choose is taken by the IT management teams once they are convinced about the security that the hybrid cloud offers. The security concerns are dependent on a variety of factors, such as the type of the industry, services to be delivered, compliance and audit requirements, and so on.

The following are the most common threats to a hybrid cloud environment:

- Lack of encryption
- Lack of compliance
- Lack of data backup and replication
- Insecure application APIs
- DoS attacks
- Data leaks

Let's look at these threats in detail and explore how we can prevent them.

Lack of encryption

When an organization starts using the hybrid cloud platform, the internal data travels to and from the public and private cloud environments. Sensitive data that travels out of the private cloud to the public cloud is susceptible to attacks and hence must be protected. Encryption is the process of transforming the data into an encoded format that is unreadable by unauthorized entities. Many cloud providers offer encryption services and also provide keys to decrypt the data.

It is a good practice to store the decryption keys away from the cloud where the data is stored.

The following techniques can be used to protect the data.

User symmetric key encryption

Public cloud providers offer encryption of the customer's data and it is essential to consider the type of encryption used. Not all encryption algorithms are completely secure. The encryption algorithms endorsed by a standard public body or by a cryptographic community should be used. In other words, proprietary encryption algorithms should be avoided.

Moreover, symmetric key encryption should be used, which involves a single key for encryption and decryption. This type of encryption is faster and more efficient as compared to asymmetric key encryption and is suitable for handling large volumes of data:

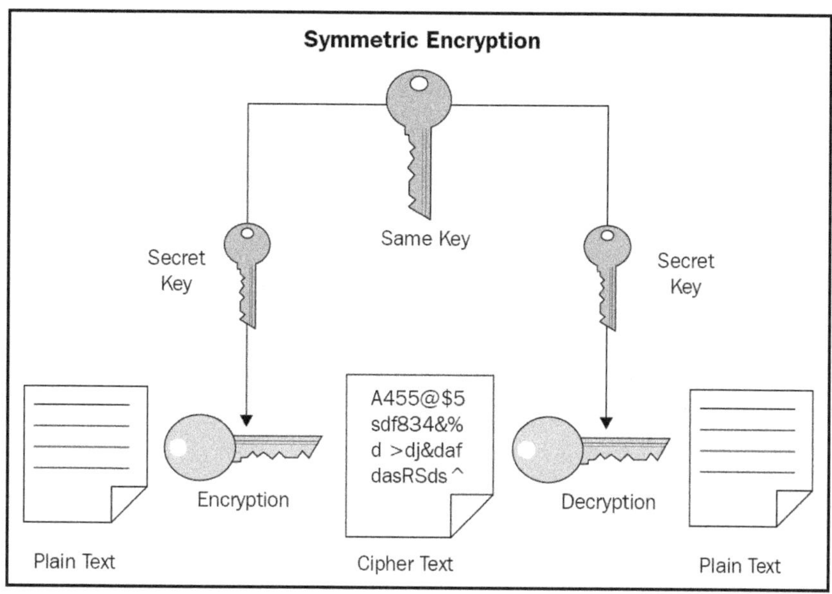

Encrypting data before uploading to the cloud

Whenever you upload data to the public cloud, ensure that it is encrypted. You may use a third-party tool to encrypt the data. A VPN connection between the private and public cloud environments generally provides protection for the data that is in transit.

AWS provides an SDK for encryption. Hybrid cloud developers must leverage this SDK when dealing with data.

Protecting data at rest and in transit with a cloud access security broker

Using a **cloud access security broker** (**CASB**) is another technique to protect and encrypt data using your own encryption keys. A CASB is a policy enforcement endpoint that provides data and threat protection on the AWS public cloud. It mediates the connections between cloud applications and the external environment through different API connectors and proxies.

Using a reliable VPN connection

Since a hybrid cloud environment involves a VPN connection between the private and public clouds, it is a good security practice to use a reliable VPN connection that offers extra security. Many non-standard VPN applications are prone to attacks; using a reputed application minimizes the risk.

Using SSH

The SSH networking tunnel protocols provide encryption for traffic over the network. When accessing host locations on the public cloud, SSH protocols must be used. You may also encrypt all transmissions using SSL/TLS to manage server authentication.

Key management

For encryption of data at rest, that is data stored on disk, one of the important security considerations related to encryption is the management of keys. In the cloud platform, you must ensure that the key management is done either by the organization itself or by a reliable third-party key management service.

It is not advisable to let the same cloud provider manage the keys that are storing or handling the data.

Lack of compliance

The term *cloud compliance* means that cloud providers must adhere to certain standards and regulations imposed by the central authority. As new technology emerges, new compliance laws and regulations come into effect. For example, the GDPR compliance law will be regulated in May 2018 and organizations who breach these compliance rules will be in trouble and may face an impact on business. It is therefore necessary that organizations adhere to the compliance policies.

When the organization's data center is migrated to a hybrid cloud platform, the cloud providers should also adhere to the policies that the organization implements for its IT infrastructure and data.

The hybrid cloud architect should understand how data is stored and processed in the cloud to ensure that the hybrid clouds are compliant with the regulations. The clouds participating in the hybrid cloud platform should be very well coordinated and must meet the industry standards for data security, especially when handling sensitive data.

For example, a hybrid cloud administrator may decide to store sensitive data on the private cloud where he has direct control over it. The administrator can decide whom to provide physical access to the storage disks. On the other hand, the non-sensitive data can be stored on the public cloud. The public cloud provides pre-developed compliance frameworks which can be leveraged:

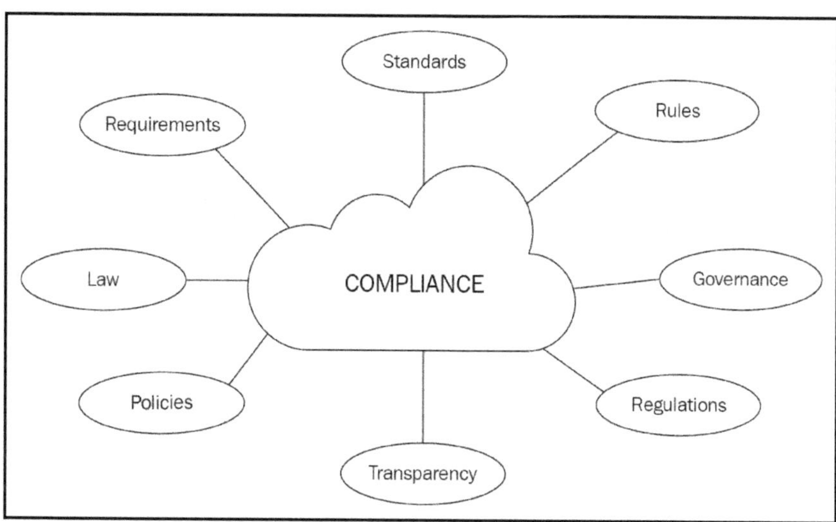

It is likely that the organization adopting a hybrid cloud may have customers around the globe. Hence, when the hybrid cloud is distributed across geographical locations, it is necessary to consider the regulations of various geographies. The requirements of each region must be checked and adapted in the hybrid cloud so that everything is aligned to the local requirements and standards.

Lack of data backup and replication

In today's cloud computing environment, protecting an organization's data and IT infrastructure is critical to ensure business continuity. Moreover, in situations of hardware failures in the cloud environment, it is essential to be able to recover from failure and restore the data by meeting the expected **recovery time objectives** (**RTOs**). It is therefore necessary to keep a backup of the critical data so that there is no data loss in case of such events.

Although cloud providers ensure the reliability of their storage resources, in the event of catastrophic disasters, it's possible that the entire IT infrastructure goes down or is destroyed. In such cases, blaming the cloud provider for the outage may not help in bringing back the business online quickly. When organizations manage their own data center, they have more control over it and can mitigate risks. However, when data is moved to the public cloud platform, very little can be done to recover data in the event of failures.

It is therefore necessary to ensure that a copy of the data is maintained at other locations from where it can be easily recovered or restored. Lack of data backups may put the hybrid cloud of your organization at risk.

Redundant copies of the data should be distributed across geographical locations. With the AWS Cloud, duplicate copies of the data should be kept in different availability zones or regions. Distributing the redundant copies in this way minimizes the damage that can occur in the event of outages in a particular data center:

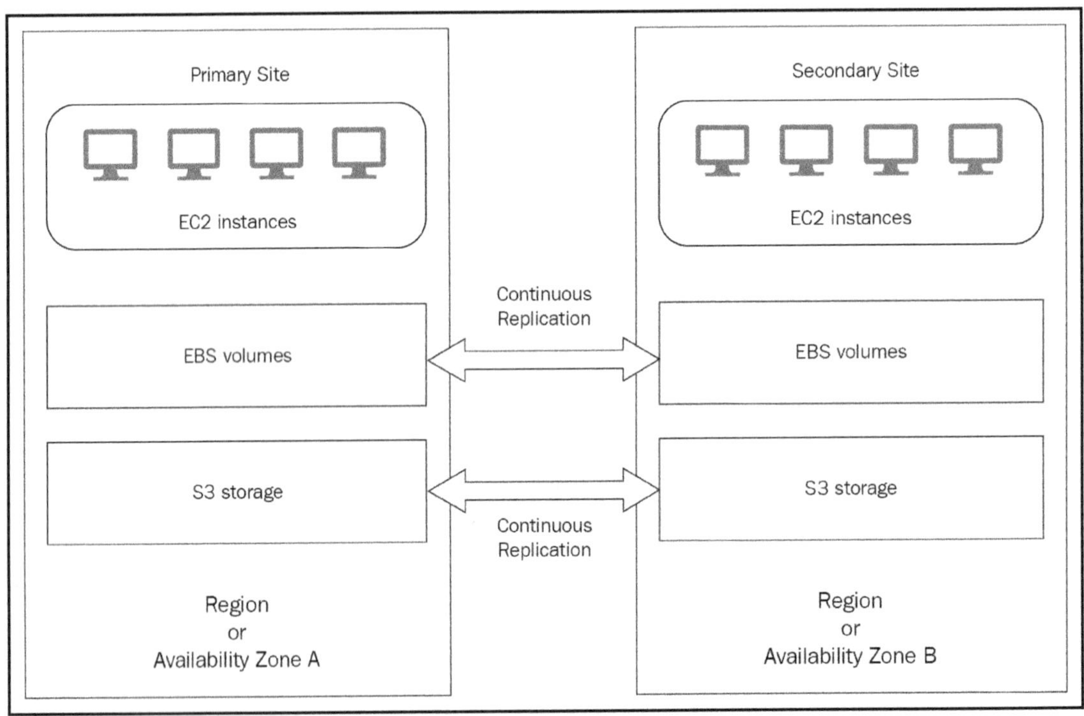

Replication techniques can be leveraged to ensure that a mirrored copy of the data is maintained and updated frequently, so that the latest copy exists on the mirror site.

Unsecure application APIs

Today, many applications provide APIs to the external developers to interact with the application. Depending on the type of services that the application offers, the API can perform simple URL-based data manipulations or even an advanced service oriented architecture model:

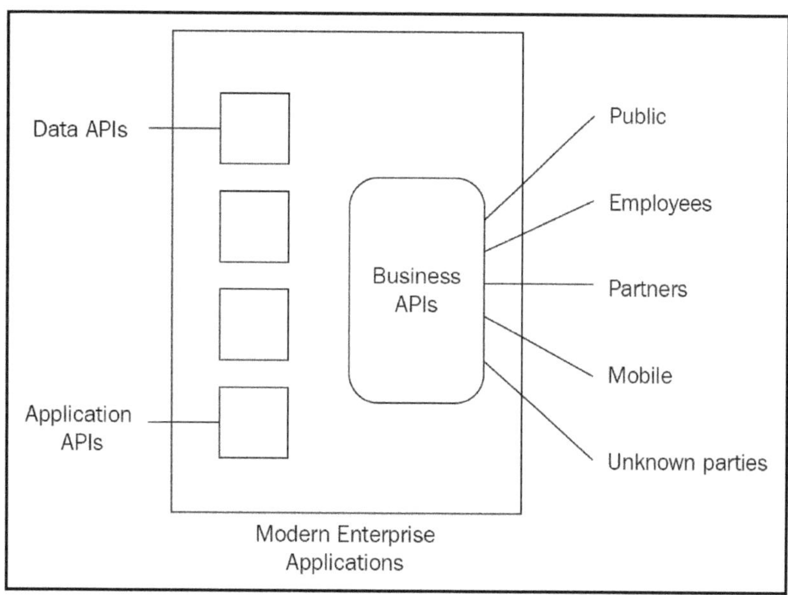

These APIs may be invoked to fetch, update, and delete data on the server or database, depending on the type of the API implementation. These APIs can simply be invoked by sending an HTTP `GET`, `PUT`, `POST`, or `DELETE` request along with the JSON representation of the resources. If these API endpoints deal with sensitive data, there is a risk of attacks from hackers or unauthorized users.

Hence, a reliable token-based authentication mechanism should be used before providing access to the APIs:

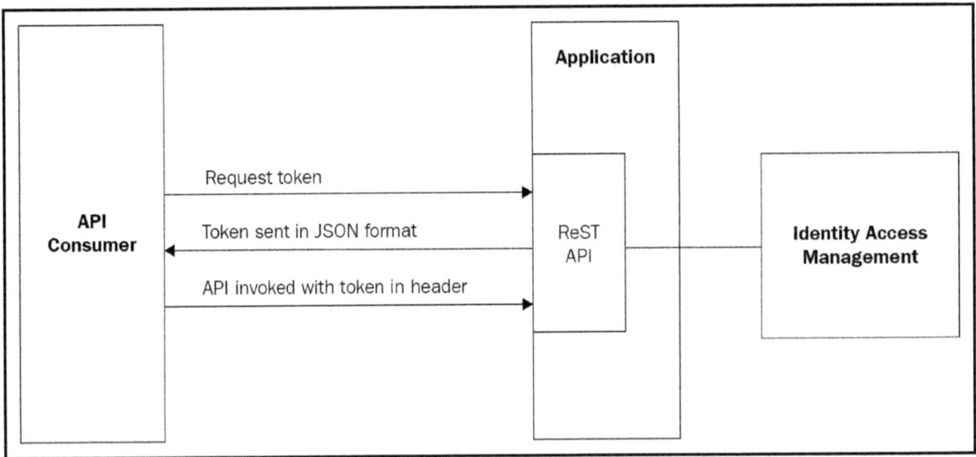

As shown in the preceding diagram, the API consumer must first request a token from the identity access management system using a token request API. Once the user is authorized, a token is granted. Once the user receives the token, he can use it to invoke APIs by specifying the token in the API request headers.

Denial of service attacks

More and more organizations are exposing APIs as a part of cloud adoption and this comes with certain security threats.

APIs are prone to DoS attacks and hybrid cloud administrators should ensure that they are able to deal with such attacks. One of the common methods that security professionals use is to disable a particular API key or access token that is used for API authentication. However, since the token or key can easily be generated by sending a simple HTTP request, this approach is not secure and doesn't solve the problem. Another common technique involves tracing the IP address of the invoker of the API and then blocking that IP address. This approach is also not a solution to the problem, as the attacker can easily send the request from a new IP address.

When the API exposes non-sensitive data, the use of access tokens and keys may be sufficient.

Although DoS attacks cannot be completely prevented, the following are some common techniques to mitigate the risks:

- **Blackholing:** This technique involves routing the offending traffic to a so-called **black hole** or a null server, where the network packets are just terminated without causing any harm.
- **Firewalling:** A firewall can be used to block the offending IP address. However, the drawback is that a legitimate request may also get blocked.

Data leaks

When organizations adopt the hybrid cloud platform, data privacy and security becomes a primary concern of the hybrid cloud administrators. An inadequate and lack of robust security protocols used by the cloud provider can compromise the data and make it prone to attacks. When data is stored on the cloud, it might get exposed to unauthorized users and may cause an impact on business. It is therefore necessary to track the movement of the data when it is stored on the cloud platform. This is can done by having some data monitoring tools that track the data store location and also where the data flows from the cloud storage.

Virtualization software security

Both public and private clouds use a hypervisor to host the virtual machines that are launched by cloud users. For example, AWS uses the Citrix XEN hypervisor, whereas OpenStack uses the KVM hypervisor by default. Hardware and operating system virtualization allows the cloud provider to share the hardware across several guest virtual machines without interfering with each other. In other words, multiple virtual machines running different operating systems can run on the same hardware simultaneously. But running several virtual machines on a single physical host has its own set of risks.

Public cloud customers who launch virtual machines have no visibility to this hypervisor or any other virtualization software that the cloud uses. On the other hand, in a private cloud, the administrator has more control over the hypervisor used. The hypervisor is a software just like any other software running on the system. If an attacker becomes aware of any loopholes or vulnerabilities of the hypervisor, he may be able to take control of it and affect all the virtual machines that are running on the hypervisor. It is therefore necessary to monitor and detect unusual activity as early as possible and perform the necessary remedies.

Most IaaS providers use a bare metal hypervisor, which is also known as a Type 1 hypervisor. These hypervisors can be directly installed on raw hardware without any operating system. For example, VMWare ESX, Citrix Xen Server, Oracle Virtual Machine, and so on are bare metal hypervisors. The cloud provider should ensure that the required security controls are in place for these hypervisors. This includes understanding the internals of the hypervisor as well as preventing or restricting physical access to the hardware machines where these hypervisors are installed.

Many of the modern hypervisors provide a feature known as *PCI passthrough*, which allows the virtual machine instance to directly get access to the hardware of the physical host where it is running. The PCI passthrough functionality is essential for virtual machines that require access to the **graphics processor unit** (**GPU**) or video cards for better performance. However, this feature poses a risk to the overall system as it allows direct memory access to the host system. A virtual machine instance must not be given access to the full memory of the underlying host, as this will give it a full view of the entire host as well as other virtual machine running on that host. To prevent this, hardware providers use the **Input/Output Memory Management Unit** (**IOMMU**) to manipulate **Direct Memory Access** (**DMA**) in such situations.

Moreover, when a virtual machine modifies the firmware of a device, it may affect other virtual machines running on the same host. This can pose a critical risk as the virtual machine can run code outside of its security limits. Hence, care should be taken to identify how a virtual machine can modify the underlying hardware state and once the virtual machine is done with the hardware, the process to reset the hardware state should be in place. For example, the firmware can be reflashed to reset the configuration.

Hybrid cloud administrators should consider the measures to ensure hypervisor security of their private cloud.

IaaS customers should understand the underlying technology and the security techniques that are put in place by the cloud provider to protect the hypervisor. This not only helps in taking additional security measures but also helps in determining any compliance gaps with respect to the organization's policies.

Virtual machine security

Once the virtual machine is launched on the cloud platform, it might be exposed to several stakeholders for access. Usually, customers are provided full access to the virtual machine. Therefore, it is the responsibility of the customer to ensure the security of the virtual machine.

A public cloud provider such as AWS offers web APIs to manipulate the EC2 instances. These APIs, when orchestrated properly using automation techniques, can provide easy scalability and elasticity for meeting the increased workload in high demand situations. Sufficient network access migration steps must be taken to restrict access to the virtual machines by configuring the firewall rules in the security groups. The virtual machine internal firewall rules should also be configured if required. For example, Linux iptable rules can be leveraged to increase the network access security. Similarly, Windows has a native firewall that can be configured appropriately to ensure that only relevant protocols and ports are allowed.

When a virtual machine is customized to meet the organization's standards and policies, it is a good practice to store hardened images of the configured virtual machine. An AMI can be created out of a a configured virtual machine instance and stored. This AMI can be used for launching more virtual machines which exhibit the same configuration settings. Similarly, on OpenStack, a Glance image can be created from a running virtual machine, which can be reused.

The following are some of the security measures to be considered for ensuring virtual machine security:

- Protect customized AMIs or Glance images from unauthorized access
- Ensure that the private keys used to access the virtual machine are safeguarded
- Avoid password-based authentication for shell access
- Require passwords for sudo or role-based access
- Configure the host firewall and allow only the required ports
- Run only the essential services and turn off the unused ones
- Enable event logging system auditing and write the logs to a dedicated log server
- Ensure that the log server is provided with higher security

The preceding measures will ensure that the virtual machine is secure.

Patch management

The hybrid cloud application may require patch updates from time to time. The underlying operating system may also require periodic patching to ensure that any recent security threats are dealt with. With an IaaS platform, the cloud users are responsible for managing patches for the entire stack, that is the operating system patches, application patches, and also database patches. For SaaS platforms, the patch management is taken care of by the cloud provider.

Security patch management is vital for the cloud applications and hence organizations must mandate this process in their change management cycles.

Intrusion detection and prevention

The distributed architecture of a hybrid cloud platform is vulnerable to potential cyber attacks by intruders. Traditional **intrusion detection and prevention systems** (**IDPs**) are not very efficient for a hybrid cloud environment. It is there necessary to consider advanced IDPs that are designed for the cloud platform:

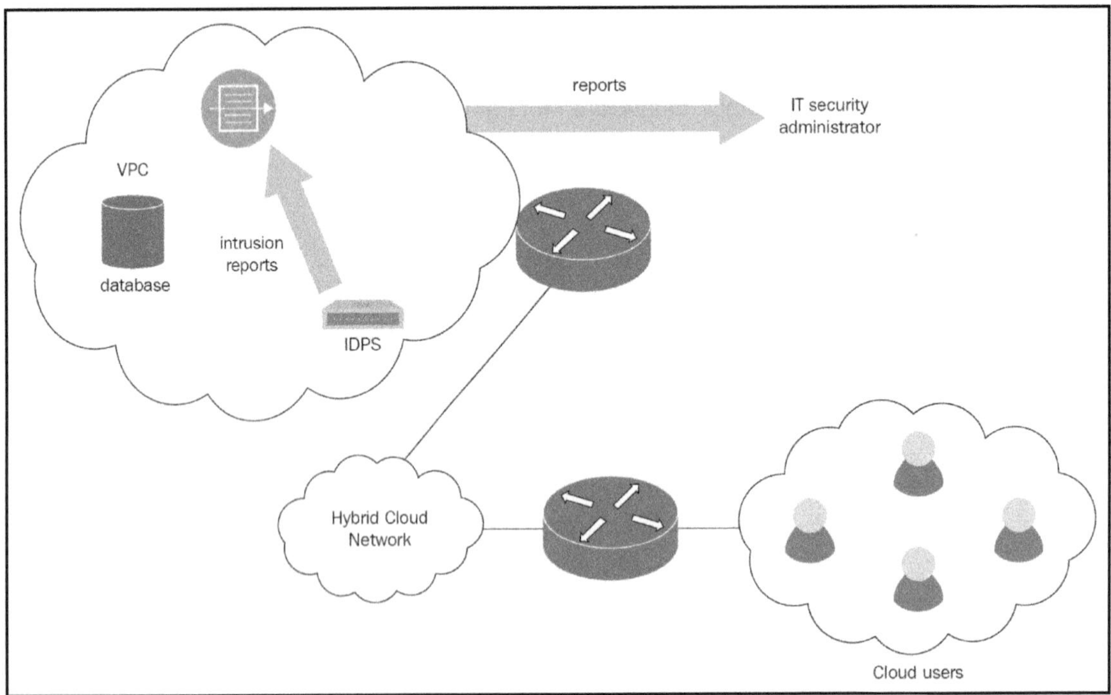

IDPs on a hybrid cloud require an efficient, scalable, and virtualization-based approach. Once the organization's data is hosted in the cloud, the IT administrators have limited control over the data and its resources. IDPs thus also become the responsibility of the cloud provider. However, it is necessary that the administration of the IDPs should be the cloud user and not the cloud provider. This gives the organization's IT security team more control over the IDPs and helps in ensuring the security of their data and resources.

The reports generated from the IDPs must be sent out to the hybrid cloud security administrators so that a risk mitigation can be done.

Identity access management

The data center in a typical organization is shielded with various security provisions. The applications, hosts, network systems, and all other data center equipment is guarded by tight security protocols and practices. The IT department has full control over the access to the infrastructure as well as the applications. External access to the organization's network is secured by providing VPN connectivity. There are also provisions for intrusion detection and intrusion prevention.

When an organization decides to adapt the hybrid cloud model, the IT department's control over the infrastructure either reduces or extends into the cloud provider's domain. This reduction of control over the IT infrastructure and applications is a challenge for organizations, as security becomes a major concern.

Thus, to reduce the security risk and compensate for the reduction of control, organizations must adapt to a higher level of application security and user access control mechanism. New techniques that perform authentication based on the a role or a claim, **single sign-on** (**SSO**), activity monitoring, and so on become important to ensure security, along with a reliable identity management system.

An identity access management system essentially provides three main features:

- **Authentication:** Authentication is a process where the identity of the user, service, or an entity is verified. For example, Microsoft Windows provides the Active Directory service which is a centralized storage of all user accounts. LDAP is another common mechanism that is used for identity verification.
- **Authorization:** Once the identity of the user, service, or entity is established, it is necessary to identify the privileges of the authenticated entity. Thus, authorization is the process of identifying the rights and privileges of the user, system, or entity so that the required access can be provided.

- **Auditing:** Every authentication and authorization performed by the IAM system must be recorded. These records are required for compliance verification. The process of recording these activities is called auditing:

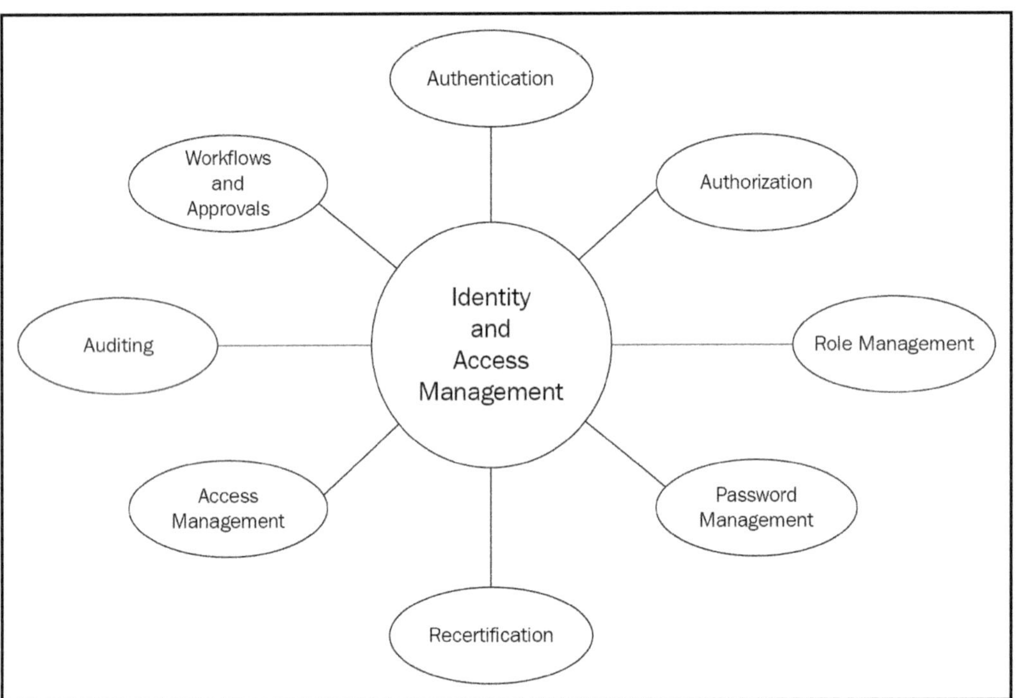

Identity management (authentication, authorization, and auditing) is indispensable when working with cloud services. A reliable identity management service must be used for resource authentication. The security data that is used by the identity management system must be synchronized with the cloud platforms participating in the hybrid cloud environment. A lack of proper synchronization may cause problems during authentication on either clouds. For cloud customers, a well-managed and synchronized IAM system along with standard practices and processes will help protect the confidentiality and integrity of the hybrid cloud data. It will also help in achieving compliance.

Developing secure applications

The application development process begins with the analysis of the requirements. For some applications, requirements may emerge as time progresses. Since application security is of prime importance, it must be taken into consideration early during the requirements and analysis phase of the software development cycle. In most cases, the tools and processes used to design and develop robust, clean, and efficient software also help in writing secure code. However, the following areas should be considered while developing secure hybrid cloud applications.

Data manipulation

A hybrid cloud application may have to handle different kinds of data. Some of it may be sensitive and requires special handling. For example, if the user's password has to be handled by the application, it should be handled with care. The following points should be considered while handling sensitive data:

- A password should not be visible on the screen when the user types it. Even if asterisks (`*`s) are displayed, you must ensure that they cannot be copied and pasted to reveal the password.
- A password or any sensitive data such as credit card information should not be transmitted from one component to another over the network, without being encrypted.
- Sensitive strings should not be passed into queries to the database. The database server may be logging all the queries and the database administrator may be able to fetch these sensitive details by looking at the logs.

Coding practices

The security of data should always be kept in mind while writing application code. For example, HTML pages and scripts that sends information to and from the cloud servers should not have sensitive information in the comments of the code. Hackers can easily exploit this information by scrutinizing these HTML scripts.

The programming language itself can be a vulnerable due to the lack of security mechanisms that it provides. For example, the C language cannot detect improper memory allocation, cannot do garbage collection, and so on. It is the programmer's responsibility to make sure that memory is allocated properly and freed up when not required. It is due to this that languages such as Java and C++ 11 have become popular.

The design of the application should be as simple as possible. A complex design elevates the possibilities of errors and makes the application more vulnerable.

A compiler warning should not be ignored and the application must be compiled with the highest level of compiler warnings to reveal the potential vulnerabilities of the application.

User input validation

Although this is a general best practice while developing any application, it is worth a mention. The hybrid cloud application, like any other application, may fetch input from the user from time to time. It is necessary to validate this input before incorporating it into database SQL queries or any other commands. If the input is not validated, it can cause content injection when the application is not able to establish a clear distinction between the user input and the command that is executed. An improper command may cause unexpected failures.

Security testing

Once the hybrid cloud application is developed by the application development teams, it should be thoroughly tested from the security perspective. Security testing should ensure that the application exhibits the following characteristics:

- The application behaves in a predictable manner
- It does not expose any security vulnerabilities
- It can handle exceptions during failure conditions
- It does not violate any security and compliance constraints

The fault injection technique should also be used by the quality assurance teams. This technique involves deliberately injecting faults in the code in order to test the code paths that handle exceptions.

Penetration testing is one of the most commonly used techniques to ensure that the application is secure. This main goal of this type of testing is to assess the vulnerabilities of the application before an attacker does. It uses different penetration testing tools that simulate real-world attacks and reveal the flaws in the applications. Application developers can then work towards fixing them and thus enhance the application security:

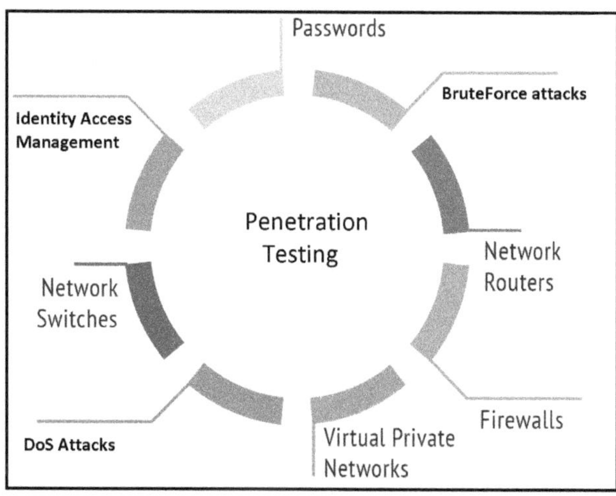

As shown in the preceding diagram, penetration testing tries to reveal the vulnerabilities of the application using various routes, such as using false IAM tokens, firewall tweaks, network switches, BruteForce attacks, and so on.

Summary

As more and more organizations are adopting the hybrid cloud platform, a large part of their IT infrastructure is moved to the cloud provider's control. This brings new challenges for the IT operations team with respect to IT security and data security. It is therefore essential that the hybrid cloud administrators become completely aware of the possible security threats and implement measures to deal with such risks.

This chapter focused on various security threats and discussed different measures to minimize the impact of these threats. With more and more organizations migrating to the hybrid cloud platform and with the cloud technology maturing, the day is not far away when traditional data centers will soon become obsolete.

Other Books You May Enjoy

If you enjoyed this book, you may be interested in these other books by Packt:

Hybrid Cloud for Architects
Alok Shrivastwa

ISBN: 978-1-78862-351-3

- Learn the demographics and definitions of Hybrid Cloud
- Understand the different architecture and design of Hybrid Cloud
- Explore multi-cloud strategy and use it with your hybrid cloud
- Implement a Hybrid Cloud using CMP / Common API's
- Implement a Hybrid Cloud using Containers
- Overcome various challenges and issues while working with your Hybrid Cloud
- Understand how to monitor your Hybrid Cloud
- Discover the security implications in the Hybrid Cloud

Building Hybrid Clouds with Azure Stack
Markus Klein, Susan Roesner

ISBN: 978-1-78646-629-7

- Gain a clear understanding of Azure Stack design
- Set up storage, network and compute services in Azure Stack
- Implement and run a hybrid cloud infrastructure with PaaS, SaaS, and IaaS services
- Get an overview of the automation options in Azure Stack
- Integrate Azure public services such as multi-factor authentication and Azure AD with Azure Stack
- Learn about the services available in the future

Leave a review - let other readers know what you think

Please share your thoughts on this book with others by leaving a review on the site that you bought it from. If you purchased the book from Amazon, please leave us an honest review on this book's Amazon page. This is vital so that other potential readers can see and use your unbiased opinion to make purchasing decisions, we can understand what our customers think about our products, and our authors can see your feedback on the title that they have worked with Packt to create. It will only take a few minutes of your time, but is valuable to other potential customers, our authors, and Packt. Thank you!

Index

B

C

D

E

F

G

P

R

S

T

U

V

W

CPSIA information can be obtained
at www.ICGtesting.com
Printed in the USA
BVHW01s1625070518
515500BV00019B/1026/P